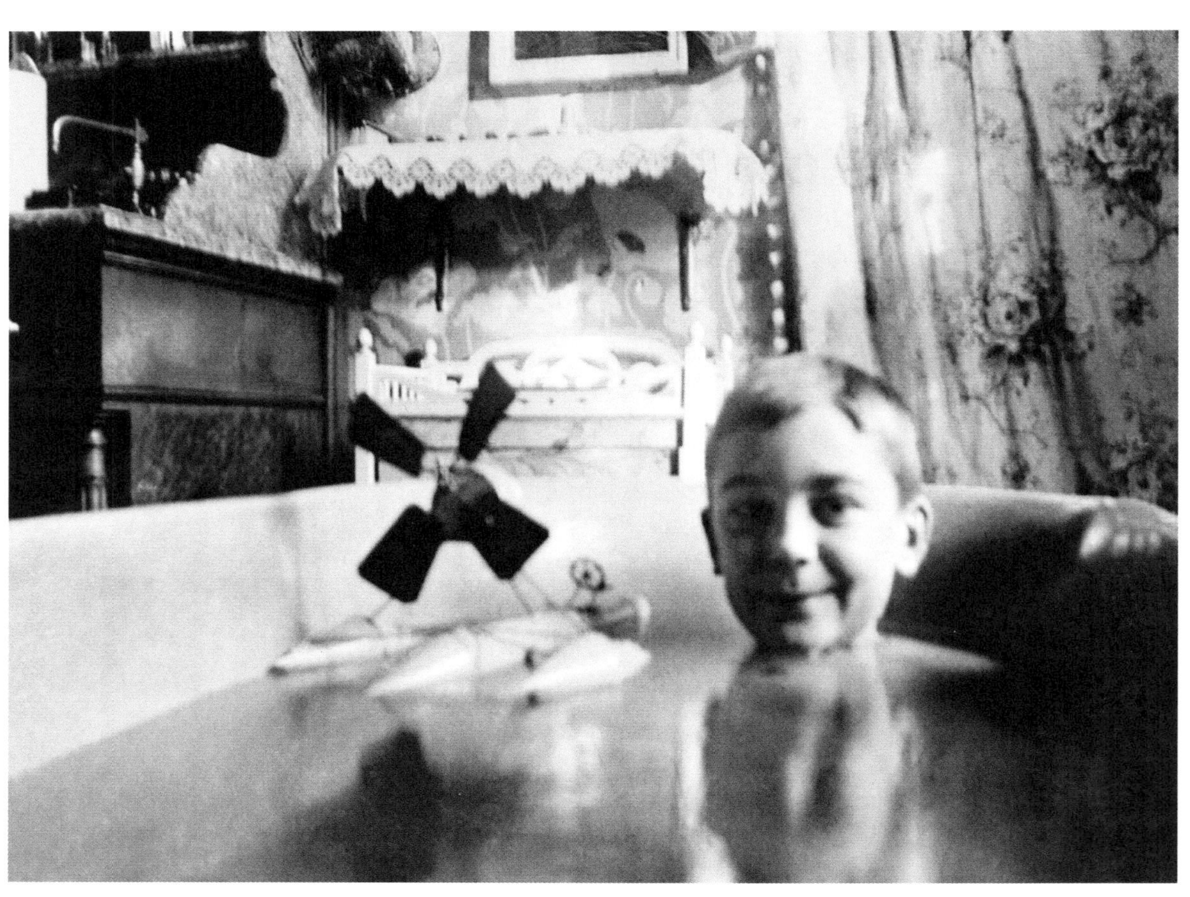

Lartigue
The Boy and the Belle Époque

Louise Baring

With 130 illustrations

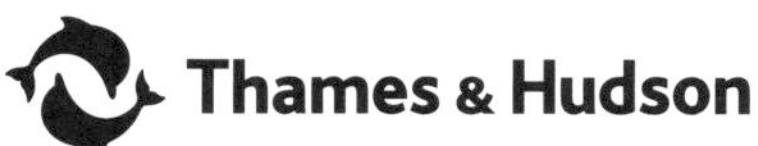

Thames & Hudson

About the author
Louise Baring has written several books on photography, including *Martine Franck* (2007),
Norman Parkinson: A Very British Glamour (2009), *Emmy Andriesse: Hidden Lens* (2013) and *Dora Maar:
Paris in the Time of Man Ray, Jean Cocteau, and Picasso* (2017).

On the cover
FRONT (clockwise from top left): Bois de Boulogne, 1912 (see p. 102); Gabriel Voisin's first
flight, 1904 (see p. 130); French Grand Prix, 1912 (see pp. 142–3); Lartigue in his bath, 1904
(see pp. 2 and 32); balloon racing, 1906 (see p. 132). BACK: Lartigue's bedroom, 1905 (see p. 33).

First published in the United Kingdom in 2020 by Thames & Hudson Ltd,
181A High Holborn, London WC1V 7QX

Lartigue: The Boy and the Belle Époque © 2020 Thames & Hudson Ltd, London

Photographs by Jacques Henri Lartigue © 2020 Ministère de la Culture – France/AAJHL

Text © 2020 Louise Baring
Written French translated by Louise Baring/Thames & Hudson Ltd
Spoken French translated and edited by Louise Baring

Designed by Fred Birdsall studio

British Library Cataloguing-in-Publication Data
A catalogue record for this book is available from the British Library

ISBN 978-0-500-02130-9

Printed and bound in China by C & C Offset Printing Co. Ltd

To find out about all our publications, please visit **www.thamesandhudson.com**.
There you can subscribe to our e-newsletter, browse or download our current catalogue,
and buy any titles that are in print.

Contents

Chapter One
An Enclosed World

'The other day Mr Szarkowski of the Museum of Modern Art in New York showed me your photographs. It was one of the most moving experiences of my life.... You brought me into your world, and isn't that, after all, the purpose of art?'[1] Thus wrote Richard Avedon to fellow photographer Jacques Henri Lartigue, who first stepped into the limelight aged sixty-nine in 1963, when MoMA's photography curator gave an exhibition of his work. Lartigue's world was Belle Époque France as it appeared in his eyes as a pampered, fun-loving boy in the years leading up to the First World War. Famously given a camera by his father when he was just seven or eight years old, he began taking photographs of his parents, his garden, his nanny Dudu throwing a ball up into the air. Aged nine, he persuaded his cousin Bichonnade to leap down a flight of stone steps in Paris, catching her in mid-flight in her long Edwardian skirt and silk jacket. He went on to photograph his older brother Zissou's whimsical inventions: a flimsy glider lifting off in a gust of wind; cousins racing round in home-made go-karts; a 'hydro-glider' atop the geometric lines of a swimming pool; the social parade in the Bois de Boulogne; a woman in furs attracting a covetous glance from a male passer-by; the gleaming lines of a racing car; winter sports in Switzerland, and summers on the beaches of Étretat and Trouville, where, he wrote: 'Nothing hinders my eyes from roaming, drifting endlessly....'[2] Motivated by a desire to catch and preserve 'happiness on the wing', a transient moment before it slips away, the young Lartigue created images now acknowledged as masterpieces in the history of photography.

MoMA promoted Lartigue as a boy genius, a precursor of modernity, raised in a photographic void. 'It is more likely that work as confidently radical as this could have been achieved only by a true primitive: one working without a sense of obligation either to tradition, or to the known characteristics of his medium. Perhaps only a greatly talented child, left to his own devices, could have made these pictures...', wrote the all-powerful

John Szarkowski in the introduction to the exhibition catalogue.[3] Lartigue was, in fact, no *ingénu*. Amateur photography was fashionable in *fin-de-siècle* France, with books and periodicals replete with instructions and examples. More importantly, Lartigue's father was not only a rich entrepreneur-cum-banker but also himself a serious amateur photographer, who shared his darkroom with his son, guiding him through the complexities of image-making. The young Lartigue was thus well versed in the art of photography. Yet his images, rooted in the spontaneity of childhood, reveal an effortless expertise that goes beyond experience. Taking consistently first-class photographs from the age of eleven (most of the images in this book were taken before he was eighteen), he seized every subject with a fresh eye, creating a rich photographic record that he took apart and remade into what he called his '*nouveau vieux*' (new-old) albums in the 1970s. Pasted into these albums are small citrate prints from the 1900s interspersed with large gelatin silver prints that Lartigue made decades later, the pages sprinkled with hand-written notes and captions. In 1979, he gave his collection of 150,000 negatives and 126 albums together with his cameras, diaries and sketches – work spanning almost eight decades – to the French state. He kept a few things to add later, working up until his death in 1986 at the age of ninety-two.

One album page shows a photograph the eleven-year-old Lartigue took of his family at dinner in 1905 (opposite). The butler proffers a dish to his mother, Marie; his father Henri, linen napkin tucked into his shirt collar, awaits his turn; and his older brother Maurice, nicknamed Zissou, pours a drink. The reflections from a glass decanter, silver settings and white table-cloth provide splashes of light in the dining room's dark opulence. The artist Gustave Caillebotte, himself an early photography enthusiast, had painted his own family in a similar, timeless, *haute-bourgeoisie* dining room interior thirty years earlier. Like Caillebotte, Jacques Lartigue (he adopted Jacques Henri only later in life) enjoyed a childhood of great privilege. Born in 1894, he spent his early years in Courbevoie on the outskirts of Paris: 'My universe is an enormous park,' he wrote. 'Above all, a vast empty sky, dazzling white through thousands of branches which form mysterious, backlit arabesques.'[4] His father, Henri Lartigue, had built up the eighth largest fortune in France. Starting out as general manager of the Compagnie Franco-Algérienne, set up in 1873 to build and operate a railway system in

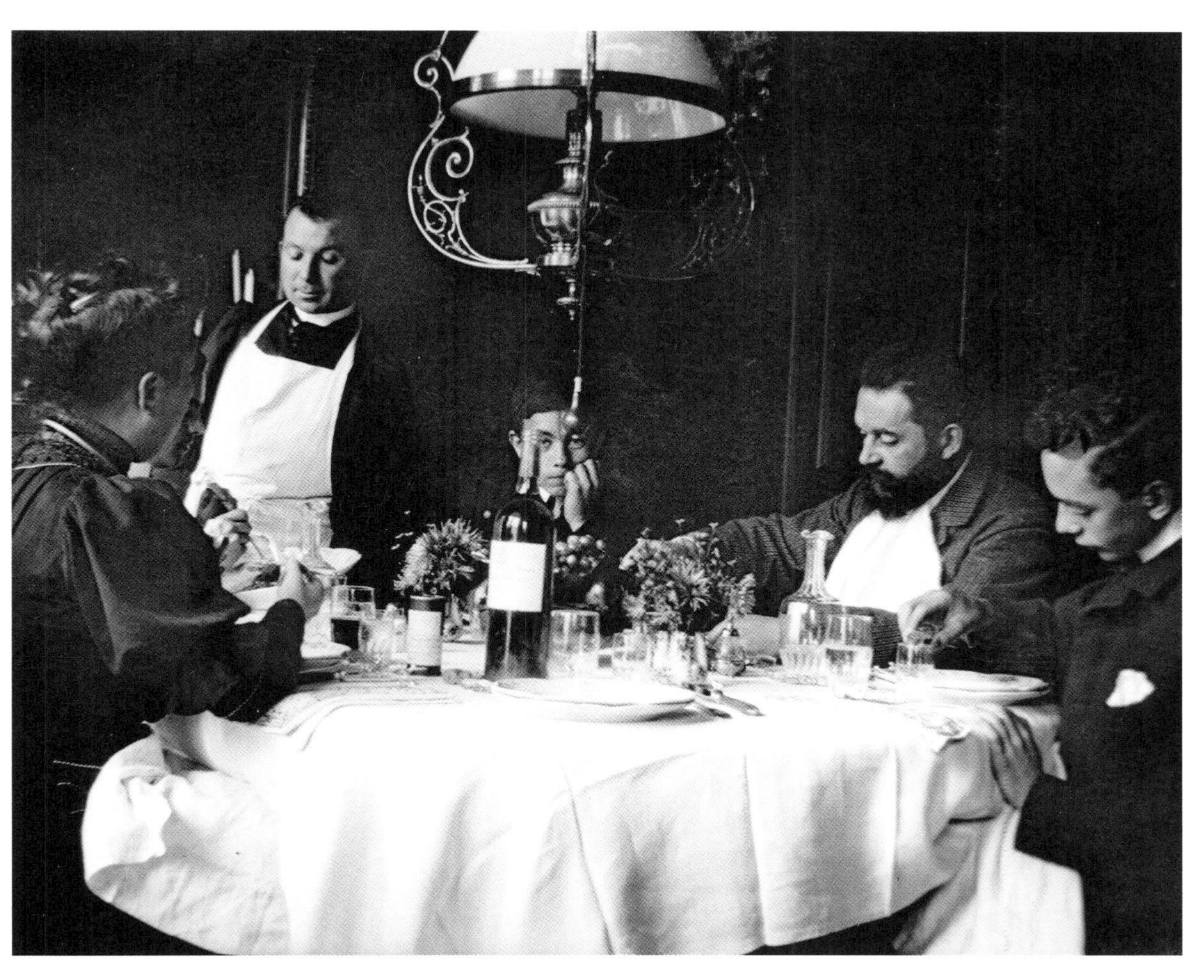

The Lartigue family at dinner: Marie Lartigue, Louis (butler), Louis Ferrand (Loulou),
Henri Lartigue and Maurice Lartigue (Zissou), 40 rue Cortambert, Paris, 1905.

the French colony, he became vice-president of the Société Française de Constructions Mécaniques and editor of a periodical, *L'Express France*, and went into banking at l'Épargne Française and, it is said, Banque Louis-Dreyfus. While Lartigue's mother Marie (whose father, Auguste Haguet, had his photographic portrait taken by the sought-after Félix Nadar) came from a family of bankers and lawyers, Henri's paternal forebears were scientists and inventors. His father, Charles Lartigue, was a mathematics professor, then an astronomer at the Paris Observatory, and later worked for the Algerian railways, developing an elevated monorail system to transport esparto grass across the desert. His uncle Henry, meanwhile, worked for the Administration des Chemins de Fer du Nord, where he was in charge of telegraphic services; his inventions included an automatic electric whistle. Henri's grandfather, Joseph Lartigue, was a mid-nineteenth-century hydro-engineer, who wrote scientific papers on air currents and atmospheric layers.

Then, as now, most hard-working bourgeois fathers sought at least to equip their sons with the *baccalauréat*, preferably followed by studies at one of the *grandes écoles* (the Third Republic was sustained by the graduates of the scientific schools and universities). Eugène Ferrand, a mayor, notary and family friend from Pont-de-l'Arche in Normandy, for example, sent his sons Robert and Louis (the latter appears in the middle of the photograph described above; see p. 11) to live with the Lartigues in Paris during the winter months, so they could attend a *lycée*. Henri Lartigue, meanwhile, envisaged a different education for his own sons. An aristocracy of money may have replaced the old order, but, as Marcel Proust attests, the nobility still retained its social potency: '[The bourgeoisie] may have differed before they reached the top, when they were climbing, but they adopted many of the nobles' values when they could,' writes the historian Theodore Zeldin.[5] Having made a fortune, Henri Lartigue taught his sons to lead carefree lives on a private income. 'I have plenty of money. My children should learn how to spend it,' he once said.[6] Neither went to school. Instead, Henri and his wife enlisted a series of tutors: Monsieur Jacommet (French history, ancient history, geography), Monsieur Blum (German, English), Monsieur Lecordier (French), Marius Aubert from the Sorbonne (maths and science); even the young playwright, Jean Giraudoux. The freedom-loving Jacques resisted conventional methods of learning: 'Throughout the lesson, Monsieur Jacommet and I look at the clock, hoping that this long, long hour will pass. French history bores me, apart from the druids in their oak forests and Charlemagne...', he wrote in the memoirs he conjured up from childhood memories and jottings, as well as the diaries he began in 1911.[7] The hapless Monsieur Blum fared no better with German. Tutors often found their lessons cancelled. Henri's only requirement was that his sons should be happy.

Both brothers, meanwhile, shared their father's fascination with the latest technology. Photography, with its increasingly fast film, emulsions and lenses, was just one example. The world outside was speeding up. The telegraph and railways had already made their mark, while the telephone, motor car and early aeroplanes began to make theirs. A French Panhard won the first international car race in 1900, averaging sixty-two kilometres an hour on the road from Paris to Lyon. The capital's last horse-drawn omnibus would make its final journey from Saint-Sulpice to La Villette in January 1913. '[Monsieur Galbrun] dislikes everything I love,' wrote Jacques of a Luddite guest at the parental dinner table. '[He] becomes furious when he speaks about the things that amuse me most: railways, electric light and, above all, motor cars.'[8] Louis Renault and his brother Marcel had

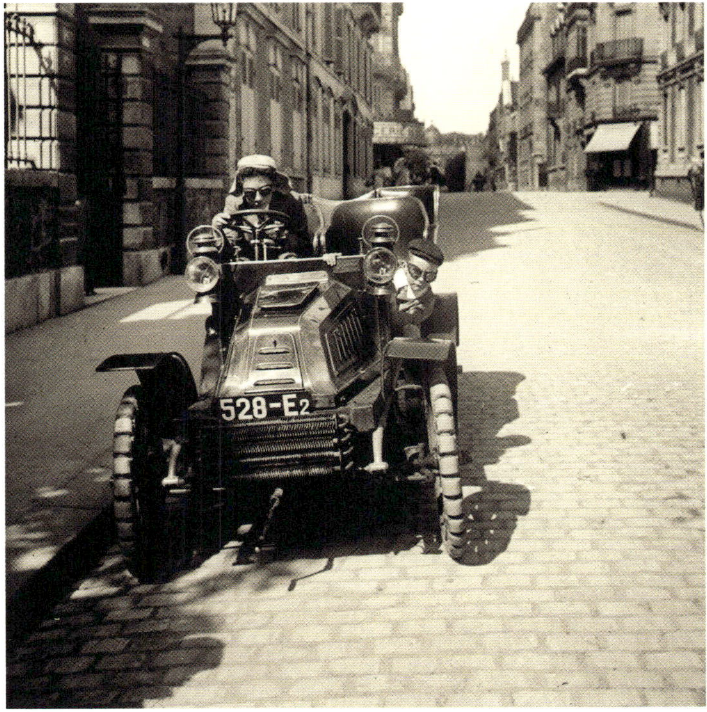

Zissou and Jacques 'driving' a De Dion-Bouton, outside 40 rue Cortambert, 1903. Photo Henri Lartigue.

built their first motor car in 1898. Within a decade, Société Renault Frères were building over 3,500 cars a year, then a great luxury, at their factory at Boulogne-Billancourt in the Paris suburbs. Renault and its twin emerging giant Peugeot were among 150 different makes that sprang up at the turn of the century (France was then the world's largest car exporter), backed by Paris banks and an abundance of skilled engineers. Henri Lartigue photographed his exuberant sons dressed as '*coureurs d'autos*' (racing drivers), complete with goggles, pretending to drive a De Dion-Bouton with puncture-proof Ducasble tyres parked in a Paris street (p. 13). The long-forgotten Delauney-Belleville factory, based in the northern suburb of Saint-Denis, meanwhile, made motor cars for Tsar Nicholas II of Russia. Henri bought the first of several cars, an electric 'Krieger' designed by electrical engineer Louis Antoine Krieger, in 1902. The eight-year-old Jacques on his bicycle struggled to follow his father's chauffeur, Yves Lecouster,

Jacques Henri Lartigue's annotations on a photograph taken by Henri Lartigue of the family home in Paris, 40 rue Cortambert, 1902 (album page).

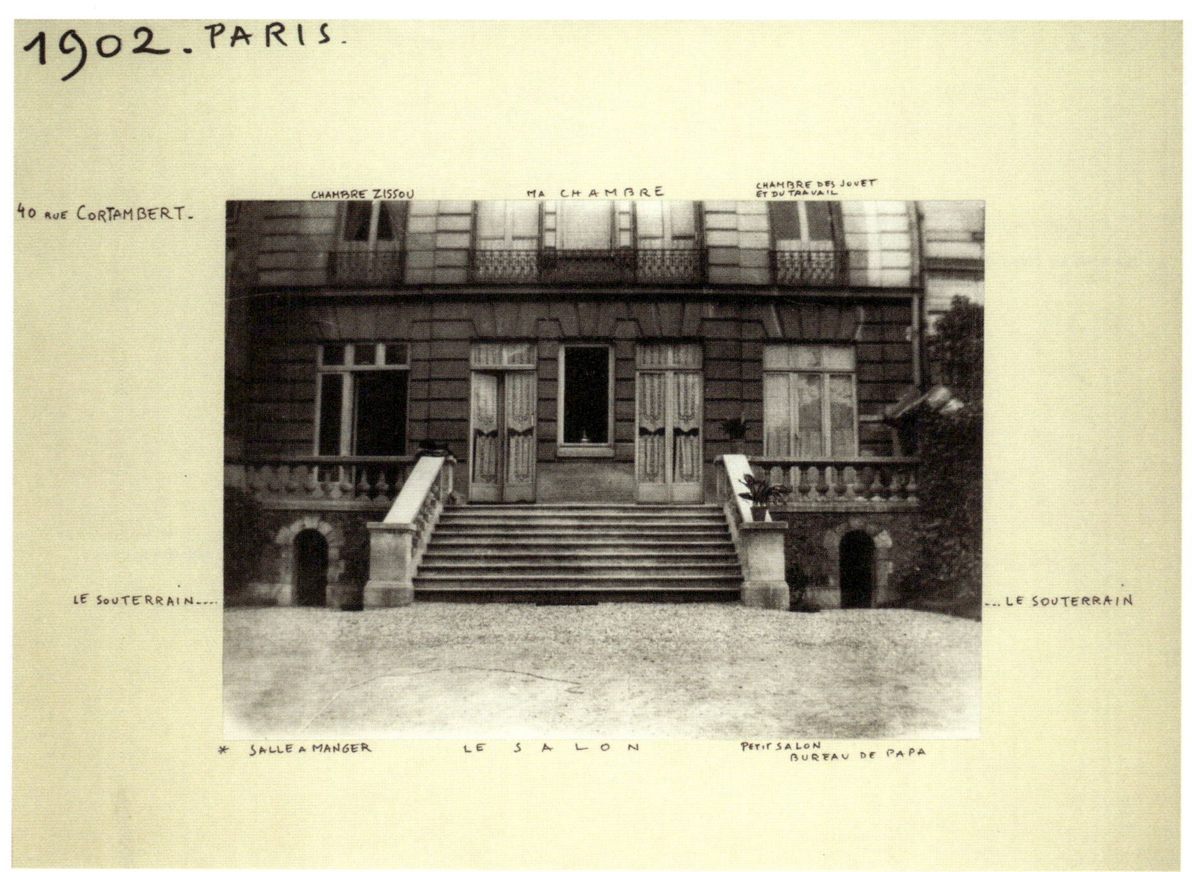

through the Bois de Boulogne, near the *hôtel particulier* at 40 rue Cortambert, where the family had moved a year earlier (see opposite).

Further to the east lay the Eiffel Tower, built in 1887–9, like a symbol of the coming age. By 1914, a mast beamed radio waves into the ether. 'The world has changed more in the last thirty years than in all the time since Jesus Christ,' wrote the poet and essayist Charles Péguy at the time.[9] In a photograph by Paul Roussel (Henri Lartigue's cousin by marriage), the iron structure dominates the 1900 World's Fair, the Trocadéro Park below lined with gleaming white Tunisian and Algerian palaces, symbols of colonial France (below). Over fifty million visited the fair, which boasted 83,000 displays: the Palais d'Electricité, lit and decorated with 5,000 electric bulbs; reproductions of a Moroccan souk, Hindu temple, Japanese pagoda and Indian pavilion. X-ray machines, wireless telegraphy, diesel engines and flying machines attracted enterprising visitors. Aviation pioneer Louis Blériot, who would go on to establish his company Recherches Aéronautique Louis Blériot in around 1906, inspected these early aircraft, later making the first flight across the English Channel in 1909. The Grand Palais, with its Art Nouveau-inspired stone, steel and glass interior, first opened its doors at the fair, as did the brand-new Paris metro line connecting the Porte de Vincennes with the Porte Maillot. Henri Lartigue took the six-year-old Jacques and Zissou, four years his senior, to the fair. Jacques

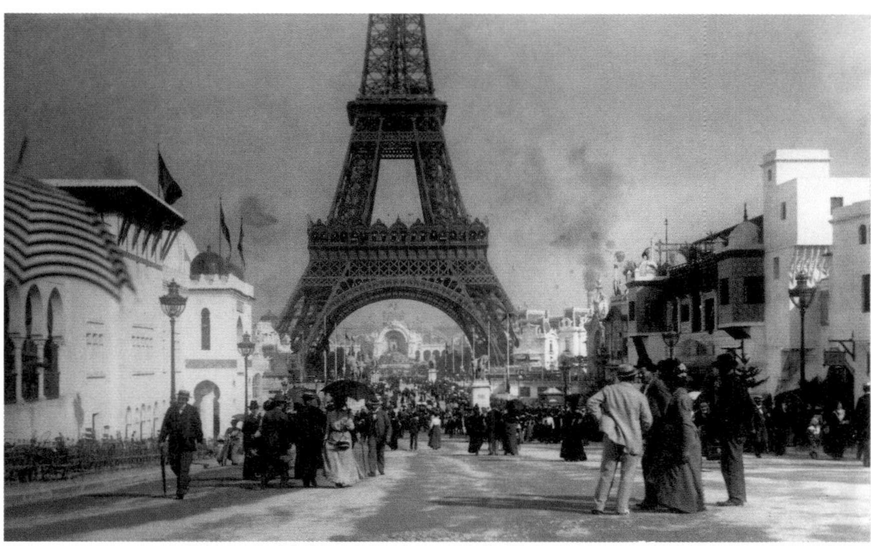

L'Exposition universelle, Paris, 1900. Photo Paul Roussel.

remembered the triumphal gateway on the Place de la Concorde, topped with 'La Parisienne', a giant statue of a woman dressed in the latest Paris fashion. Best of all was a two-kilometre *trottoir roulant*, a moving wooden 'pavement' that ferried visitors from one point to another: '[It's a bit] like a dream when you stay still yet keep moving quickly, quickly…. Zissou even tried running.'[10]

The first sound-synchronized film projections, comprising brief ballet and opera excerpts, proved another highlight at the fair. The Lumière brothers (Auguste and Louis) had already made history five years earlier in December 1895, when their revolutionary moving pictures took their Parisian audience by surprise with the first public screening of their film *La Sortie des ouvriers de l'usine Lumière à Lyon* (Workers Leaving the Lumière Factory in Lyon), at the Salon Indien du Grand Café on the Boulevard des Capucines. The Lumière brothers deemed their invention of scientific interest, with scant commercial value. But in 1897 Georges Méliès, a young entrepreneur, set up a studio in Montreuil, an eastern suburb of Paris, making hundreds of short films, including the 1902 Jules Verne-inspired *Le Voyage dans la lune* (Trip to the Moon), which follows six astronomers travelling to the moon in a cannon-propelled capsule. Rival early French cinema pioneers and producers, Charles Pathé and Léon Gaumont, also built their own studios in Vincennes and in the rue des Alouettes near the Parc des Buttes-Chaumont in the 19th *arrondissement*.

The young Lartigue first watched Méliès' *Le Voyage dans la lune*, among other short films, at Les Grands Magasins Dufayel, an opulent furnishings department store in the Goutte d'Or neighbourhood that included a winter garden, a theatre and a cinema with wrought-iron seats. With some 7,000 employees in its heyday, Dufayel offered a catalogue ordering service as well as credit, taking advantage of the consumer craze sweeping Paris. Lartigue often accompanied his mother to the Grands Magasins du Louvre or its rival, Le Bon Marché, on a Thursday, electric light extending the pleasures of shopping during the winter months. By the 1900s, visiting Le Bon Marché, a Belle Époque landmark that inspired the luxury emporium in Émile Zola's 1883 novel, *Au Bonheur des dames* (The Ladies' Paradise), had become an adventure in itself. Inside its entrance on the rue de Sèvres with its three sweeping staircases, up to 15,000 shoppers a day were greeted with extravagant displays, whether a profusion of silks, chiffon and velvets, an Eastern bazaar selling oriental carpets, or a scene from an Arctic expedition. By 1914, motor cars and even aeroplanes were displayed inside the store, highlighting French technology and progress. It was at Le Bon Marché that Jacques bought his first diaries and photograph albums in which he classified, arranged and labelled his photographs like an obsessive lepidopterist, noting in his diary that he had taken 1,097 photographs in 1912 alone.

Unlike the daredevil Zissou, who excluded him from the games he organized with cousins and friends, Jacques was a sensitive child who became a lifelong spectator. A photograph by Eugène Atget, who created a photographic portrait of Paris on the cusp of the modern age, by chance caught the brothers watching a *guignol* puppet show in the Jardin du Luxembourg in 1899, the five-year-old Jacques' face rapt with attention (below). Though exuberant, he was frail and prone to protracted bouts of ill health. His parents feared tuberculosis. The disease remained endemic in early twentieth-century France, killing 10,000 adults and children a year in Paris alone. Beyond the dashing boulevards that epitomized the Belle Époque lay quarters like Montmartre or the area below the Gare d'Austerlitz (now the 13th *arrondissement*), where entire families lived on the streets or in crumbling, overcrowded housing with little light and no sanitation. Tuberculosis thrived there, even travelling to the well-heeled neighbourhoods to the west, known as *les beaux quartiers*.

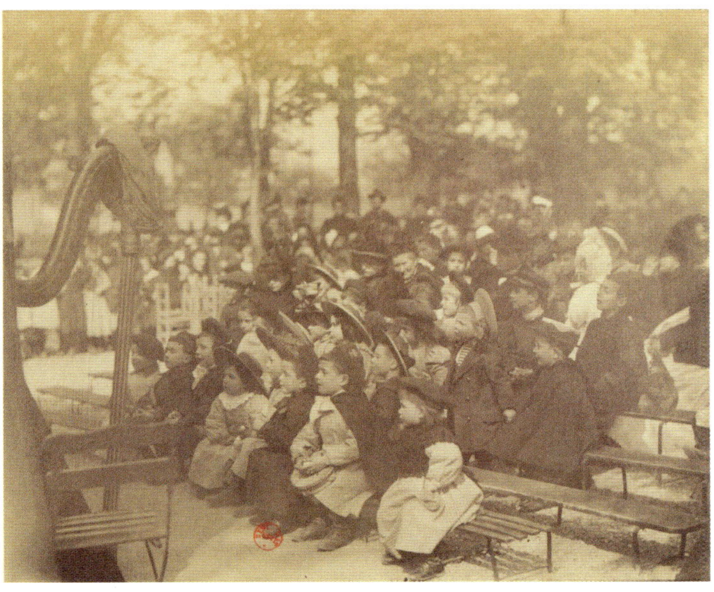

Jardin du Luxembourg, Paris, 1899, with Jacques Lartigue standing up, second from right, in the third row. Photo Eugène Atget. Bibliothèque nationale de France.

Jacques spent days in bed drawing or with his mother at his side, singing or reading to him. Marie Lartigue, whom Jacques later photographed with his Irish wolfhound, Rags, in the Bois de Boulogne in 1911 (below) was a practical woman, who offered her younger son structure and stability. Wedded to routine, she organized the Lartigue household (Ernest and Noémie Boudisseau, the valet and cook remained with the family for thirty-five years), counting out linens and preserves, writing out menus for kitchen staff, or negotiating the fare for a Renault taxi cab known as a *taximètre*, 1,500 of which appeared on Paris streets by 1907. The art of being 'correct' included an 'at home' every other Friday, dinner parties, the appropriate dress for each stage of mourning (black, grey or mauve), and outings to the theatre, concerts or operettas. Lartigue's boyish, unconventional father

Marie Lartigue with Rags, Allée des Acacias, Bois de Boulogne, 1911.

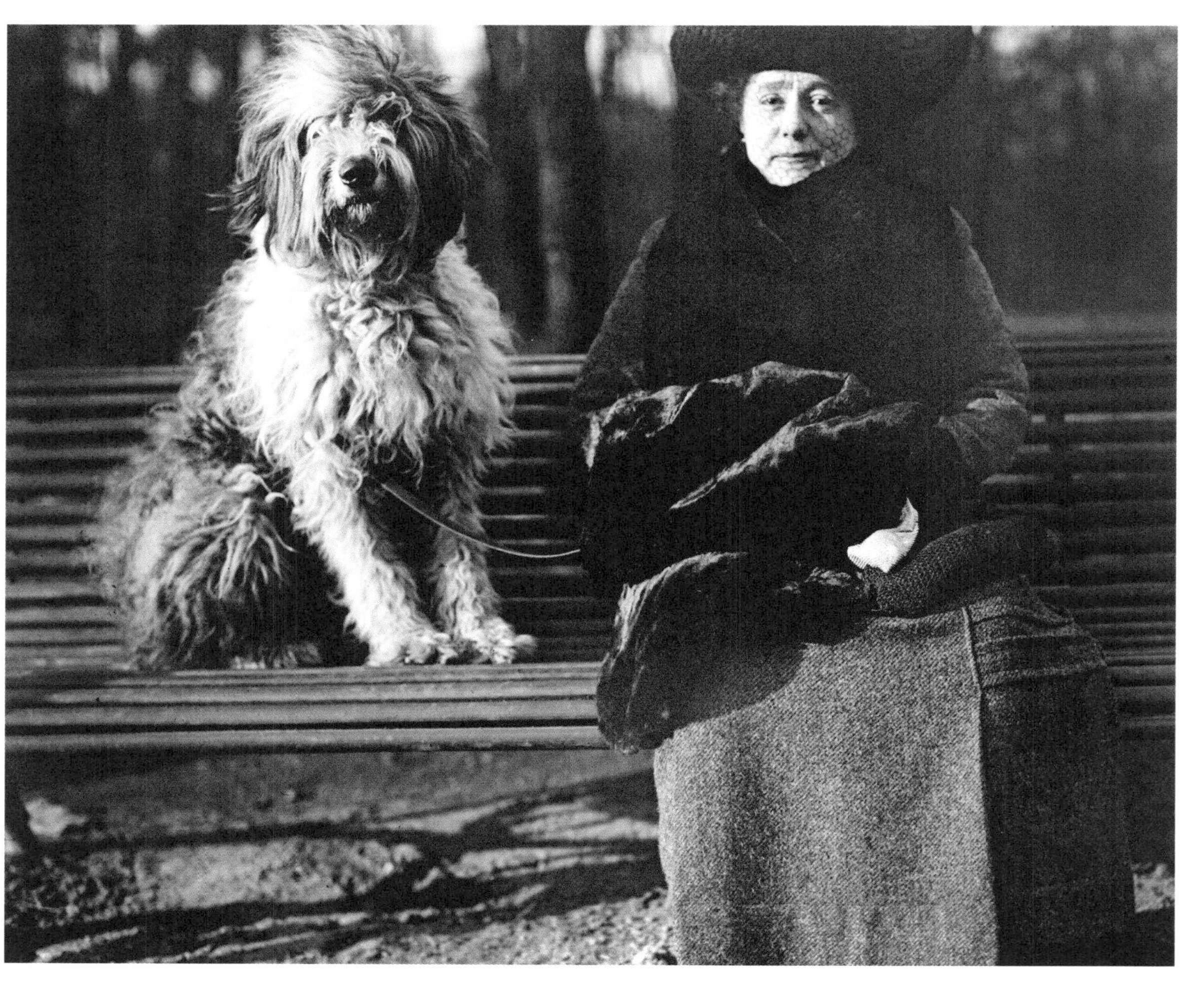

Henri (below), with whom he enjoyed a deep bond, shared with both sons his love of motor races and early attempts to fly. He showed his sons how to make kites and miniature hot-air balloons, or brought home scooters, bicycles, a phonograph and, of course, an ever-evolving series of cameras (he owned at least six), lenses and other photographic equipment.

Given to flights of fancy, Jacques first preserved thoughts and memories he called '*les choses*' (things) by scribbling signs and messages on scraps of paper, secreting them in the cracks between floorboards, in seashells or inside the nostrils of his mechanical horse at the Lartigue country house at Pont-de-l'Arche, to be rediscovered the following year. In Paris he awoke early to draw (even his early sketches reveal a grasp of spatial depth) before anyone came to help him dress. More importantly, he believed that by blinking his eyes he could freeze-frame any image in the world that so delighted him, inventing his famous 'eye-trap' at the age of six or seven: 'I was looking around, enjoying myself.... Suddenly an idea began dancing in my head, an invention straight from fairyland, as a result of which I thought I could never ever be bored or sad again. I open my eyes, then shut them, then open them again, then open them wide, and whoosh! I catch the picture with everything in it: colours! Actual size! And what I see is living things that are moving and feeling.'[11]

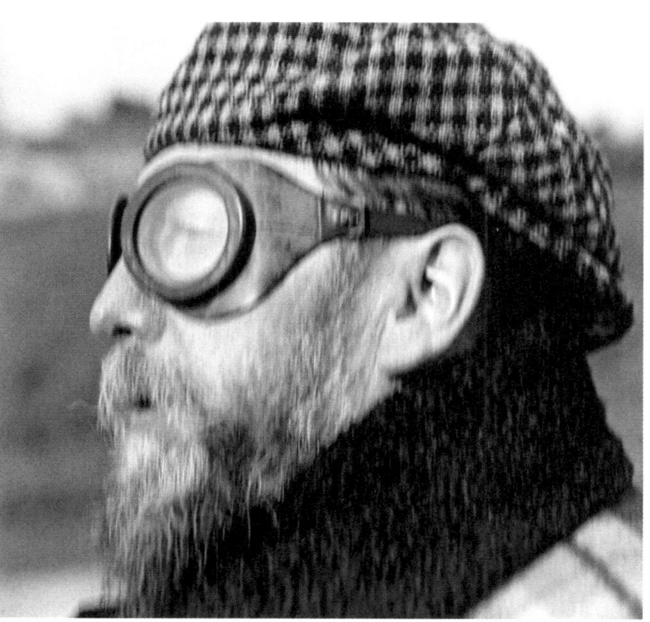

Henri Lartigue, driving at eighty kilometres per hour, 1913.

The human eye has, of course, much in common with a camera. Light bounces off the surface of an object into the eye, the pupil dilating or constricting in response to variations in light. The camera, in turn, has an aperture that must be adapted along with shutter speed to ensure perfect exposure. But, as Lartigue soon realized, the image the camera produces lasts far longer than memory. A couple of days later, he discovered his 'eye trap' did not work: he could no longer recall the images he captured. His father – a bearded, God-like figure in his eyes – came to the rescue: 'For many years now, Papa has done photography. Photography is a magical Thing. A thing that has mysterious odours, a little strange and frightening, something one quickly grows to love,' Lartigue recalled in a childlike voice in his memoirs, published in 1975.[12] 'Under the black veil, Papa lifts me up so that I can see the image that he is going to take: a marvellous little picture, with all the colours, dazzling, alive, but upside down. A small image, lovelier and clearer than the little bit of reality one sees. When I'm the one posing for Papa, I can't move at all while he counts: "One, two, three, it's done!" Each time, though, my eyes disobey and seek amusement by wandering.'

His retrospective account goes on to describe the mysteries of photographic development. 'Afterwards, in the darkroom, under a little red light, I watch Papa's hands as he puts the large green plate, now almost white, into the basin. We wait, and suddenly it starts: we see the image appear! Slowly, then much more quickly. The plate darkens, and one can no longer see anything. Papa rocks the basin continuously in order to agitate the liquid: this annoys me and keeps me from seeing very well. Finally, the plate is moved to the basin in the middle, then it is placed in the third basin. Papa says: "It's a success". And we wait in the dark, with nothing to do, unless we begin right away to develop another photograph.'

Recognizing the camera as the perfect tool to express himself, Jacques first persuaded his father to photograph whatever caught his imagination: 'Photograph this, and this, and this,' he ordered. Then, in late 1901 or 1902, Henri Lartigue gave the boy his own camera: a hefty polished wood 13 × 18 cm plate camera, made by J. Audouin, with no shutter, affixed to a tripod. Lengthy exposure was made by lifting and replacing the lens cap by hand. Henri's often-reproduced photograph of Jacques in the Bois de Boulogne from 1903 shows the nine-year-old clutching a Jumelle hand-held box camera with 9 × 12 cm glass plates, his mother and maternal grandmother in tow

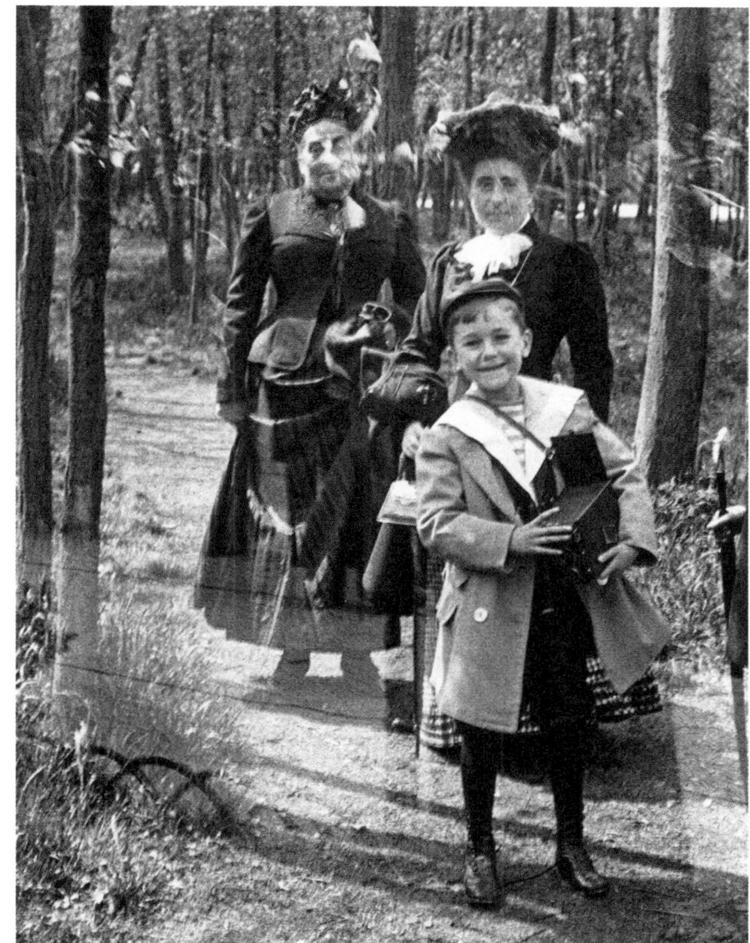

(above). His impish yet curiously adult face is recognizable even in a documentary made eighty years later, his deft hands demonstrating how to use a folding Gaumont Block-Notes camera his father gave him in 1904.

Lartigue's first photograph (developed by his father), which Marie Lartigue pasted into a lined black notebook she entitled *Photographies Diverses 1894–1903*, shows a posed family portrait at Pont-de-l'Arche in the summer of 1902 (p. 22). Though Henri and Marie Lartigue enjoyed the pleasures of the rich, they showed scant interest in the beau-monde. Jacques grew up amid a swarm of aunts, uncles and cousins, many of whom appear in his photographs, including his maternal grandmother, Eugénie Haguet, a short bundle of a woman who covered the page in alarm when he showed her a photograph of herself. His mother had three brothers, two of whom

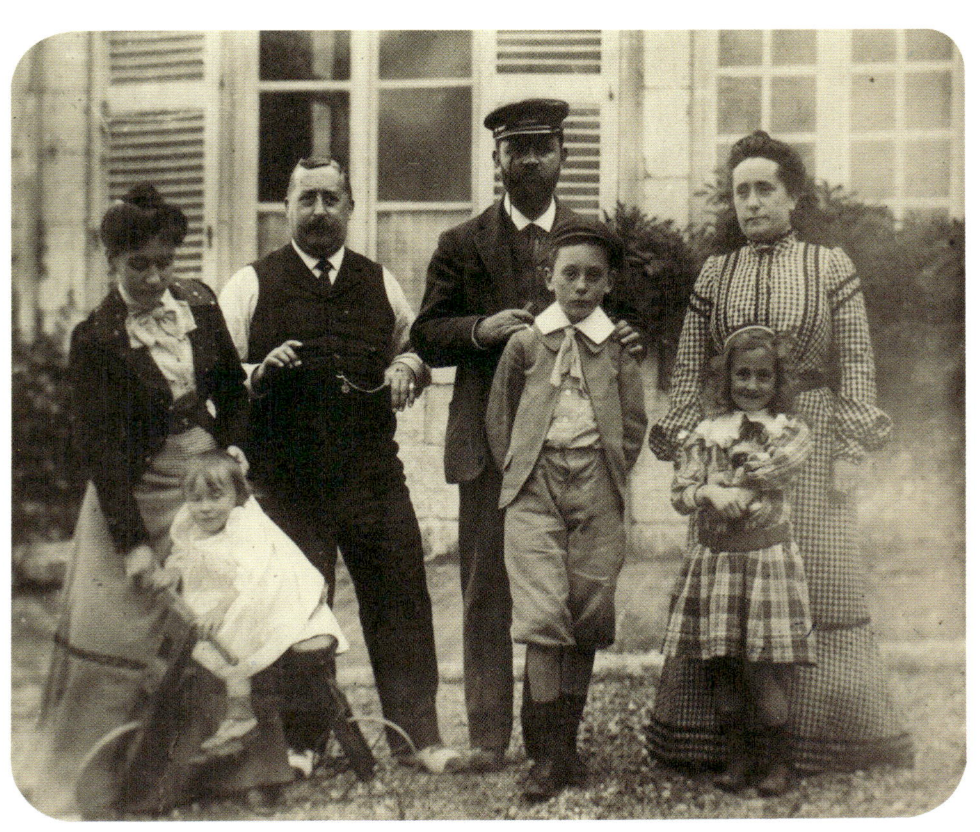

married two of his father's sisters, Marguerite and Geneviève (Tante Yéyé to Jacques), the latter of whom obliged her precocious nephew by writing down his dreams in a notebook entitled *Livre des rêves de Coco* (Coco's Book of Dreams; 1903). A photograph Jacques took in his bedroom at 40 rue Cortambert shows Yéyé's well-fed husband, Nononcle Auguste (Jacques' maternal uncle), a parody of bourgeois contentment, filling the frame, his son Dédé perched on his knee (p. 24, left). Jacques' bedroom, with its intricate wallpaper, features in several early photographs, whether of Jacques in bed with his cat Zizi (the shutter released by his nanny Dudu; below), a portrait of Dédé's sister Marcelle (p. 25), or a homemade glider strewn on the floor by Jacques' bed (p. 26). The painter Édouard Vuillard, known for his small-scale turn-of-the century domestic interiors, was among the first artists to use the camera as an aide-memoire to catch everyday moments. He then used his snapshots as a reference point or to reflect a mood, his abbreviated figures almost swallowed by the vibrant décor. Even the wallpaper pattern in one Vuillard interior (p. 24, right) is similar to that in Jacques' bedroom at rue Cortambert.

Lartigue's first photograph. From left to right: Geneviève Haguet (née Lartigue, known as Tante Yéyé), André Haguet (Dédé), Auguste Haguet (Nononcle Auguste), Henri Lartigue, Maurice Lartigue (Zissou), Marie Lartigue (née Haguet) and Marcelle Haguet. Pont-de-l'Arche, Normandy, 1902.

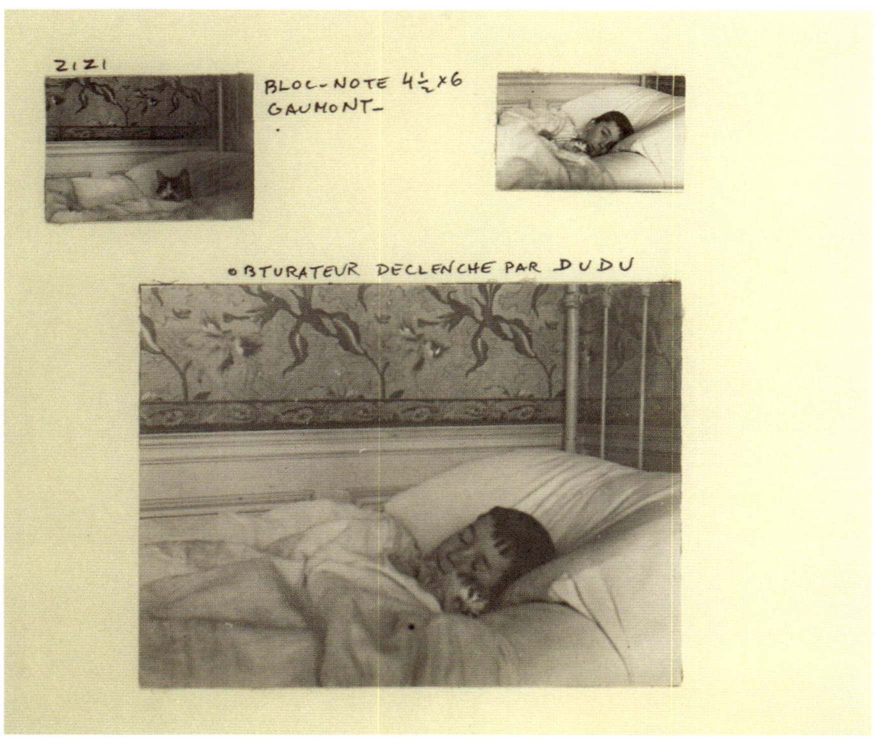

Lartigue in bed with his cat Zizi (album page detail, shutter released by Dudu, the Lartigue family nursemaid), 40 rue Cortambert, 1904.

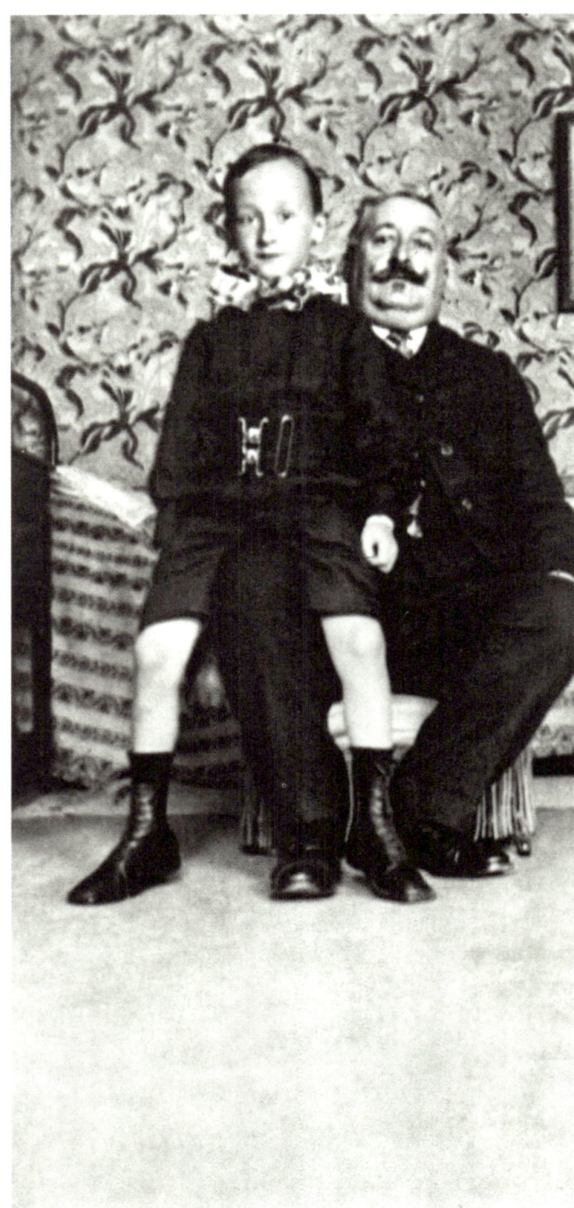

Nononcle Auguste and André Haguet (Dédé) in
Lartigue's bedroom, 40 rue Cortambert, 1906.

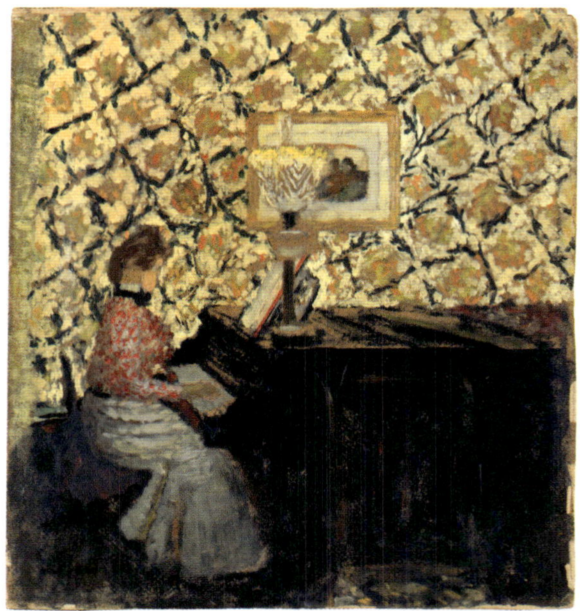

Édouard Vuillard, *Paris Interior (Misia at the Piano)*, oil on cardboard, 1895.

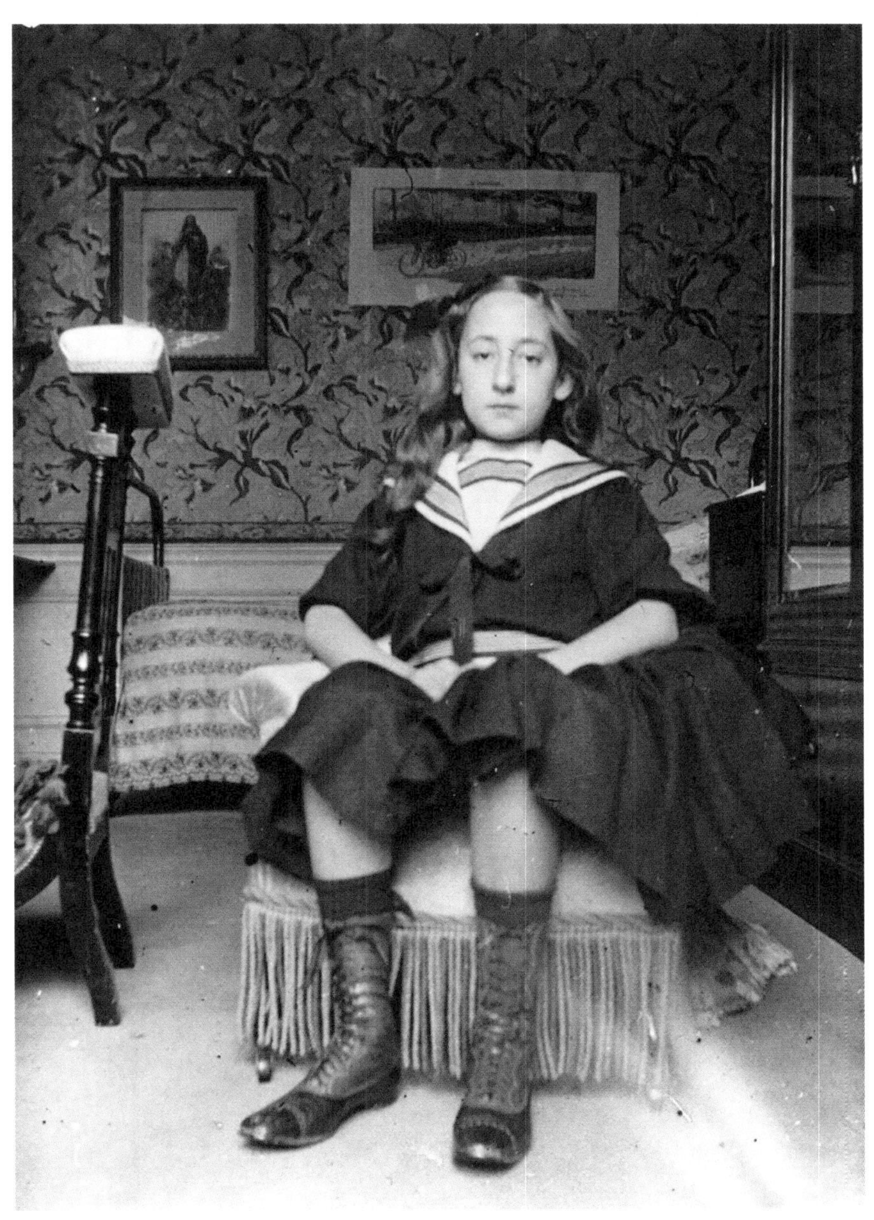

Marcelle Haguet in Lartigue's bedroom, 40 rue Cortambert, 1906.

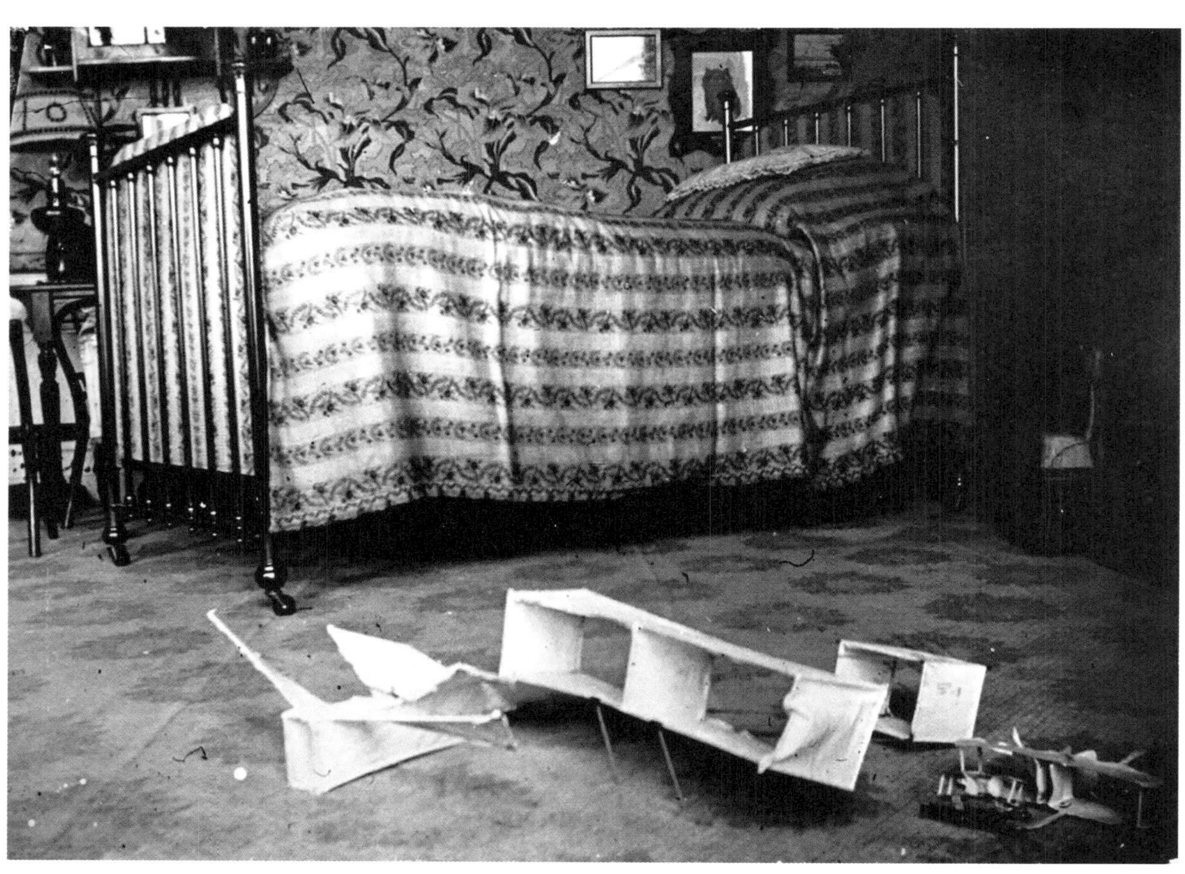

Lartigue's bedroom, 40 rue Cortambert, 1906.

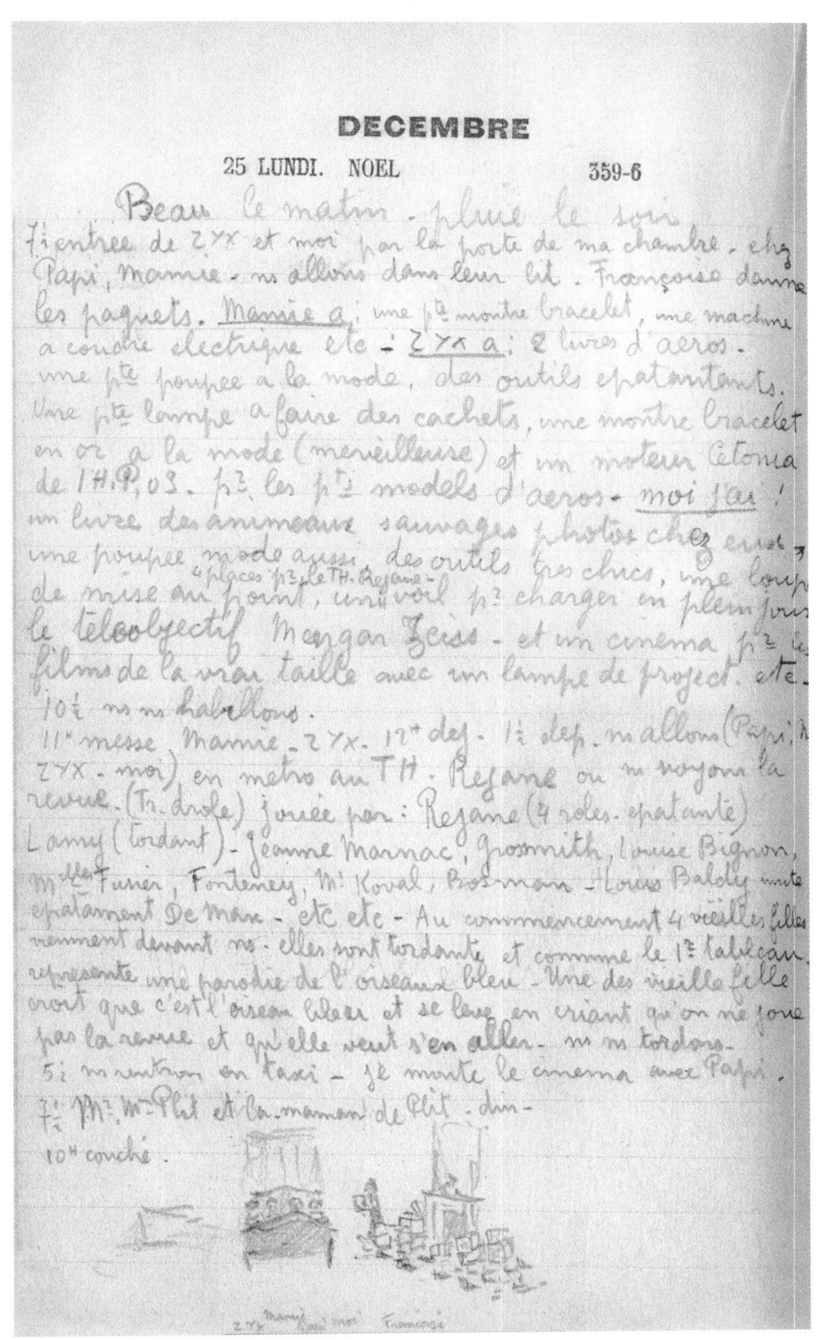

Page from Lartigue's diary, Christmas Day 1911, showing Lartigue and his family in bed.

The advent of the gelatin silver emulsion dry-plate process in the 1880s revolutionized photography. Its flexibility of use, combined with greater sensitivity, allowed enthusiasts to photograph from life, rather than from a stiff, static pose. The invention ushered in further improvements, enabling Henri to experiment with multiple cameras and techniques. Independent-minded as he was, Henri never joined any of the amateur photography clubs that sprang up in France in the late nineteenth century. While both Vuillard and fellow painter Pierre Bonnard, with whom he shared a studio, favoured the simple hand-held Kodak, first introduced in 1888, using flexible film instead of glass plates, serious amateurs like Henri saw photography as a branch of science. They purchased top-quality Krauss-Zeiss lenses and shutter releases, in addition to the latest cameras. With an eye for composition, Henri photographed landscapes, family portraits, stop-action images of motor cars or friends and family at play, as well as developing and printing his own photographs in his own darkroom. He subscribed to instruction manuals, periodicals with names like *L'Amateur Photographe* and *Photogazette* and reviews, exchanging ideas with fellow photography enthusiasts. Their numbers included his cousin Caroline's husband, Paul Roussel, whose photograph of the Eiffel Tower at the 1901 World's Fair appears on page 15 of this book; his friend, Hubert Laroze; the young Lartigue's tutor, Marius Aubert, who in addition to being a mathematics professor at the Sorbonne was assistant to Gabriel Lippmann, one of the inventors of colour photography; and the Swiss-born Monsieur Folletête ('Plitt' to Jacques), Henri's private secretary, who favoured a Vérascope Richard, a small stereoscopic camera.

Henri gave the quick, inquisitive, young Lartigue a series of cameras in varying formats, increasingly lightweight, smaller in size and faster in speed, starting in 1904 with the 4.5 × 6 cm Gaumont Block-Notes, the one Lartigue used the most: 'It was very modern for its time,' he explained.[13] The following year his father gave him a Folding Kodak Brownie No. 2 with roll film producing 6 × 9 cm images, which involved commercial rather than darkroom development. He sometimes borrowed his father's Gaumont Spido stereoscopic camera with its three-dimensional effect,[14] photographing aviation pioneer Gabriel Voisin taking off from the top of a sand dune in his Archdeacon glider in 1904 (see p. 130) or making a carefully constructed image of Zissou as he leaps arms outstretched from a boat hull at low tide

in imitation of his hero (below). Aged sixteen in 1910, Jacques received a
9 × 12 cm Klapp Takyr with Krauss-Zeiss lenses and a relatively fast shutter
speed of 1/1000 of a second, with which he took many of his perceptive, often
humorous photographs of women in the Bois de Boulogne (see Chapter
Four), using the buffer that a camera provides to frame moments which
might otherwise pass unnoticed. Towards the end of 1911, he acquired his
own Klapp Nettel stereoscopic camera (see note 14 on p. 181), favoured by
sports photographers with its shutter speed of 1/1200 of a second, far faster
than Lartigue's original Block-Notes with only 1/100 of a second. As with his
father's Gaumont Spido stereo, the Klapp Nettel's twin lenses converted to a
single 6 × 13 cm format with the flip of a lever, its elongated frame allowing
Jacques to take panoramic images.

Aided by his father, Jacques mastered both technical and aesthetic challenges, such as lighting and composition. The fledgling photographer also
learned various photographic tricks then popular among serious amateurs:

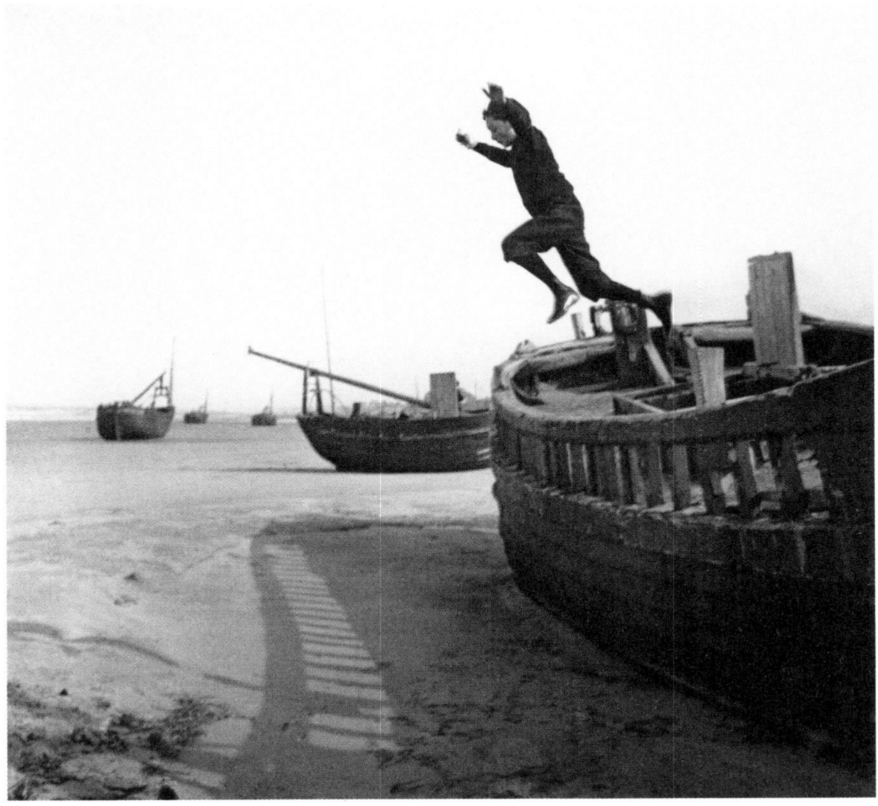

Zissou takes off, imitating
aviation pioneer Gabriel
Voisin, Merlimont, Pas-de-
Calais, 1904.

tilting a photographic print to steepen the horizon line for dramatic effect in a cycling image, for example, or using a double-exposure technique to create a 'spirit' photograph, like his image of a semi-transparent, ghost-like Zissou draped in a bedsheet as he closes in on a reclining boy, whose arms are outstretched in horror. More important were '*instantanés*', stop-action photographs that captured a world of people and objects in motion, spurred by Eadweard Muybridge and Étienne-Jules Marey's scientific investigations into the nature of movement in the 1870s and '80s. In an early photograph shot with his Brownie No. 2, Lartigue catches the moment his nanny throws a ball up into the air, and another with his cat Zizi springing up to catch a ball in the garden (below), and family friend Georges Bourard leaping over a cross-leg table perched on the front lawn at Pont-de-l'Arche in 1905 (opposite). The collaboration between father and son was undeniably close.

Dudu and Zizi in the garden at 40 rue Cortambert, 1904 (album page).

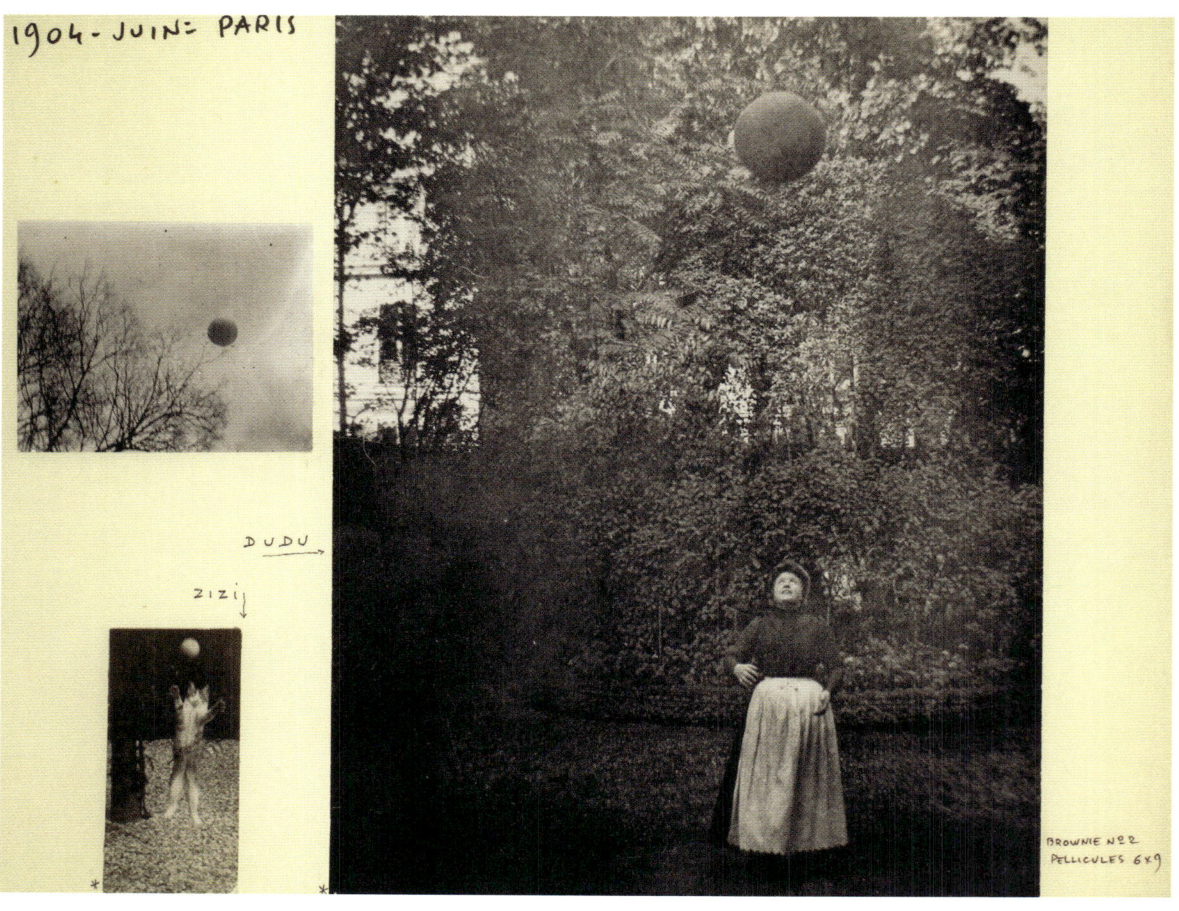

Indeed, Lartigue was happy to appropriate the odd Henri Lartigue photograph as his own. Martine d'Astier, former director of the Donation Jacques Henri Lartigue, has identified an image of Zissou leaping up at an angle, his beach ball suspended in mid-air, as one example. The full negative reveals crop lines excising the diminutive Jacques on the left, thus only his father could have taken the photograph.

The young Lartigue's ever-active imagination injected magic into his surroundings, without which he found mundane life inconsequential, even suffocating. Rarely without one of his cameras, he documented everything he enjoyed most: 'Every lovely, curious, strange or interesting thing gives me such pleasure that I am mad with joy! Even more so, since I can preserve so much, thanks to photography!'[15] Other children took photographs, particularly with the introduction of the simple, inexpensive, roll-film Kodak Brownie in 1900 that eliminated the task of developing and printing negatives, but none with the same drive or excitement in the creative process.

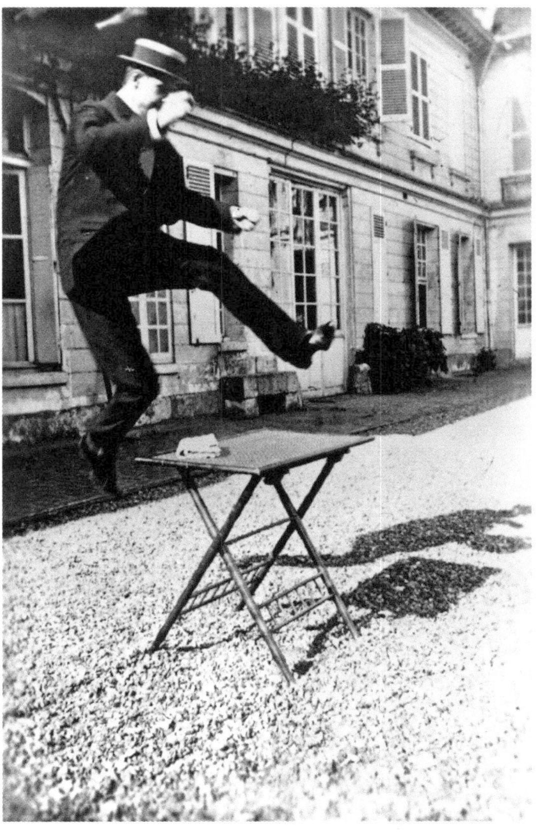

Georges Bourard, Pont-de-l'Arche, Normandy, 1905.

In 1904, the ten-year-old positioned his camera on a board placed across one end of his bath, setting the focus and exposure. He then asked his mother to press the shutter release, photographing him with the still water up to his neck, his toy hydro-glider floating next to him (below). A year later, he photographed a toy racing car rally on his bedroom floor (opposite). This time he placed his camera low down to give a child's-eye view of the scene, his cars dwarfed by a tall chest of drawers, the mantelpiece shrouded with a sheet. The mirror above reflects the far ceiling, adding to the mysterious, almost dizzying atmosphere. Another precise, original photograph taken from a low angle shows a spindly model aeroplane, its wheels balanced on a wooden floor like a runway. 'In my view, you cannot claim to have seen something until you have photographed it…', Émile Zola once said in an interview.[16] A talented, experimental photographer, the novelist took thousands of photographs, making his own prints in the years leading up to his death

Lartigue in his bath with his hydro-glider model (shutter released by Marie Lartigue), 40 rue Cortambert, 1904.

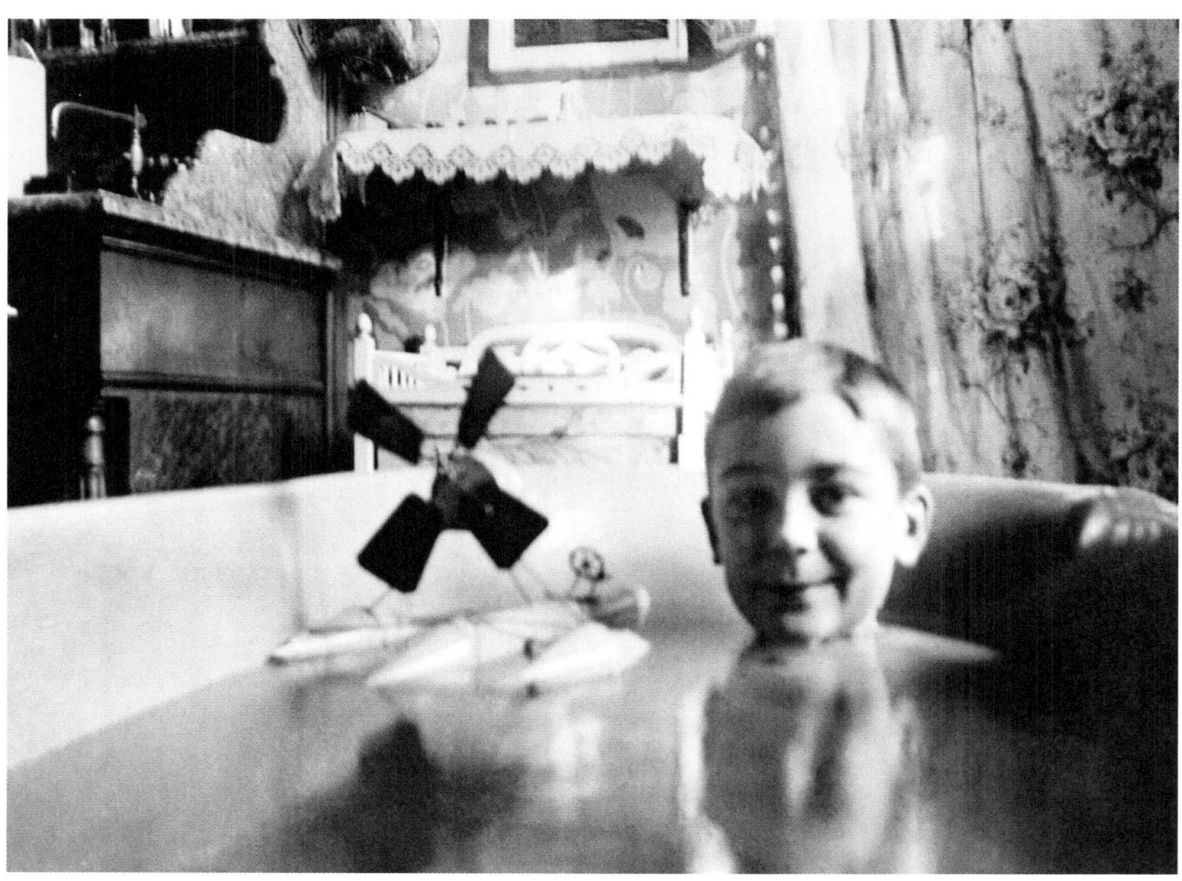

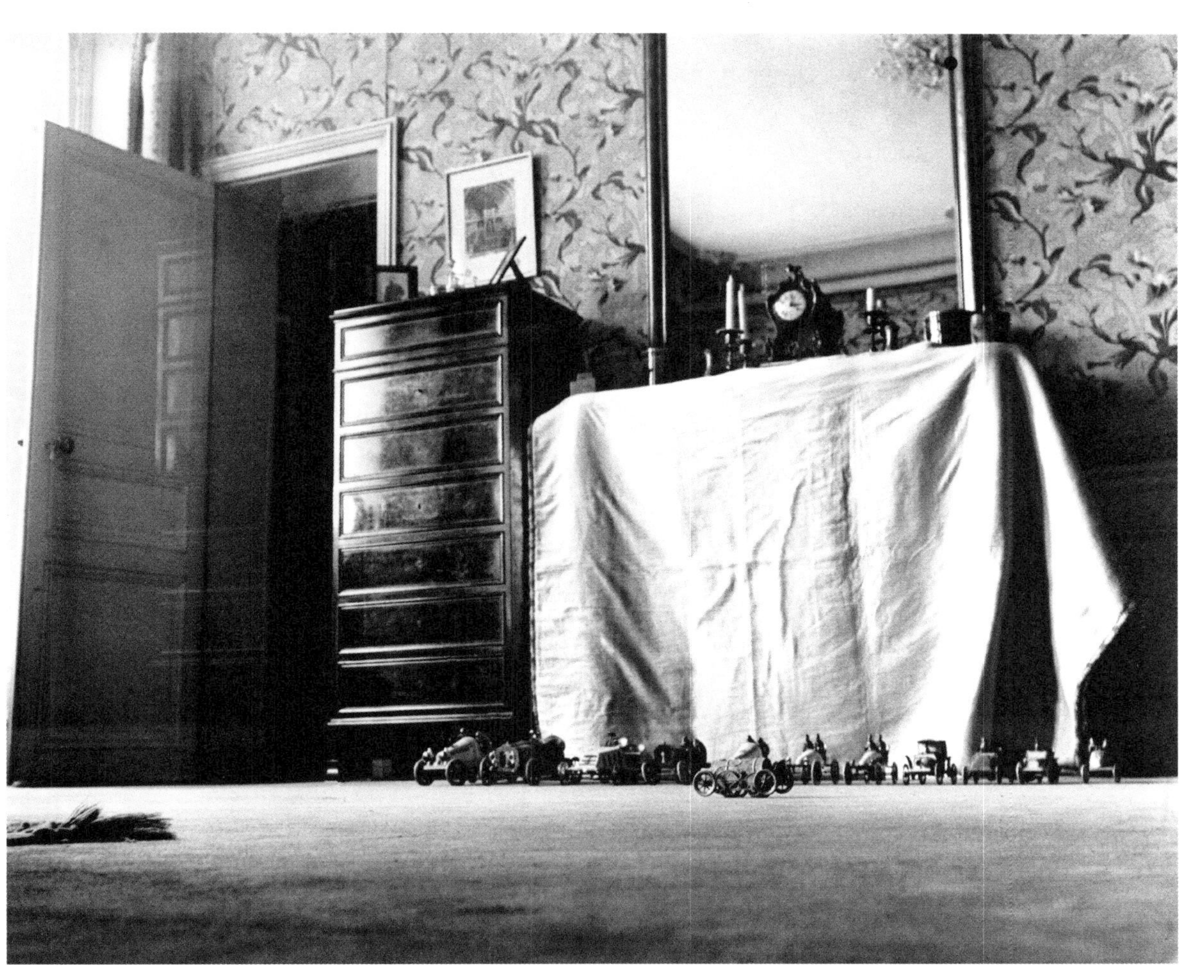

Lartigue's bedroom, 40 rue Cortambert, 1905.

in 1902. Lartigue might have expressed the same sentiment, as he examined and re-examined his own photographs, in his case partly to assuage his anxiety about the passage of time.

By the time Lartigue reached his late teens, Henri's private secretary, Monsieur Folletête, had started acting as his companion. Fellow enthusiasts, they often photographed together at the aerodrome at Issy-les-Moulineaux, the horse races at Auteuil, the Grand Prix at the Circuit de Dieppe in Normandy, and the Bois de Boulogne. They spent time developing photographs in the darkroom at rue Cortambert, or arranging them in the albums that Lartigue began in 1911, at the same time as his diaries, in which he noted the number of photographs he took per day and per month. Though he often developed his own negatives, Lartigue also ordered new, enlarged prints, as well as darkroom chemicals, from Poulenc Frères on the rue Vieille-du-Temple. 'When are you going to stop? You are going to ruin me at this rate!' pleaded his mother, to which Lartigue retorted in his diary:

Page from Lartigue's diary, 24 March 1912.

'Without telling her, I've decided to carry on until I'm almost eighteen!'[17] Lartigue would order new prints from old negatives throughout his life, working on his albums almost up until his death.

'I don't think he [Folletête] minds that Papa often tells him to spend time with me, instead of working as his secretary in the office,' wrote the teenager who photographed his companion in his suit and bowler hat as he sent his Jack Russell Tupy flying across a stream in the Bois de Boulogne (below), drawing the sequence in his diary that evening as an aide-memoire in case of a darkroom disaster (opposite). Blessed with a powerful visual memory, Lartigue sketched some of his best-known photographs even before he developed them. Folletête, who was fond of listening to the

Henri Lartigue's secretary, Monsieur Folletête (Plitt), with his dog Tupy, Bois de Boulogne, 1912.

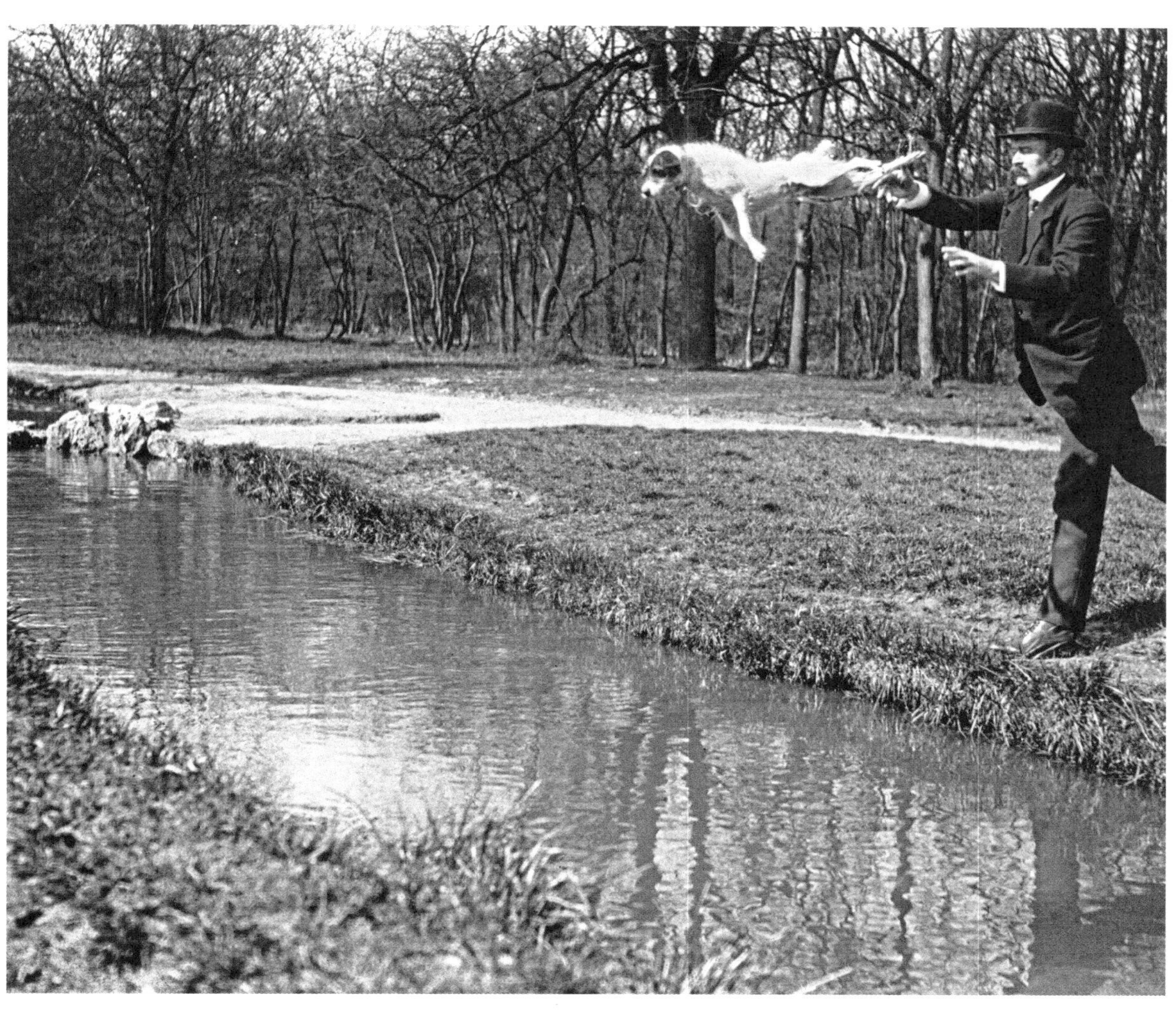

Barcarolle from Offenbach's operetta, *The Tales of Hoffmann*, photographed with his own Vérascope Richard. '[He] has been taking photographs for a long time…', wrote Lartigue, who sometimes borrowed the Vérascope. 'But what I find strange, and what annoys me a little, is that he always tries to take the same photo as me.'[18]

In 1911, his father gave him a Cinématographe, followed by a Pathé Professionnel for Christmas 1912 – both film camera-projectors, manually operated by a hand-crank. Over the next couple of years, Lartigue devoted time to filming (see p. 167). In April 1913 he even made a short dramatic film, set in the Bois de Boulogne, starring Jean Baldoni, an aspiring actor and cousin of the Roussels, and again at Rouzat in 1914. He also filmed fashionable women in the Bois de Boulogne, but more often he filmed sports such as tennis, skiing or skating, often printing individual frames as photographs. He screened these films at home, often after dinner parties, even selling several reels to Pathé, who showed them in cinemas.

The diary he began in 1911 details the countless films he saw (sometimes twice), whether short comedies, romances, detective stories or newsreels, often at the Cinérama on the Avenue de la Grande Armée, complete with a four-piece musical ensemble. With 260 film theatres in Paris alone by 1914, other forms of popular entertainment including street fairs and music halls dwindled. The Cirque d'Hiver (Winter Circus) became the Cinéma Pathé in 1907, and Léon Gaumont turned the Hippodrome on the rue Caulaincourt in Montmartre into Gaumont Palace in 1911, with over 3,000 seats. Lartigue visited the latter with an American friend, Henry S. Broadwater (Rico), to watch an early talking movie, both film and sound then recorded on separate equipment. Synchronization proved a limited success: 'On screen there's a singer. He makes operatic gestures, opens his mouth…. But sometimes the words come out when the gentleman's mouth is closed, and other times there's silence when his mouth is wide open.'[19]

On Fridays, the entire Lartigue family went to Les Vendredis de Fémina, a variety show at the Théâtre Fémina on the Champs-Élysées housed in offices owned by Pierre Lafitte, a publisher who exploited the burgeoning market for illustrated magazines as well as running a photographic studio and gallery. Henri Lartigue read *Excelsior*, Lafitte's illustrated daily newspaper first published in 1910, his wife favoured *Femina* magazine, while Jacques and Zissou subscribed to *Je Sais Tout* and *La Vie au Grand Air*, both illustrated with photographs. The latter magazine published a photograph that Lartigue took of an aeroplane swooping in the sky above Issy-les-Moulineaux on the front cover in February 1912 (see p. 139), the first of half a dozen images they used, including one of a paddle boat designed by Zissou at Rouzat the previous summer. That month, the family went to see the sixty-seven-year-old Sarah Bernhardt at Les Vendredis de Fémina, though Lartigue was unimpressed by her tremulous voice. While his maternal grandmother enjoyed family outings to open-air *café concerts* at Les Ambassadeurs or L'Alcazar d'Été, his mother, who subscribed to a Lafitte periodical entitled *Musica*, also took Jacques and his cousin Simone Roussel to a performance of Igor Stravinsky's *The Rite of Spring* by Diaghilev's Ballets Russes (conducted by the composer) at Auguste and Gustave Perret's early Art Deco masterpiece, the Théâtre des Champs-Élysées, in June 1913. 'What a cacophony!' said Madame Lartigue. '[But] I find it exciting to watch the dancers leap up like animals...', wrote her son, regretting that he was unable to photograph Nijinsky. 'The orchestra makes a deafening sound that fills me up, like all the great noises I love: aeroplane engines at Issy-les-Moulineaux, racing cars....'[20]

In addition to Les Vendredis de Fémina ('the most amusing day of the week'),[21] the family went to plays at La Renaissance and the Comédie Royale, as well as the cabaret music hall, the Folies Bergère, where spectators – a mix of aristocrats, rich bourgeoisie and skilled workers – could indulge in unpretentious tastes. A wide *promenoir* allowed visitors to stroll around or order drinks at the mirrored bar that Édouard Manet had already immortalized in his 1882 painting, *A Bar at the Folies Bergère*. There Lartigue, accompanied by Zissou or Monsieur Folletête and his wife, watched trapeze artists, bicycle acrobats, jugglers or short ballets. One evening he saw the Spanish-born actress, dancer and courtesan La Belle Otéro miming a mini-drama, followed by Dranem, a comic singer admired by Lartigue. On another occasion, he watched a performance by Régina Badet, an actress and dancer who was also a star at the Opéra Comique.

'I was only little', said Lartigue, describing a photograph he took of Régina Badet with his Klapp Takyr in the Bois de Boulogne in 1911 (see p. 103), though he was almost seventeen.[22] The prospect of leaving childhood filled him with dismay: 'Sometimes I find myself full of sorrow because I'm growing up. I would like to be able to stay as I am.... I often cried because I was growing up...this happiness won't last forever.'[23] Facing up to the hateful realities of adult life threatened the physical, emotional and intellectual flight he expressed in so many of his photographs. Sheltered from the outside world, he knew nothing of social or political unrest or the fierce conflict over the church that resulted in the 1905 law separating church and state. Nor, closer to home, was he aware of his father's business dealings. In early 1914, a Monsieur Chevallier-Kurt shot at Henri Lartigue in public, near the Arc de Triomphe: '*La Drame de la Place de l'Étoile*' (Drama on the Place de l'Étoile) wrote *Le Figaro* on 3 February. On his arrest, the gunman insisted he was not mad, claiming Henri Lartigue had ruined him – the incident hinting at a certain ruthlessness in Henri's quest for riches. 'The assailant is a man half-crazed. He asked Papa for a business paper that doesn't exist and, as Papa didn't give it to him, he shot him in the back at close range,' wrote the nineteen-year-old Lartigue in his diary.[24] 'Everything will continue as before,' he added on his father's return home from hospital three weeks later, a couple of bullets having been extracted from his torso. Sensitive and self-centred as Lartigue was, his ability to disconnect from reality if it became too threatening grew into a lifelong habit. 'Does hiding one's head in the sand like an ostrich mean being happy? Yes! Then let's hide our heads in the sand,' he argued.[25]

American academic Kevin Moore writes that Lartigue thought of photography as a chic, popular entertainment, like bicycling.[26] Yet the photographer's insouciance cloaked an underlying seriousness about his work, a restless desire for self-expression. Disciplined and capable of intense concentration, he kept a strict timetable, often rising at 6.30 a.m., at peace only if he had his photographs: 'I told myself this morning, before I left for the Bois with Zissou, that I was too tired to take my big camera, always so heavy... and that the weather wasn't good...that there wouldn't be many people...', the seventeen-year-old wrote in 1911. 'What it is to be lazy. Now I am truly sorry. I could have taken at least two photographs, if not more. (Two empty spaces in my album.)...'[27]

Lartigue later eked out a meagre living as a painter. His father lost a hefty chunk of his fortune after the First World War, then the remainder in the 1929 Wall Street Crash. Armed with a year's training at the Académie Julien in Paris, Lartigue often painted flowers and portraits of women, his colourful style influenced by his friend, the Fauve painter Kees van Dongen, who later became a popular society portraitist. Like van Dongen, Lartigue designed decorations for balls and galas at casinos on the rich Riviera in the 1930s. Though invited out by *le tout Paris*, he found it hard to make ends meet, particularly after the Second World War, sometimes exchanging a painting for a hotel room. '[People] imagine I'm very rich, when I'm not at all...', he told the critic Hervé Guibert for a series on photography for *Le Monde*, published in the 1980s, that included Henri Cartier-Bresson and Eugène Atget.[28] 'On the one hand, I was completely accustomed to Paris with all its luxuries...I would be invited to dinner at Maxim's, yet I had no money to pay for the *métro*.... I suffered terrible tortures when clients [for my paintings] didn't come along,' he added.

Despite Lartigue's early success selling images to *La Vie au Grand Air*, a career as a professional photographer was then deemed unsuitable for a young man from a good family. Critics also disparaged the medium as an art form. When French and British rare booksellers published beautiful volumes celebrating one hundred years of photography in the 1930s, the books sank without a ripple. By mid-century everyone was so inundated with photographic images that, even among collectors and experts, the simplest principles of evaluation threatened to get lost. After the war, Lartigue sold a handful of his photographs to Catholic periodicals such as *Fêtes et Saisons*. Then, in September 1954, *Point de Vue – Images du Monde*, a society and royalty magazine, published an article entitled *Aux Temps Heroïques d'Automobiles*, illustrated with Lartigue's images of pre-1914 car races (see Chapter Five). 'No one questions [Lartigue's] value as a painter but, who knows, he may one day be more famous as a photographer, he who took photographs for personal amusement alone,' wrote Albert Plécy, the magazine's editor.[29] Photography came sharply back into focus as television took over many of the medium's practical roles. But Lartigue never managed to persuade French museums or the Cabinet des Estampes at the Bibliothèque Nationale to interest themselves in his Belle Époque photographs: 'Yes, yes, we already have lots of pictures from 1910,' Jean Adhémar, at the latter institution, is said to have argued.[30]

It was only when the Hungarian-born Charles Rado at the Rapho press agency in New York famously introduced Lartigue to MoMA's John Szarkowski that the sixty-nine-year-old's life changed almost overnight. Szarkowski's exhibition of Lartigue's Belle Époque photographs at MoMA in 1963, followed by a ten-page spread in LIFE magazine in November that year, garnered praise, and his talents were then called upon by fashion magazines such as *Harper's Bazaar*. Georges Tourdjman, a French photographer enlisted to retouch a handful of Lartigue's images for a television advertisement for LIFE, recalled his astonishment at their quality, given that few had ever heard of the photographer. He also remarked upon the dapper Frenchman's 'extraordinary youthfulness'. *Diary of a Century*, a volume devoted to Lartigue's sixty-year oeuvre, edited by Richard Avedon, appeared seven years later, in 1970. Enthralled by his work, the American photographer helped seal Lartigue's reputation as a twentieth-century master. The French art establishment, meanwhile, embraced the ageing photographer as a part of their cultural heritage, rewarding him with his first museum exhibition in Paris at the Musée des Arts Décoratifs in 1975, followed five years later by a retrospective at the Grand Palais entitled 'Bonjour Monsieur Lartigue'.

Kevin Moore describes Lartigue as a 'natural self-promoter, and nostalgic raconteur'.[31] Somewhat disingenuous, Lartigue knew that part of the enchantment of his images lay in the nostalgia that clung to the Belle Époque, in an era then overshadowed by the tumultuous events of the twentieth century. An elastic view of time in his memoirs and interviews also reveals a wish to enhance his image as a child genius. Yet taking photographs was for much of his life a solitary project, done for his understanding and fulfilment alone. Alive with boyish vision, combined with a formal beauty, his photographs defy classification. 'For my father, happiness was a constant battle. To overcome his chronic anxiety, he needed to prove to himself, through his indelible images, that this happiness buried deep inside of him was his raison d'être,' explained his son, Dani Lartigue, in April 2003.[32] There is also a lingering assumption in some quarters that, because these photographs were taken by a privileged amateur, about his own world, away from lofty theories of creation, they remain somehow trivial or irrelevant. 'His work upsets both the status of the artist as photographer and the definition of photography itself,' argues the French photographic historian Michel Frizot.[33] All spectators need to do is stand back and admire.

During the nineteenth century, an 'irresistible awakening of a collective desire for the shore' took hold among well-heeled Parisians.[1] Fashionable seaside resorts such as Deauville first sprang up under Napoleon III, who drove a railway network through France in the 1860s. Seaside visits became an annual fixture for the rich Belle Époque *bourgeoisie* for whom remaining in Paris in July and August was, in any case, unthinkable. While Jacques' mother, Marie Lartigue, enthused about *'le bon air'* outside Paris, Docteur Variot, the family physician, believed there was nothing better to relieve the headaches that plagued her younger son: 'Happy migraines, thanks to which I'm so often allowed to swap "dull ramblings about the past" in my history lessons with a marvellous reality, filled with the unknown, with light, with the future...', remembered Jacques, who baulked at having his liberty curtailed by timetables.[2] The seaside, in particular, caught his imagination: 'The beach is the most enormous place in the world. You can run there "without limit", and no one shouts at you to be careful. Nothing hinders my eyes from roaming, drifting endlessly into the distance, any more.'[3]

The Lartigue family travelled to the coast by train or, later, in Henri's series of open-topped motor cars, including a red 24 HP Panhard et Levassor he purchased in 1906. Uncles, aunts and cousins joined them. The family first visited Ambleteuse in 1897, a village between Calais and Boulogne then popular with visitors from Paris eager for the cold, turbulent seawater, deemed beneficial to the health, as well as fresh oysters from local beds built to enhance the *bourgeois* ambience. 'Ambleteuse. The sea! Despite my travelling shoes, which prevent me from running into the water, I go quickly, quickly to see the beach before anyone stops me...'[4] Henri Lartigue and his wife's cousin, Marcel van Weers, accompanied the children to the rocks at low tide, where pools of water with waving seaweed reflected the sky: 'When the sun comes out from behind a cloud, it illuminates the bottom of a pool,

and you can even surprise a fish…which swims off at the speed of lightning
to hide in the crevices of rocks or under plants.'[5]

Lartigue took a series of seaside photographs seven years later, in 1904.
Anxious to preserve all that captured his interest, the ten-year-old now
rarely left the house without his new folding Gaumont Block-Notes made
in Paris with glass plates, 4.5 × 6 cm in size. With a surprisingly sophisticated grasp of composition, he captured a group of paddlers at low tide, the
girls in dresses and enormous hats, giving the viewer a feeling of being able
to walk straight into the photograph, or Zissou in mid-flight jumping off
a fisherman's boat on the sand (see p. 29). Another image, taken that same
year at Villerville, a seaside village in Normandy, shows his cousin and
first love, Simone Roussel, standing alone on the beach with a dog, her
ringlets topped with a *broderie anglaise* cap (below). Bored by boys his own
age, Lartigue found in Simone an ideal playmate. In his 1951 memoir,

Simone Roussel, Villerville,
Normandy, 1904.

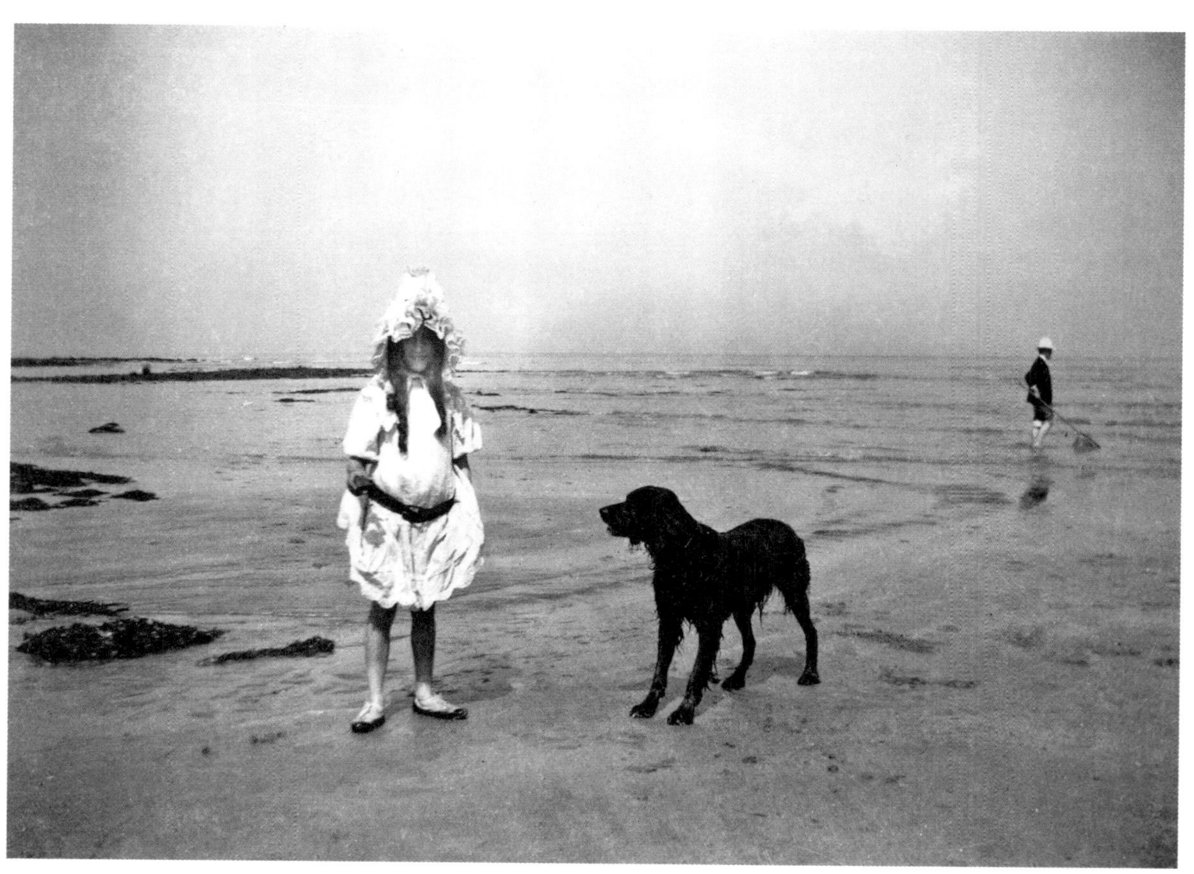

Speak Memory, Vladimir Nabokov describes his own boyhood love for a ten-year-old Parisian girl on the beach at Biarritz, where he travelled with his family from pre-revolutionary St Petersburg in 1909: 'Since my parents were not keen to meet hers, I saw her only on the beach; but I thought of her constantly…', recalled the novelist. 'One day, as we were bending together over a starfish, and Colette's ringlets were tickling my ear, she suddenly turned toward me and kissed me on the cheek.'[6] Nabokov describes the beach at Biarritz almost like a Lartigue photograph: 'Along the back line of the "*plage*", various seaside chairs and stools supported the parents of straw-hatted children who were playing in front on the sand.' Lartigue visited the Basque resort with his parents in 1905, photographing a garden party in honour of Edward VII through the railings of the Hôtel du Palais overlooking the sea. His image of the beach, taken with his Block-Notes camera, shows clusters of children, the boys in sailor suits, standing

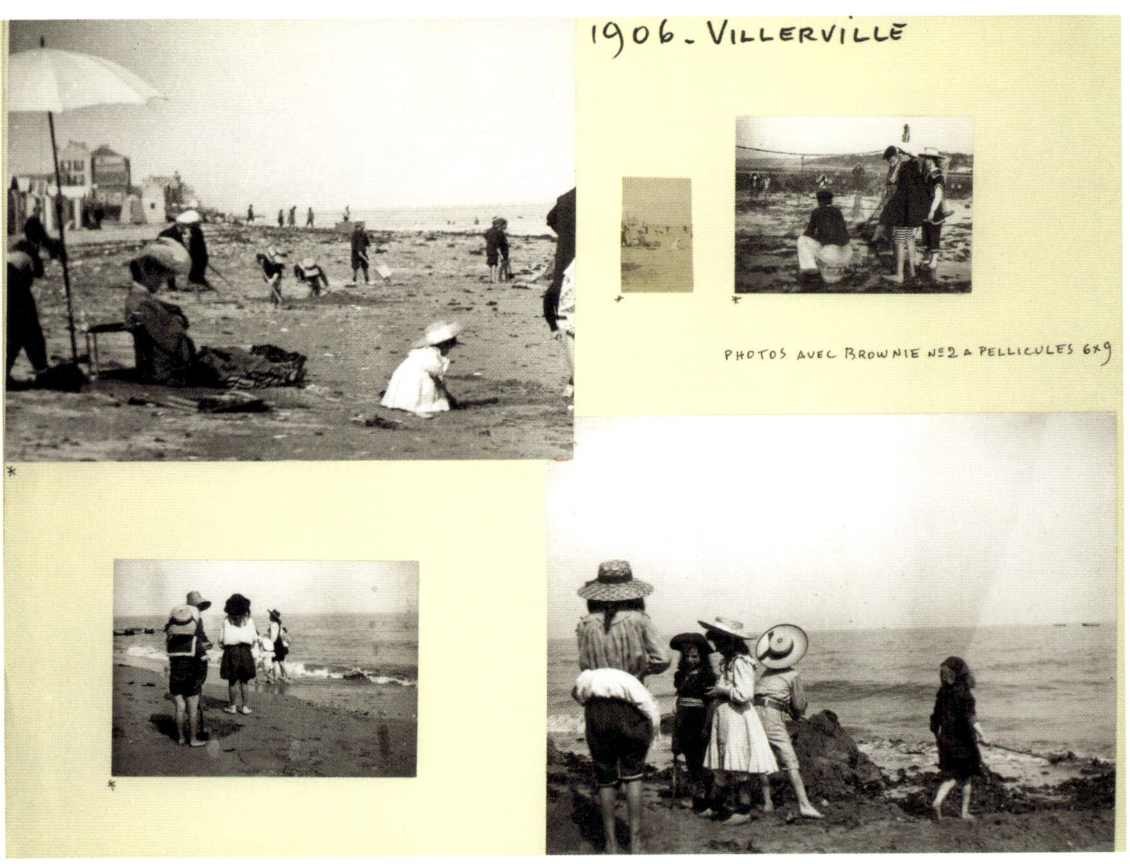

transfixed as they watch a man flying a giant winged box kite in the stiff sea breeze (opposite).

Back in Villerville, the bearded Monsieur Plantevigne, a family friend, immaculate in his white suit and cap, strides into the frame casting a sharp shadow in the sand, while Lartigue's cousin Caro Roussel (Simone's older sister) gathers the skirts of her narrow-waisted dress from behind as she stands looking out to sea, her angled parasol providing a perfect compositional counterpoint (pp. 48–9). Photographing this time with a Kodak No. 2 Brownie, with roll film producing images 6 x 9 cm in size, Lartigue seizes the moment with a click of a button, the fleeting scene frozen forever in time.

Plantevigne doubtless enjoyed nearby Trouville, with its half-timbered Belle Époque villas perched almost on the beach. Once a fishing village, it turned into a resort in the mid-1860s when a train line opened from the Gare Saint-Lazare in Paris. *Le tout Paris* fled the capital in early July to gather at Trouville or its racier neighbour, Deauville: 'The boring vexations of modern life take on a particular intensity in summer, at that moment when the Parisian remaining in Paris is given over to solitude and is no longer taken away from himself by dinners, parties, visits – the contact at every moment of bustling humanity,' wrote the critic Edmond de Goncourt of the tedium of Paris in high summer, when even theatres and opera houses closed their doors.[7] At both resorts, the upper-crust enjoyed the same life as in the capital: *salons de thé*, where women gathered in the afternoon; open-air dinners; performances by stars from the Folies Bergère or Opéra Comique, including Régina Badet (see pp. 103 and 107), tennis, golf, swimming or the races at the hippodrome in Deauville. Even the reclusive Marcel Proust planned a holiday near Trouville with various distractions, including outings in a hooded motor car. The trip fell through, leaving only the memory of a holiday that had never taken place.

Over thirty-five years after Claude Monet painted Trouville's Hôtel des Roches Noires with figures promenading along the seafront below, Lartigue captured the hotel from another angle (p. 50), with steps leading down to rows of striped bathing huts, a man standing, arms akimbo in his striped bathing suit. Most stylish women, known as '*les élégantes*', did not swim, preferring to take in the sea air perched bolt upright on folding chairs (see pp. 51–3). Feathered hats, veils, gloves and parasols protected their skin from the sun. Lartigue photographed them on the white-pebbled beach at nearby

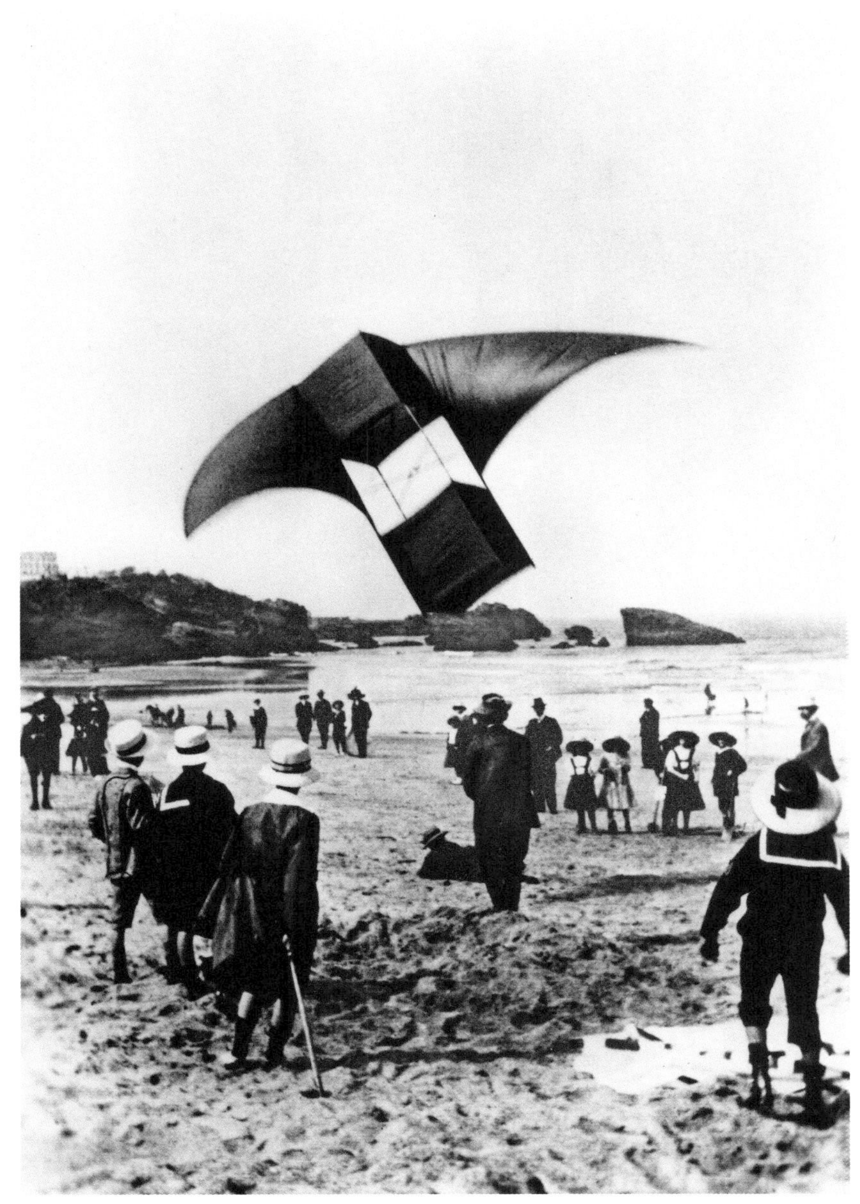

Biarritz, 1905.

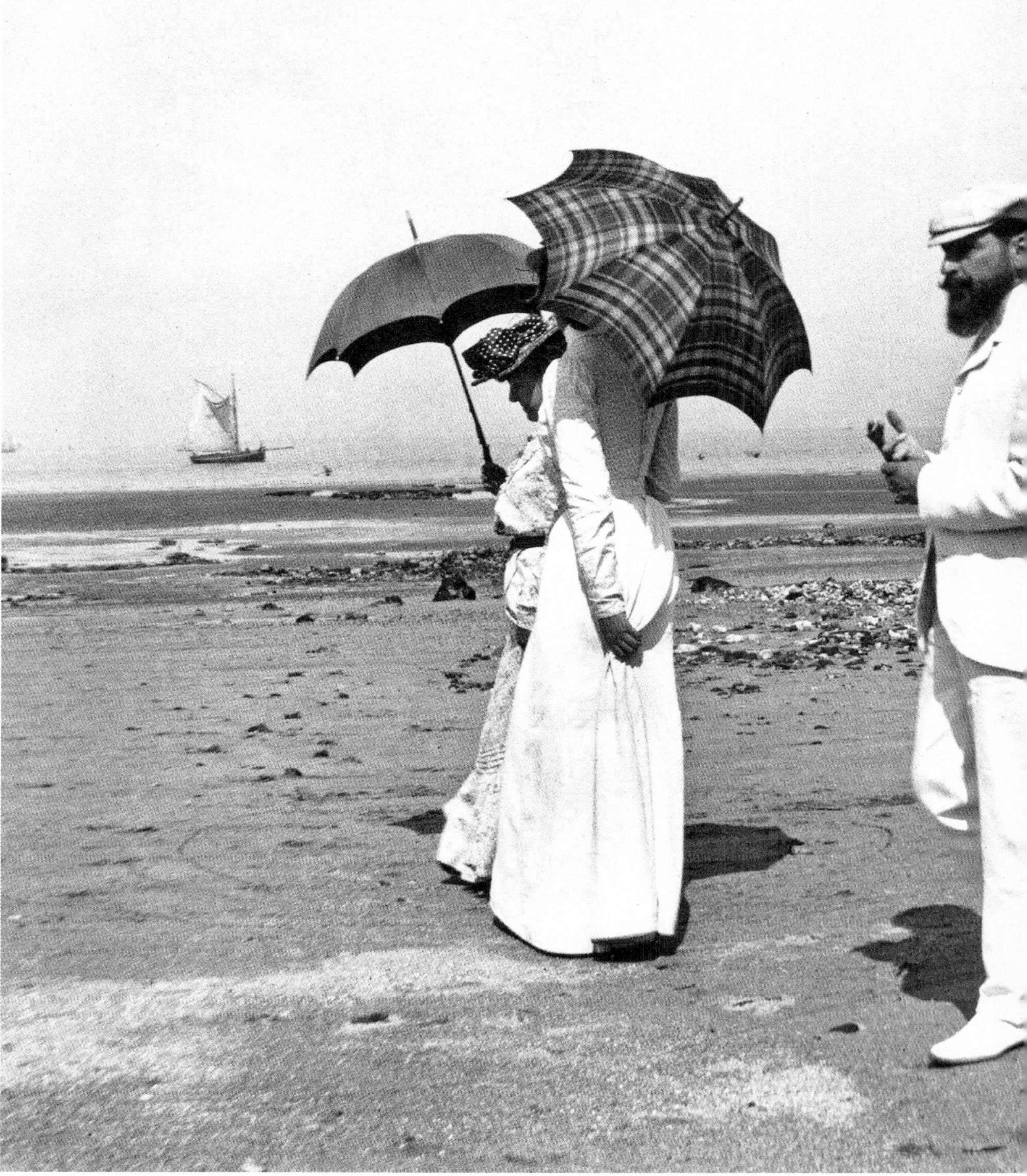

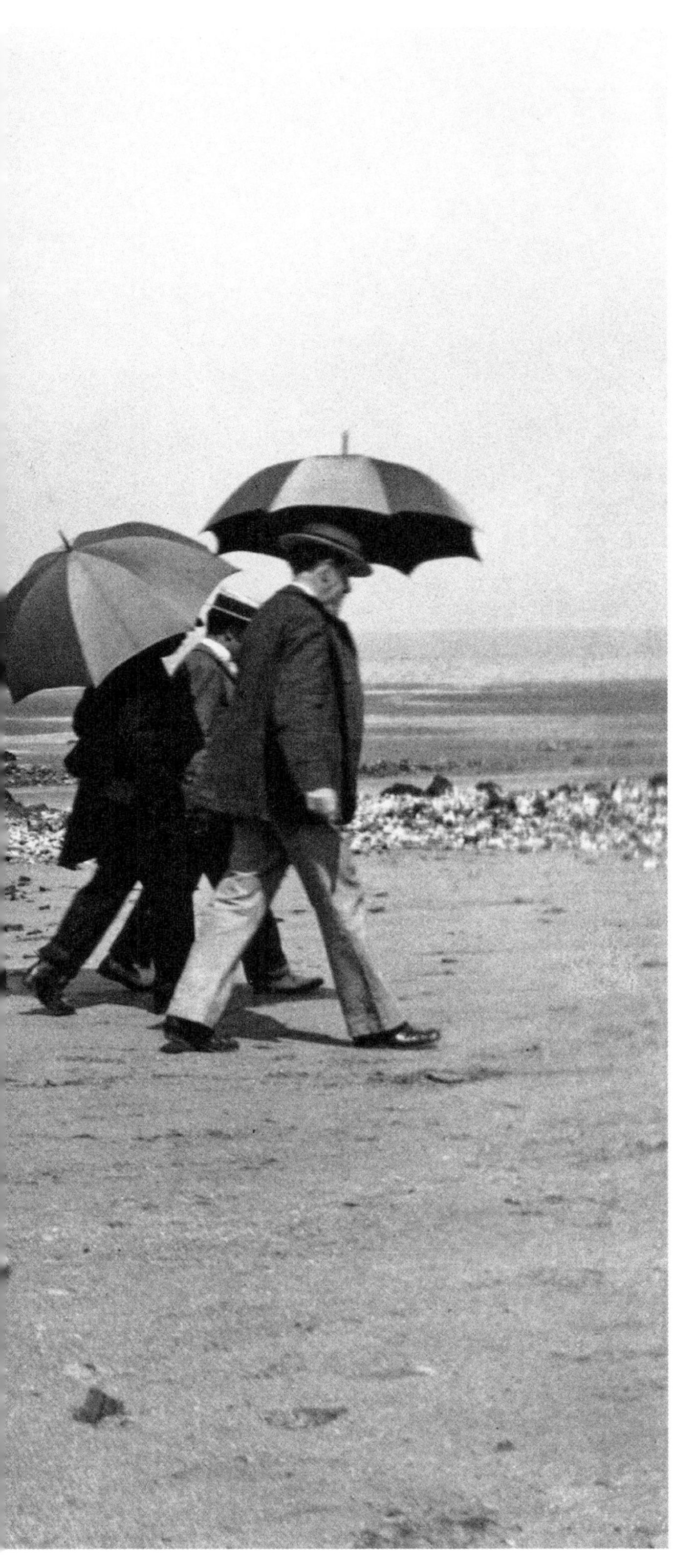

Caroline Roussel (Caro) and Monsieur
Plantevigne, Villerville, Normandy, 1906.

Étretat, its white chalk cliffs carved by the sea into arches and needles, familiar from Monet's paintings. The Parisian literary periodical *Gil Blas* describes a scene at Étretat in 1901: 'Seated in convivial groups on the shingle, spectators, lorgnettes in hand, watch that ever-appealing summer spectacle: a pretty young woman entering the water to emerge a few minutes later like Amphitrite, goddess of the sea.'[8]

One of Lartigue's photographs taken at Étretat in July 1907 shows a stocky man, his bearded profile visible as he sits facing the sea, his back to the camera (p. 53). A seated matron dominates the foreground, her giant feathered hat jutting out like the prow of a ship. 'I think this is the great musician Claude Debussy,' Lartigue wrote in his 1907 album, in which he pasted an enlarged print of his snapshot. In his book *Debussy à la plage* (2018),

Trouville, Normandy, 1906.

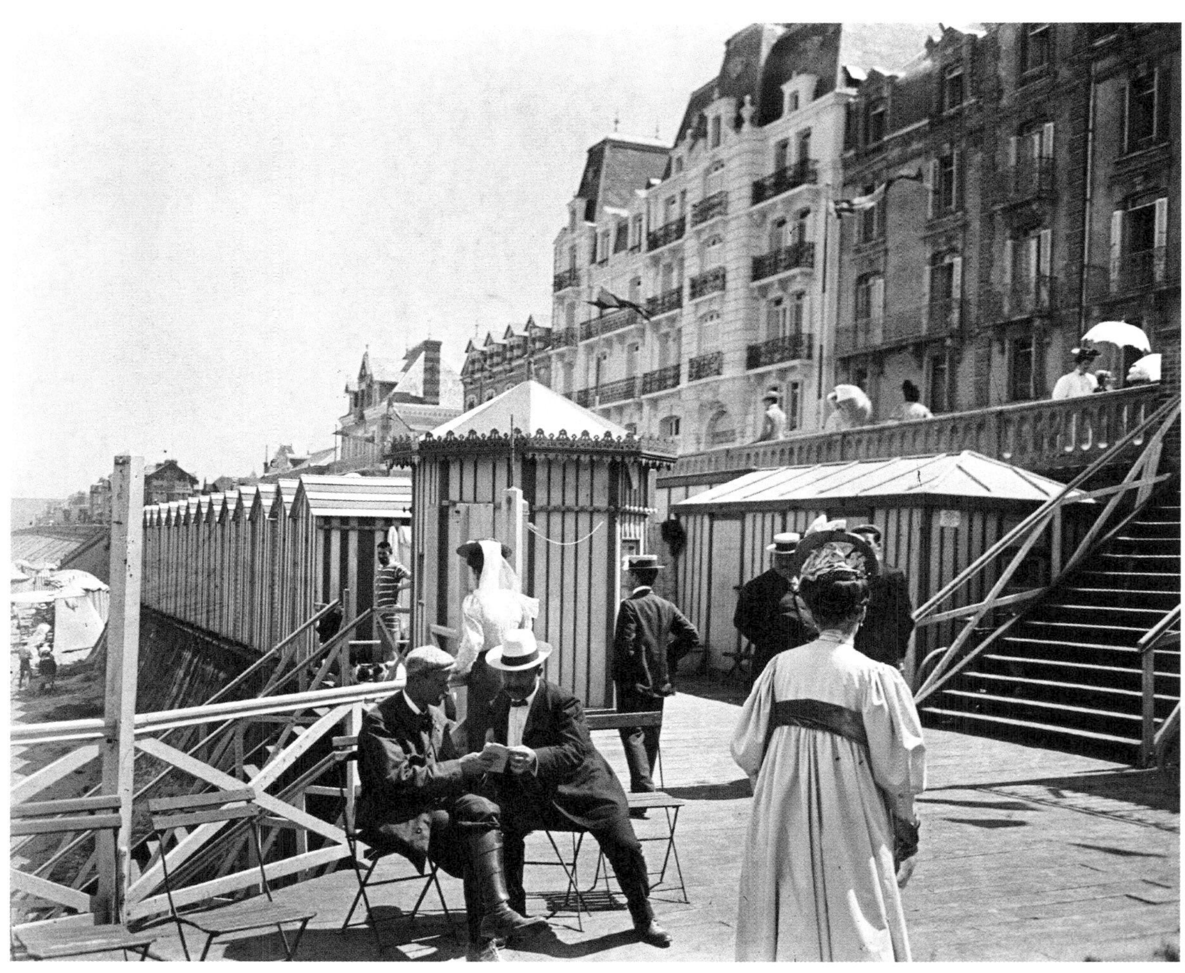

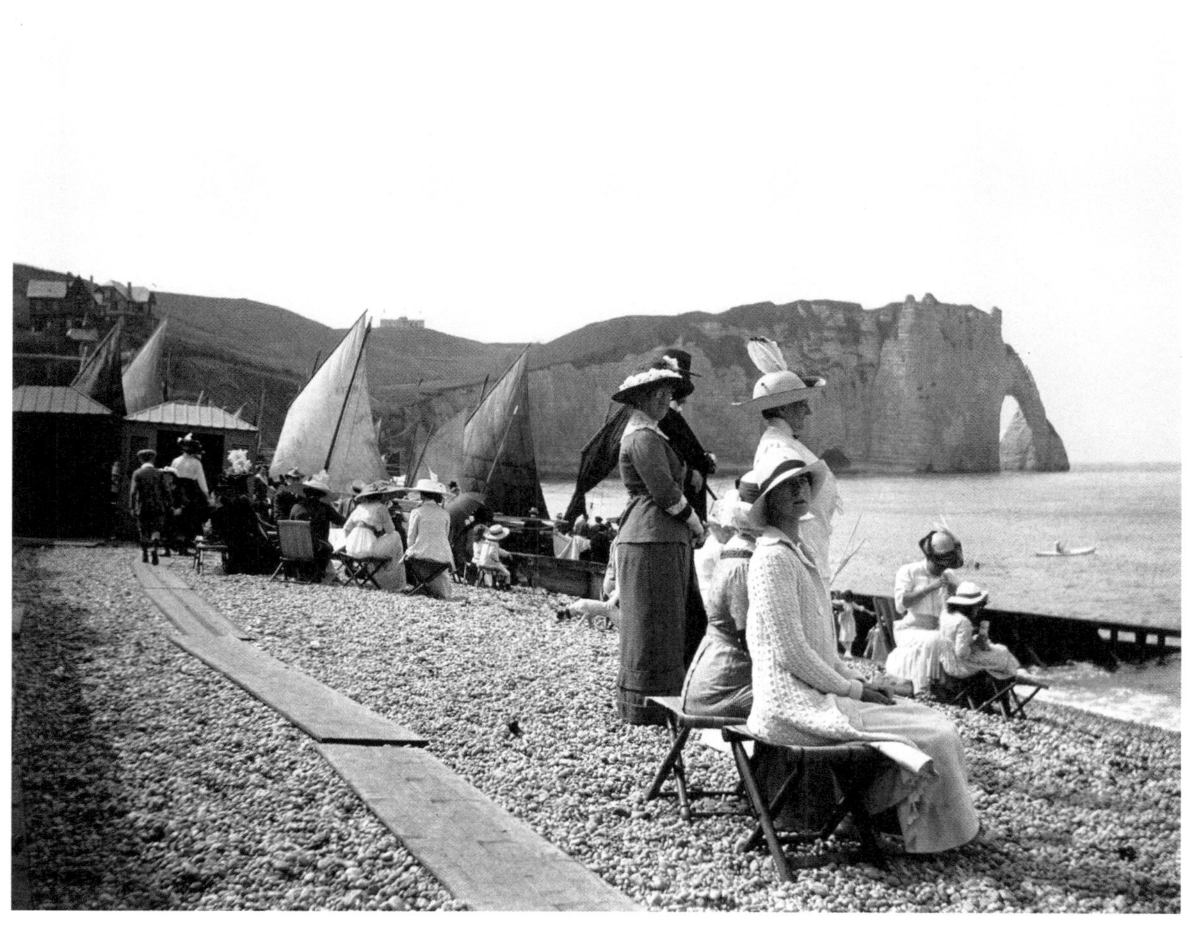

Étretat, Normandy, 1913.

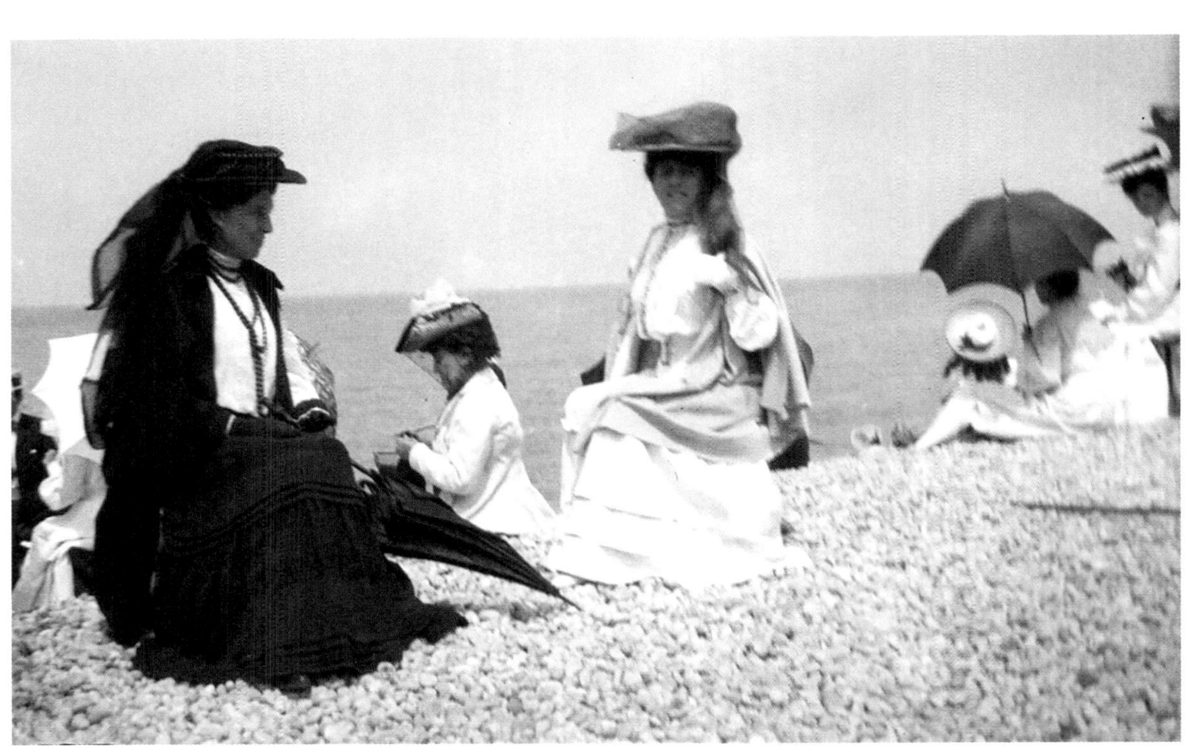

Rémy Campos, music history professor at the Conservatoire de Paris, confirms the identity of the French composer whose groundbreaking music ushered in the twentieth century. Debussy's mistress Emma Bardac, whom he married in 1908, sits to the composer's right. Back in Paris, Debussy lived a stone's throw from the Lartigues at 80 Avenue du Bois de Boulogne (now Avenue Foch) in a *hôtel particulier* set back from the street. Lartigue, who began photographing women parading past his lens in the Bois de Boulogne in 1910, again unknowingly captured Emma Bardac, this time together with Chouchou, her daughter with Debussy, in May 1911. As Campos points out, 'People [in fashionable places] were already being photographed regardless, caught in the lens of innumerable snapshot cameras.'[9] Though he never played an instrument, Lartigue owned a pianola, a self-playing piano, with pre-programmed music recorded on perforated paper, popular in early

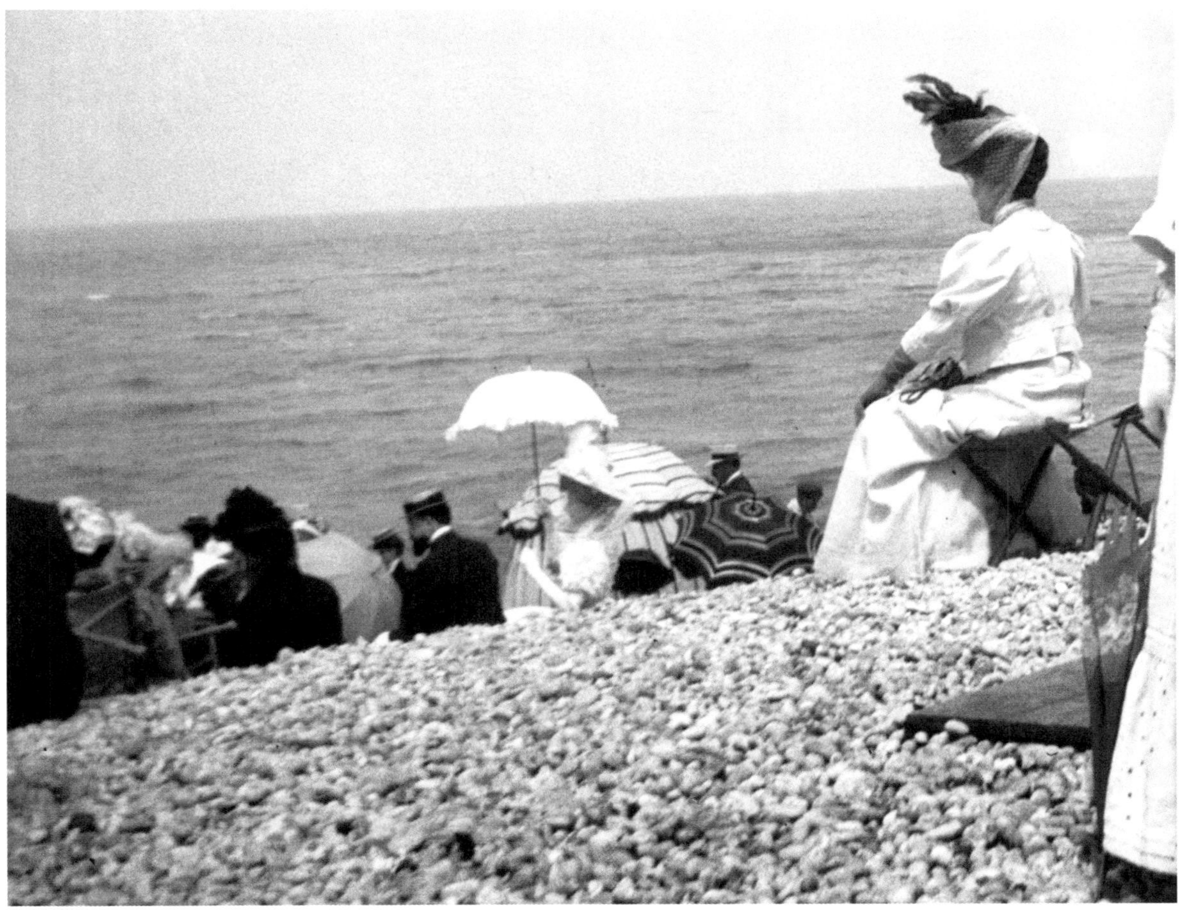

twentieth-century Europe. His collection included work by Debussy. 'I've just received [a] new parcel [of recordings],' he wrote in his diary. 'Scheherazade by Rimsky-Korsakov and the Petite Suite by Debussy.... I've just tried them out. It's marvellous: when my brain receives a shower of music, I imagine, imagine, imagine everything that I'm going to do, and everything that I would like to do but that is impossible....'[10]

While Debussy and his wife remained in Paris during the winter, Paris society travelled south from January to March to the heated hotels and villas of Nice, Cannes, Antibes and Monte-Carlo. As with the summer resorts of Trouville and Deauville, the arrival of the railway in the mid-1860s helped develop the Riviera as a winter destination. By 1900, new train services brought travellers via Paris from all over Europe. What the trains lacked in speed (the night express from Paris to Nice took over twelve hours), they made up for with opulent, dark blue *wagons-lits* and dining cars. According to a periodical entitled *La Grande Vie*, Parisian ladies of 'both great and easy

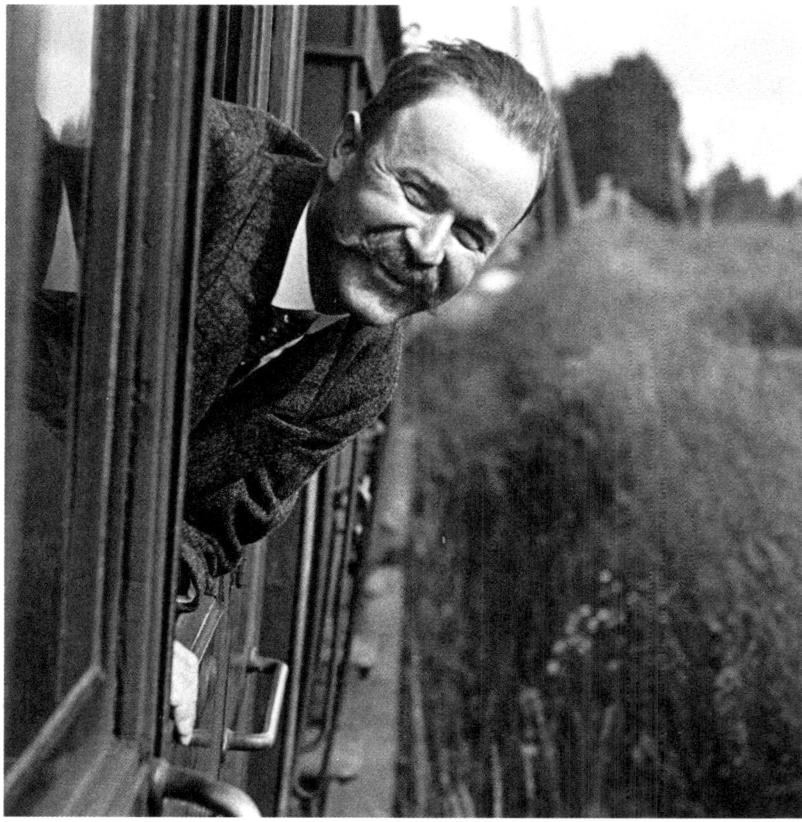

Monsieur Folletête (Plitt)
on the train to Tréport,
Normandy, 1912.

virtue' arrived in Nice with trunks replete with 'beach dresses all in white, dresses for the villa…yachting dresses with sailor-collars in lace, décolleté evening dresses, and leather costumes with "musketeer" gloves for driving in motor cars'.[11] Anxious to preserve their pale skin, the pre-1914 smart set shunned the Riviera during the summer months.

In April 1911, as winter visitors (known as '*les hivernants*') were returning to Paris, the sixteen-year-old Lartigue took the night express train at 7.30 p.m. from the Gare de Lyon to Nice, accompanied by his parents, grandmother, Zissou and cousin Raymond (known as Oléo) van Weers, as well as Robert and Louis Ferrand. Lartigue carefully loaded his camera in advance, his albums now expanding to two volumes per year. At 8 a.m. the following morning, the photographer stood in the train corridor to watch the Mediterranean landscape rushing past: 'I look at the sea, the reflection on the horizon, the red rocks, and everything, everything, everything! In Paris it was all a bit grey; here, it's the opposite of grey.'[12] Jacques and Zissou hurried

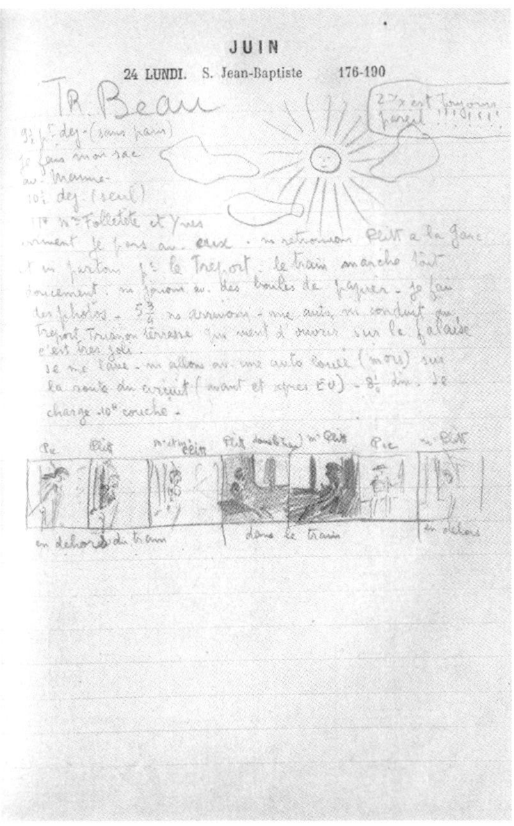

Page from Lartigue's diary, 24 June 1912.

to Monte-Carlo by train to see a motor-boat race, though Jacques was in the end too high up to photograph the sprays of seawater. At an aerodrome by the sea near Nice, he snapped one of his heroes, aviation pioneer Gabriel Voisin, experimenting with his new 'Voisin' bi-plane, hovering just above the sea, then flying up again to land next to Jacques. Henri Lartigue rented a 15 HP Panhard et Levassor motor car for excursions to the hills above Nice and Monte-Carlo, where his son photographed Zissou and his friends, their figures silhouetted against the sea far below.

By the early 1900s, Nice boasted bright new villas, apartment blocks, offices, banks and galleries of shops decorated with ornate plasterwork and cupolas. Electrified trams had replaced horse-drawn models, while winter entertainments included an indoor skating rink and a cinema. There, Jacques, Zissou and their friend Georges Bourard saw their first talking movie, shown on the '*chronophone Gaumont*'. Film pioneer and inventor Léon Gaumont first demonstrated this synchronized film and sound system in Paris in 1910. But, as with his visit to the Gaumont Palace in Paris with Henry S. Broadwater in January 1912, Lartigue was disappointed: poor recording quality rendered the sound scratchy and too fast. At night, he photographed Nice's brightly lit Casino de la Jetée-Promenade, a Belle Époque landmark perched at the end of a pier, seeming to float on the dark sea. There the actress, dancer and courtesan La Belle Otéro, who was also a compulsive gambler, lost eight million francs over just a few weeks in 1910, selling off jewelry to pay off her debt.

During the day, Lartigue loaded and reloaded his camera in a window-less bathroom at his Tante Amélie's rented villa, walking to photograph the palm tree-lined Promenade des Anglais overlooking the sea. The Mediterranean blue skies offered a sharp contrast to the changeable weather and watery reflections in Normandy, in Biarritz, or even amid the trees of the Bois de Boulogne. The young Jacques announced, '[I've already taken] a fashion photograph. It's brighter, but less mysterious....'[13] After the First World War, he photographed pedestrians struggling along the storm-lashed Promenade des Anglais, its palm trees bending in the wind, lending an uncharacteristic tinge of melancholy. In Biarritz he focused his lens on a lone man seen from behind as he watches the sea lashing against the rocks. 'Wind, rain, waves are the only three things that can find a little door into my memory,' he wrote in 1927.[14]

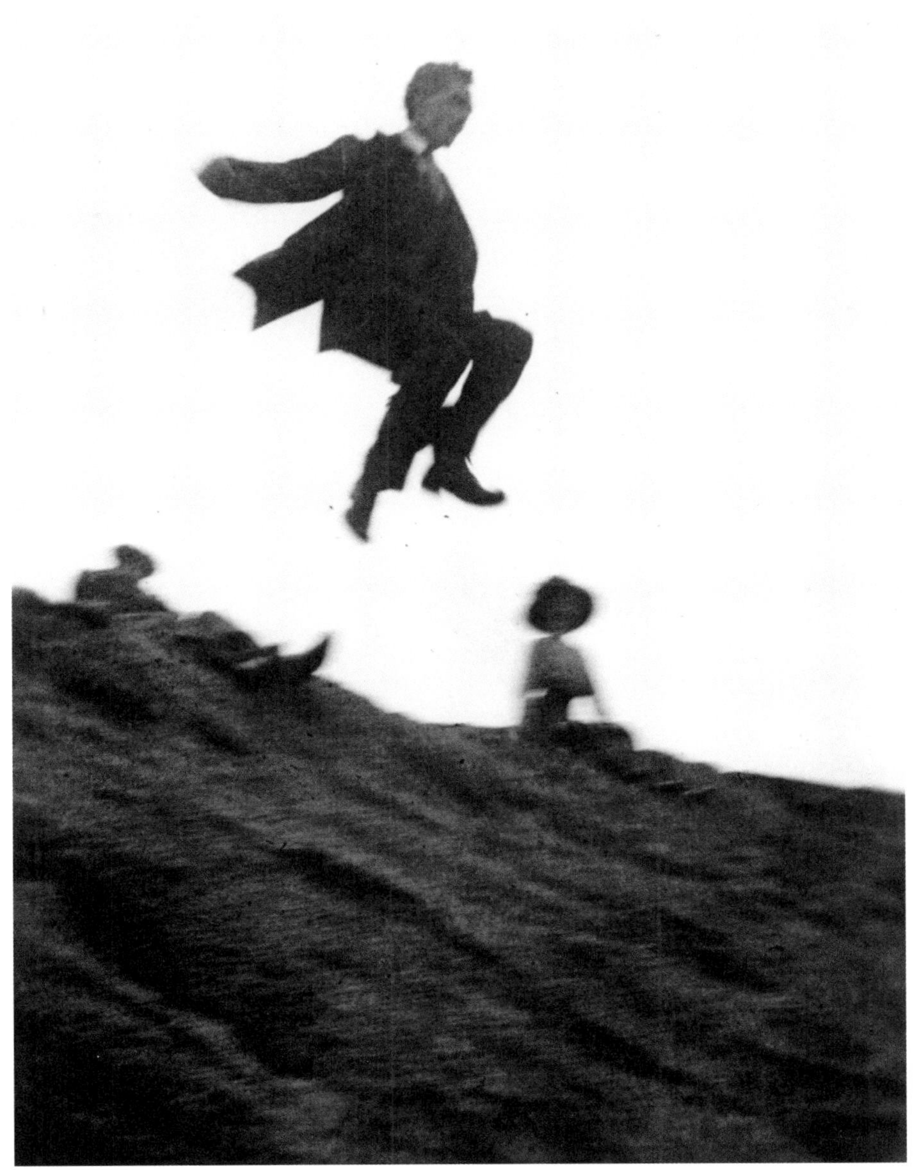

Zissou, Biarritz, 1909.

A younger Lartigue, sitting with his parents outside the Hôtel de Paris in Monte-Carlo one afternoon in April 1911, prior to watching a firework display that night, lifted his camera to snap a young woman dressed in cream-coloured silk *jupe-culottes* – then a controversial new fashion – jerking her head away from his lens as she hurries towards the steps of the casino (see p. 120). Best of all is a photograph he took of Kätchen, a family maid who accompanied the family on an earlier trip to Menton in 1908 (below). Shaded by her umbrella, she peers over to inspect the Mediterranean – a reminder of how, in the early 1900s, seventy-five per cent of the population in France had never seen the sea, which remained a wild, unpredictable place in the popular imagination.

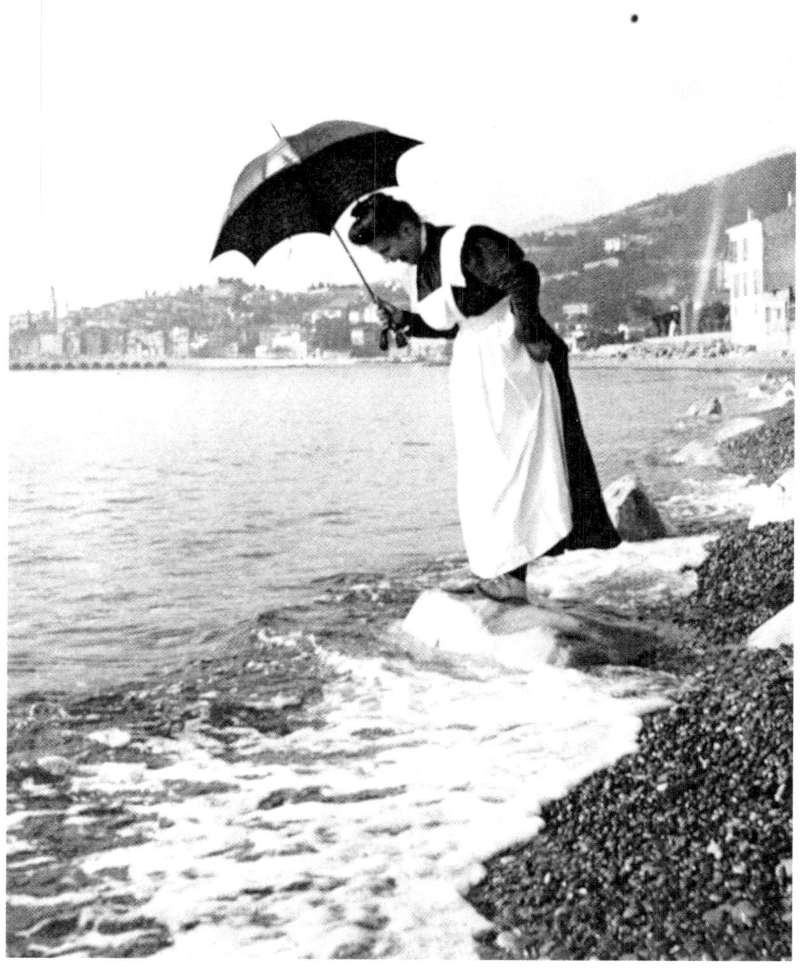

Kätchen inspecting the sea, Menton, Côte d'Azur, 1908.

Chapter Three
La Vie du Château

'I have so many wonderful memories of Rouzat that I'd need an entire note-book to describe them,' wrote Lartigue.[1] 'Arriving at Rouzat, even before the carriage has stopped, I jump out and run to pee in a corner of the park, to listen to the vast, heavy silence that envelops you like happiness.'

As with many Belle Époque *haut-bourgeois*, Henri Lartigue's patrician tastes included the purchase of a country property. 'Their ideal was…to have a house in the country, and to divide their time between it and the town in exactly the same way as the aristocracy,' writes Theodore Zeldin, in his *History of French Passions*.[2] Henri's first purchase, from the composer Jules Massenet in 1901, was the house at Pont-de-l'Arche in Normandy, with a terraced garden leading down to the Seine, which served as the setting for some of Jacques' earliest photographs (see, for example, pp. 22 and 31). Four years later, in 1905, Henri bought and restored the Château de Rouzat in the Limagne, a large plain in the Puy-de-Dôme region of the Auvergne, about fifty kilometres from the spa town of Vichy. Having subscribed to *Fermes et Châteaux*, one of the many illustrated periodicals published by Paris press baron Pierre Lafitte, Henri added a wrought-iron gate and railings at the hillside entrance to the park, four kilometres off a main road, to complete the look. There the Lartigue family travelled, despite the odd puncture (see p. 62), in Henri's new Panhard et Levassor motor car in mid-July, returning to Paris in late September.

Lartigue often photographed his exuberant family circle at Rouzat, his father setting up a darkroom in an outbuilding opposite the chapel: 'I'm well settled here: more space than in Paris. I've got good weighing scales [for darkroom chemicals], glass plates, filter papers (useful for avoiding dark specks on photos).'[3] Henri, whose interest in photography dwindled in favour of the Cinématographe (the film camera-cum-projector invented by the Lumière brothers), gradually left the darkroom to his son. Now able to make his own prints, the young Lartigue enlisted his cousin Bouboutte

(Marthe van Weers) as his darkroom assistant. In one of his early Rouzat photographs from 1908, he catches a headless Bouboutte in mid-flight jumping off an outside wall in a blur of petticoats (opposite). Bouboutte's older sister Bichonnade falls off her bicycle with its puncture-proof tyres, while another cousin, Marcelle Haguet, is caught at an awkward moment as she clambers onto a donkey. 'I enjoy little mishaps,' Lartigue confessed decades later. 'They happen quickly but the photo preserves them.'[4]

Four years Zissou's junior, Lartigue remained excluded from the fast-paced antics at Rouzat. Only his first cousin and lifelong friend, Dédé (André Haguet), who later enjoyed a career as a screenplay writer and film producer, was younger. Lartigue photographed the seven-year-old Dédé on the drive at Rouzat, pushing a curious-looking homemade 'glide bike' (p. 64). Perplexed by his brother's obsession, first with his 'eye trap' then with his cameras, Zissou would ask what he was doing, 'standing there, rooted to the spot like an idiot'.[5] However, Jacques, with his growing technical prowess, was happy to remain a spectator, creating his *instantanés* that froze motion in time.

'The Rouzat property seemed to be well suited to every invention,' wrote Lartigue's third wife, Florette, in her memoir, *La Traversée du siècle*.[6] 'The

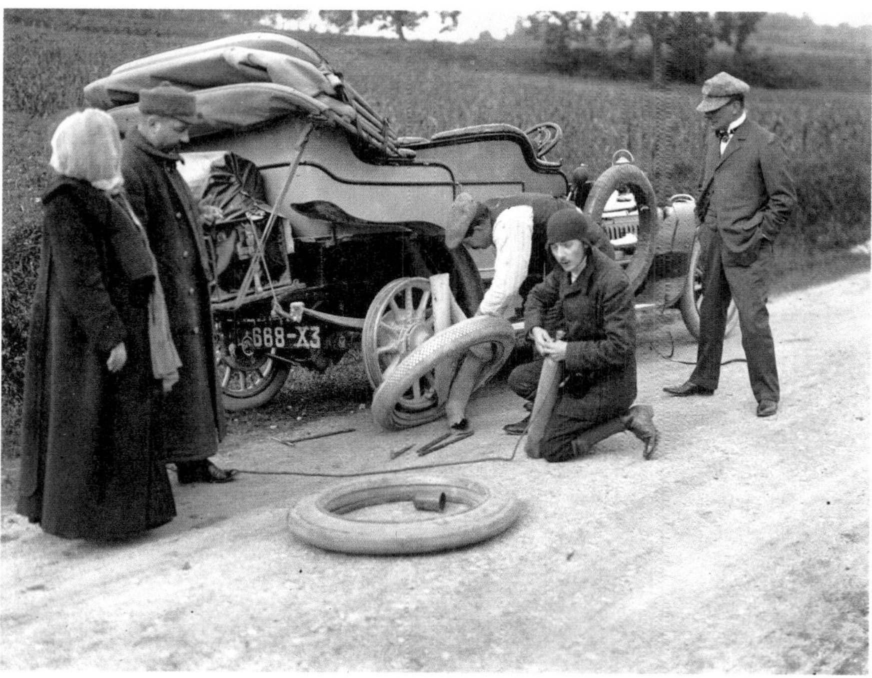

Marie and Henri Lartigue, Yves Lecouster (family chauffeur), Zissou and Hubert Laroze, Rouzat, 1911.

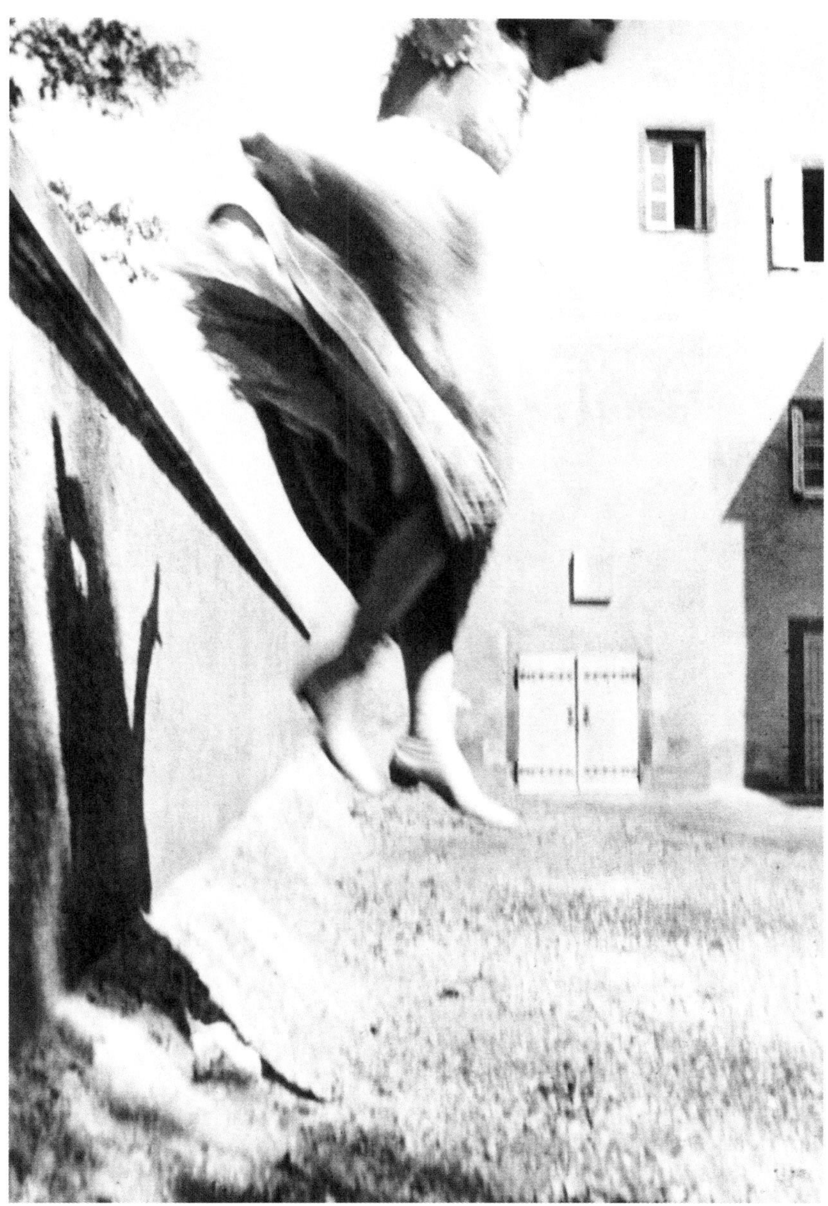

Marthe van Weers (Bouboutte), Rouzat, 1908.

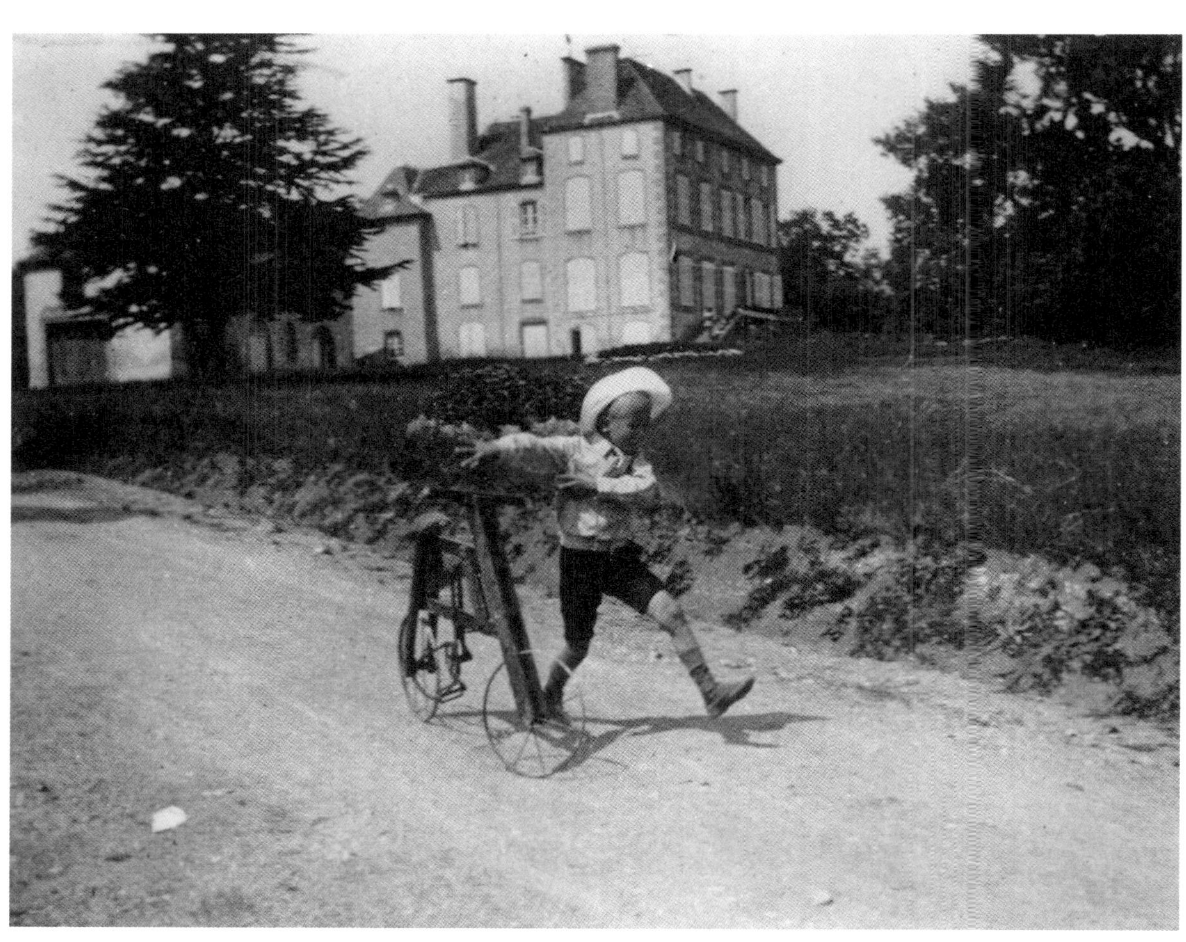

[five-kilometre] hill gave the boys the idea to build a type of four-wheeled go-kart with no pedals that hurtled down the hill at high speed...' (below and p. 66). In one race, Lartigue's hefty cousin Jean Haguet and family friend Louis Ferrand shoot past, trailing clouds of dust and gravel. On other occasions, by then in his late teens, Lartigue joined his cousin as a passenger, noting that his German camera with a shutter speed of 1/1000 of a second allowed him to take very sharp images. Handicapped as he was by crude, somewhat inaccurate early viewfinders, Lartigue found himself obliged to crop away extraneous foreground in order to create his final image. Anticipating a mishap, he waited, shutter cocked, for his sports-loving cousin Simone Roussel to tumble off a homemade scooter as she turned a corner, sprawling with her black-stockinged legs in the air (p. 67): 'She was very good natured,' he later recalled.[7]

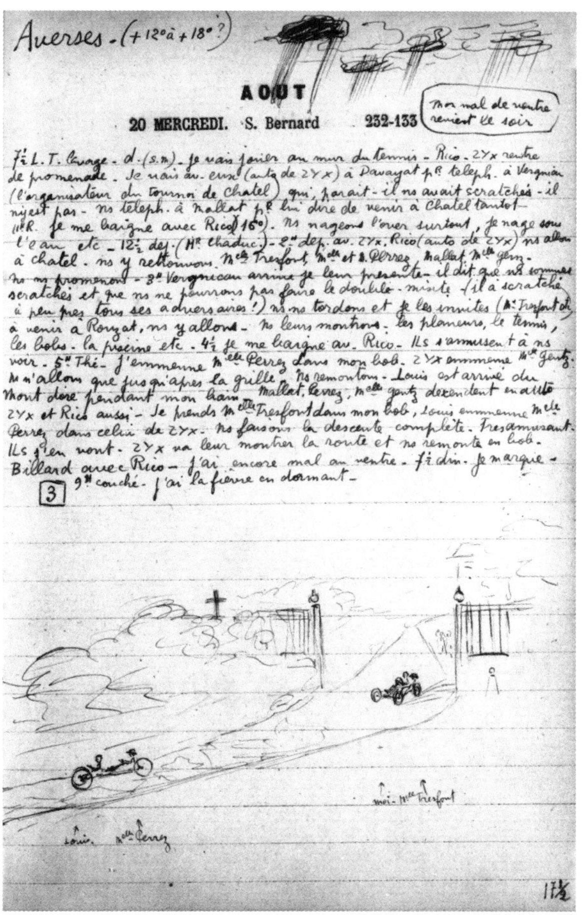

Page from Lartigue's diary,
20 August 1913.

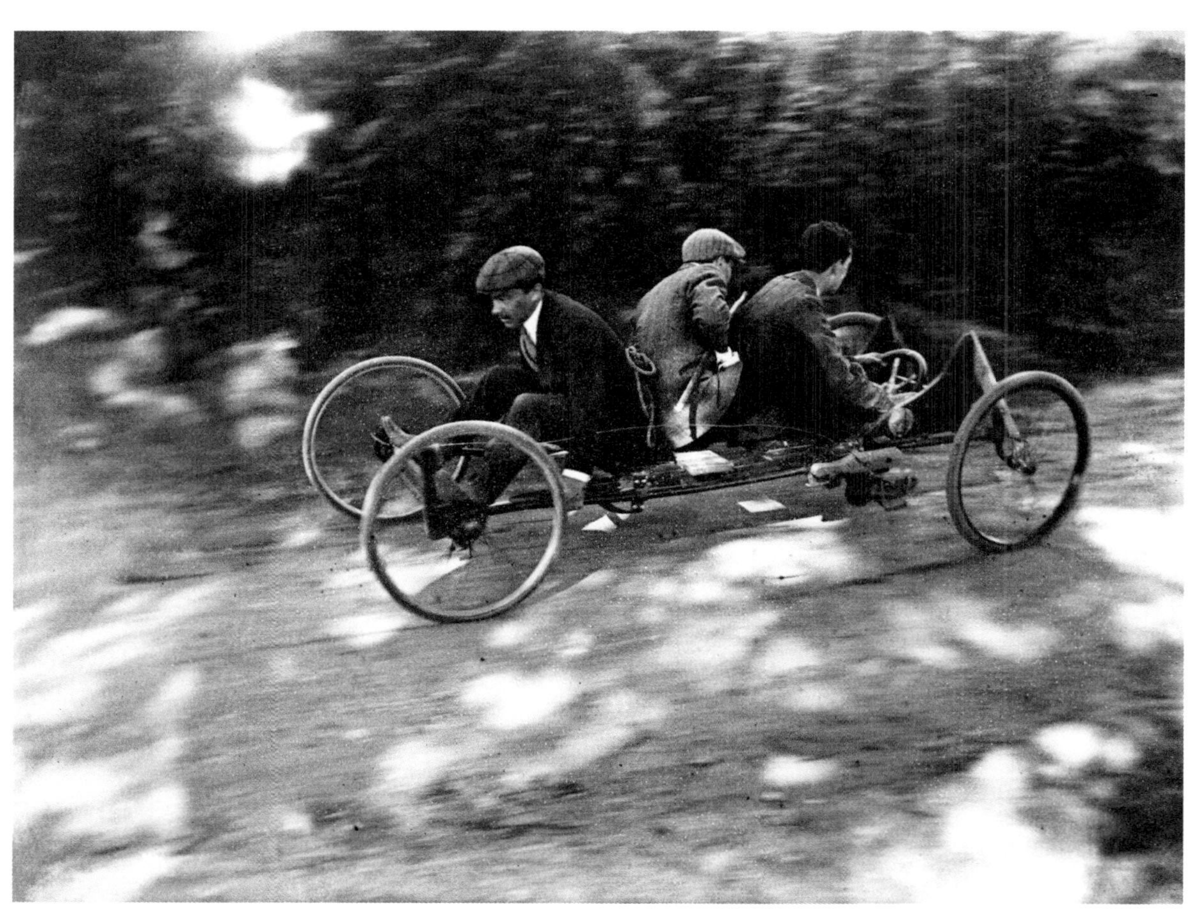

Louis Ferrand (Loulou), Lartigue's cousin Raymond van Weers (Oléo) and Zissou, Rouzat, 1910.

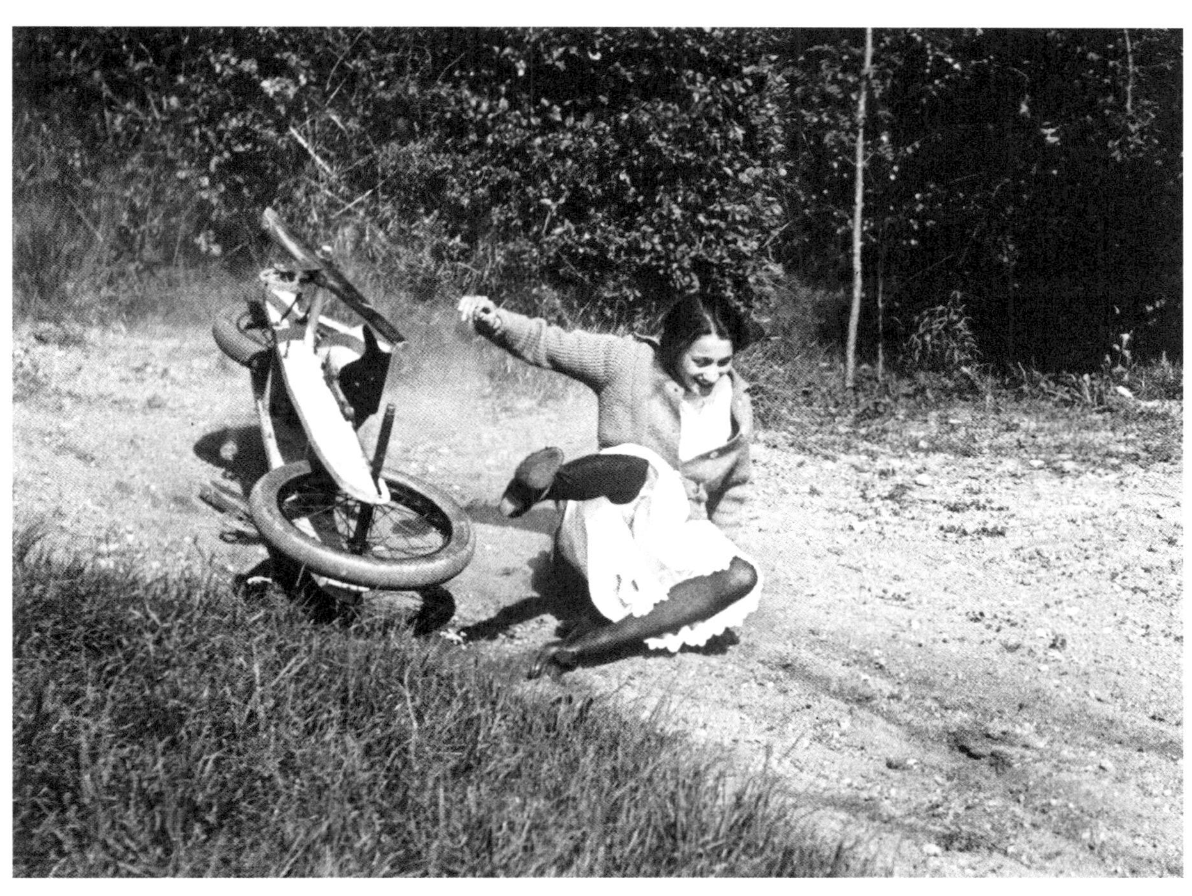

Simone Roussel, Rouzat, 1913.

In one unforgettable photograph (opposite), the nineteen-year-old Zissou dressed in a buttoned jacket, white trousers, flap cap and dark goggles, perches on a go-kart he designed with a wooden board, four bicycle wheels connected with steel pipes, plus a car steering wheel, his serious expression adding to his comic eccentricity. Zissou dressed as a dandy, whatever the occasion: 'To go to the Bois [de Boulogne] he puts on beige spats over made-to-measure shoes from the rue des Petits-Champs...I see him from afar, with his little cane which is very light and serves no purpose.'[8] Knowing what was 'correct' was an essential attribute for the well-heeled. Entire books were written on various ways to knot a tie. The aim was to exude effortless elegance, even deep in the French countryside. At Rouzat, Zissou and his cousin Oléo van Weers leapt a row of chairs, Oléo in white trousers and straw boater proving to be the champion (below; Zissou never wore his own boater until after the Grand Prix at Longchamp in late June), or performed the cakewalk, the high-stepping, back-arching African-American dance craze that crossed the Atlantic to Paris in 1902 when the

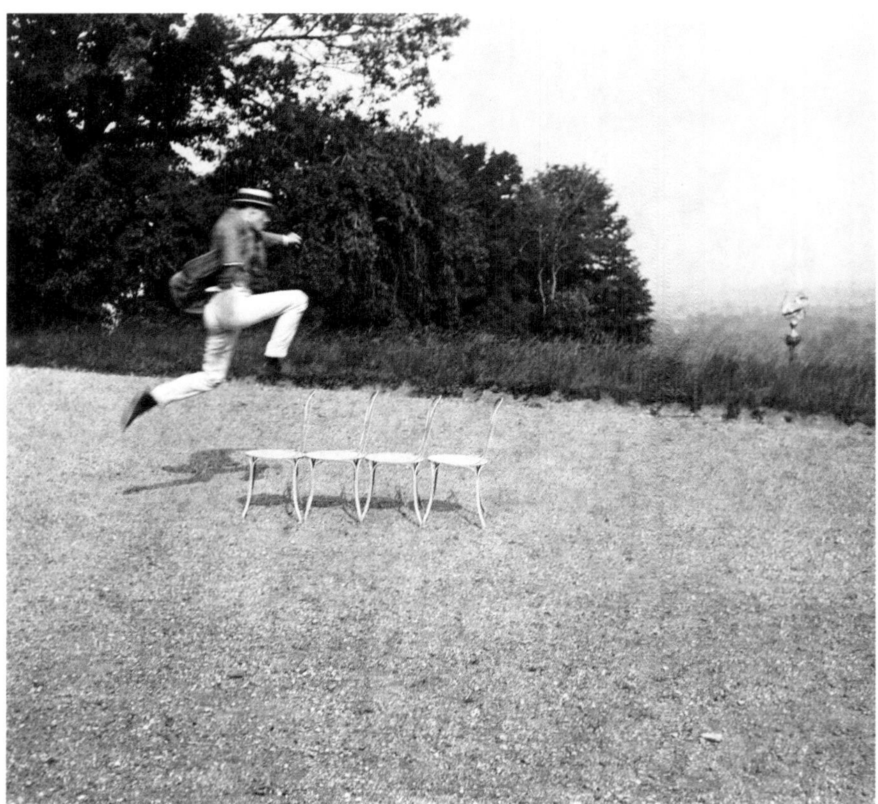

Raymond van Weers (Oléo), Rouzat, 1908.

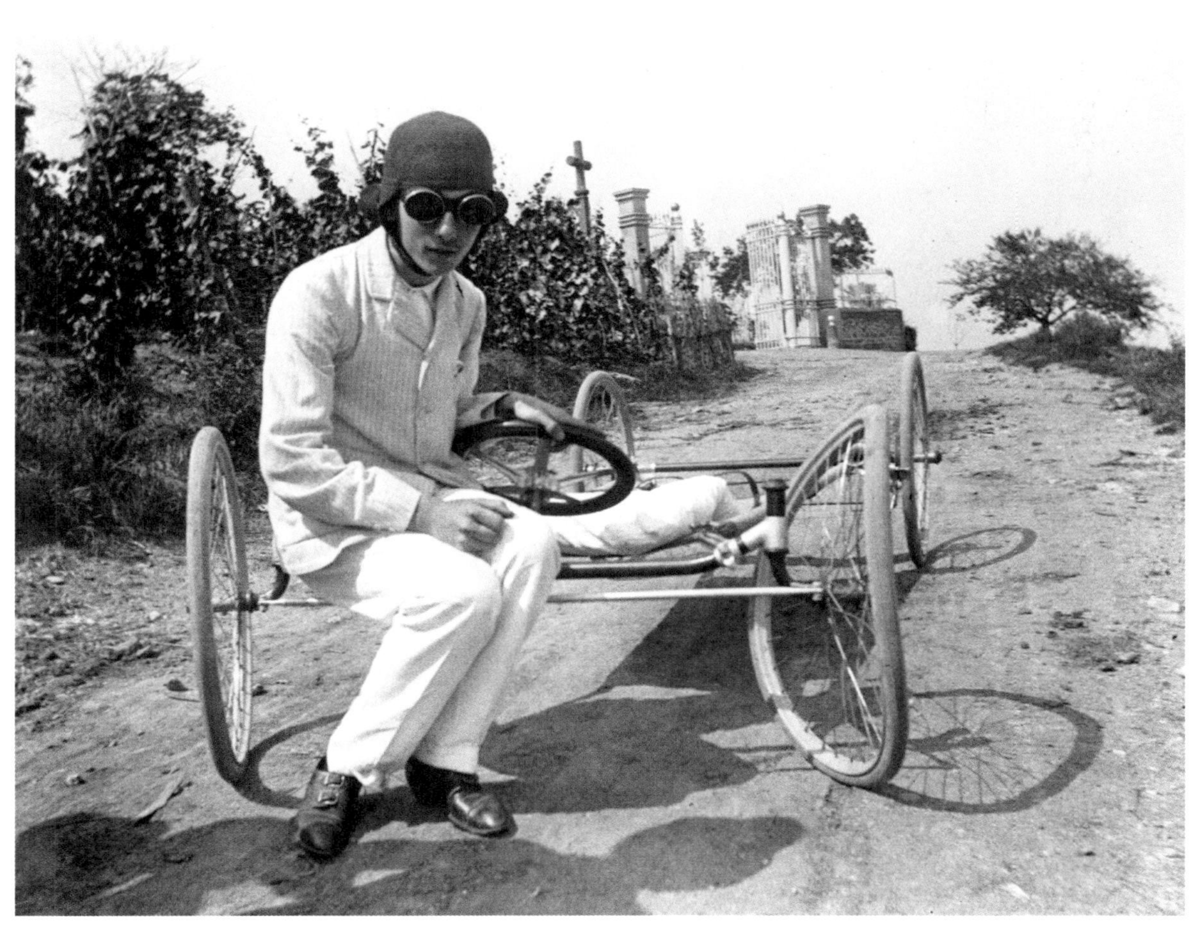

Zissou, Rouzat, 1909.

Lumière brothers filmed *Les joyeux nègres* at the Nouveau Cirque. Zissou and
Oléo aped the young Maurice Chevalier, who, like other French stars, incor-
porated the cakewalk into his cabaret act at the Folies Bergère.

Henri Lartigue, meanwhile, transformed a muddy garden pond into
a concrete-lined swimming pool, the setting for an armada of whimsical
boats, rafts, ramps and hydro-gliders (see below and opposite), prompting
neighbours to dismiss the family as a 'curious lot'. In one game, partici-
pants propel themselves along the water in empty wine barrels with garden
spades, aiming to capsize an opponent. Even Monsieur Folletête, Henri
Lartigue's private secretary, enters into the spirit of things, floating in
his barrel ready for battle in his shirtsleeves, tie and braces (p. 72, above).
Lartigue's paternal uncle Raymond and friend Robert Ferrand wage a pillow
fight straddling a fir tree trunk placed across one end of the pool, its sharp
lines framing the image. The latter's brother Louis, meanwhile, experiments with Zissou's propeller-driven raft, bringing an oar to help push
himself along (p. 72, below). In one image from 1911 (p. 74), Zissou, complete with hat, sunglasses and the three-piece tweed suit and silk tie he had
worn to Mass that morning, floats in a miniature rubber dinghy designed
for duck shoots with waders attached, which the brothers purchased from a

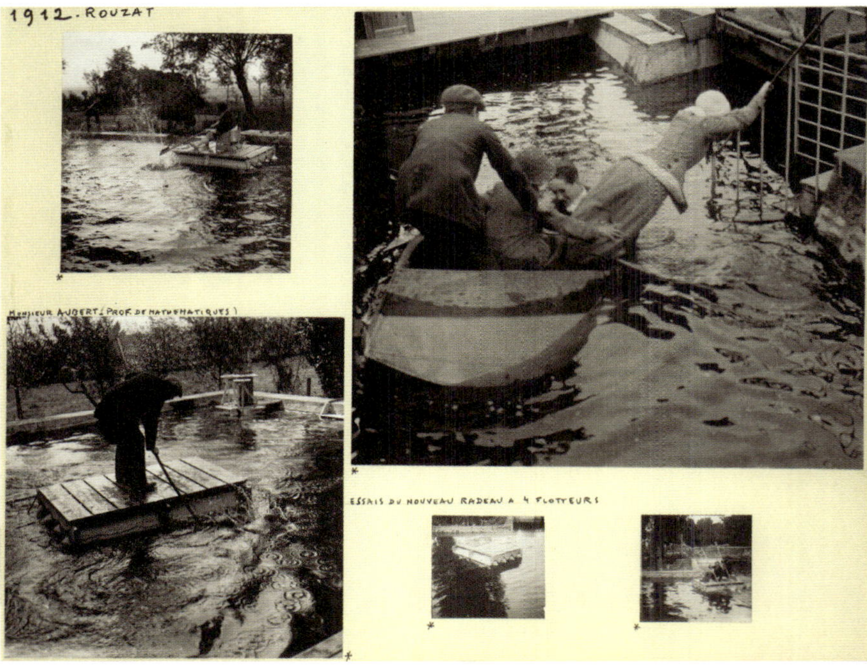

Rouzat, 1912 (album page).

catalogue. Earlier that year Lartigue began writing his diaries, detailing his daily activities in a neat hand, often adding illustrations of his photographs. The entry for that day includes a sketch of Zissou in his dinghy (see p. 75).

Jacques in turn asked to be photographed jumping into the pool fully dressed, his mother insisting on old clothes. Jumping and diving were ever-popular subjects among amateur photographers in pursuit of 'instantanés'. Jacques catches Dédé suspended in mid-air, straining with effort as he attempts a dive, his hands clasped in prayer position (p. 76, above). The brothers' American friend, Rico (Henry S. Broadwater) tries out a new wooden water slide, his torso reflected in the mirror-like surface of the pool. Rico appears again a couple of years later in September 1913, seated cross-legged in front of the geometric shapes of new changing huts (improvements to the pool were made each year), as he watches skating star Charles Sabouret just before he hits the water, breaking up with ripples and reflections (p. 77).

Page from Lartigue's diary, 27 August 1912, showing the Lartigue household boating.

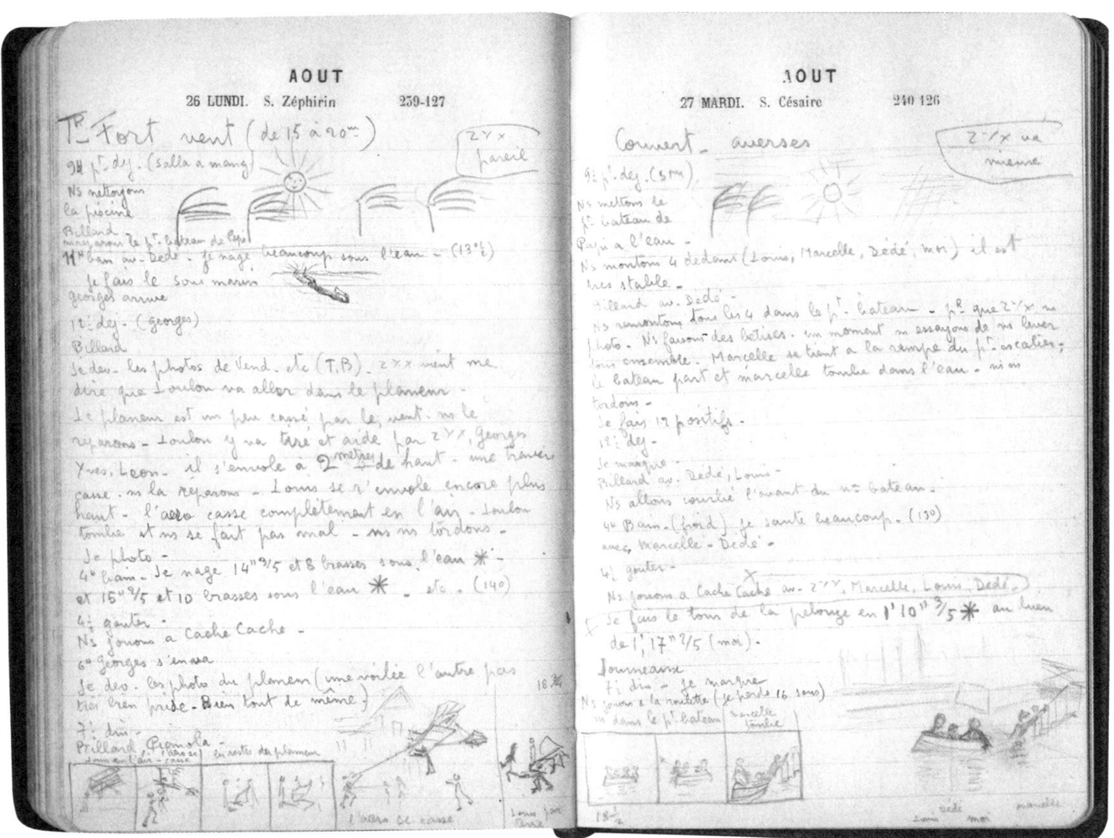

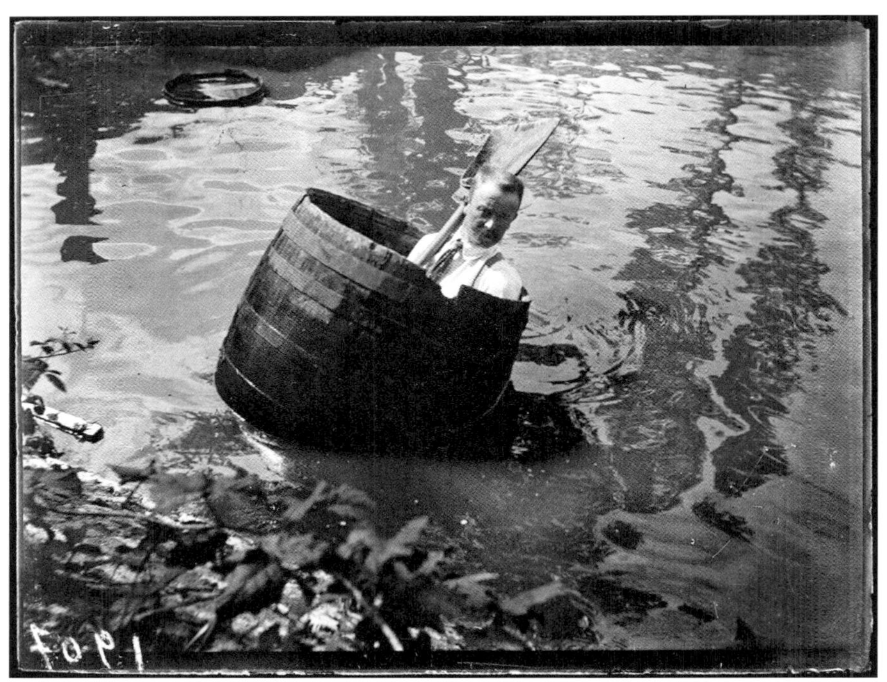

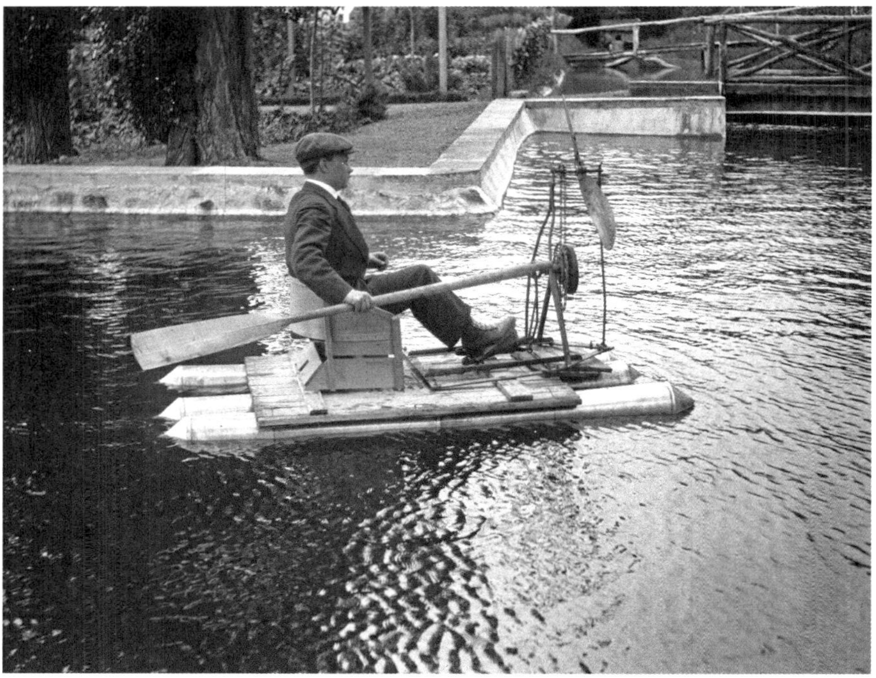

Monsieur Folletête (Plitt), Rouzat, 1907.
Louis Ferrand (Loulou) on one of Zissou's inventions, Rouzat, 1912.

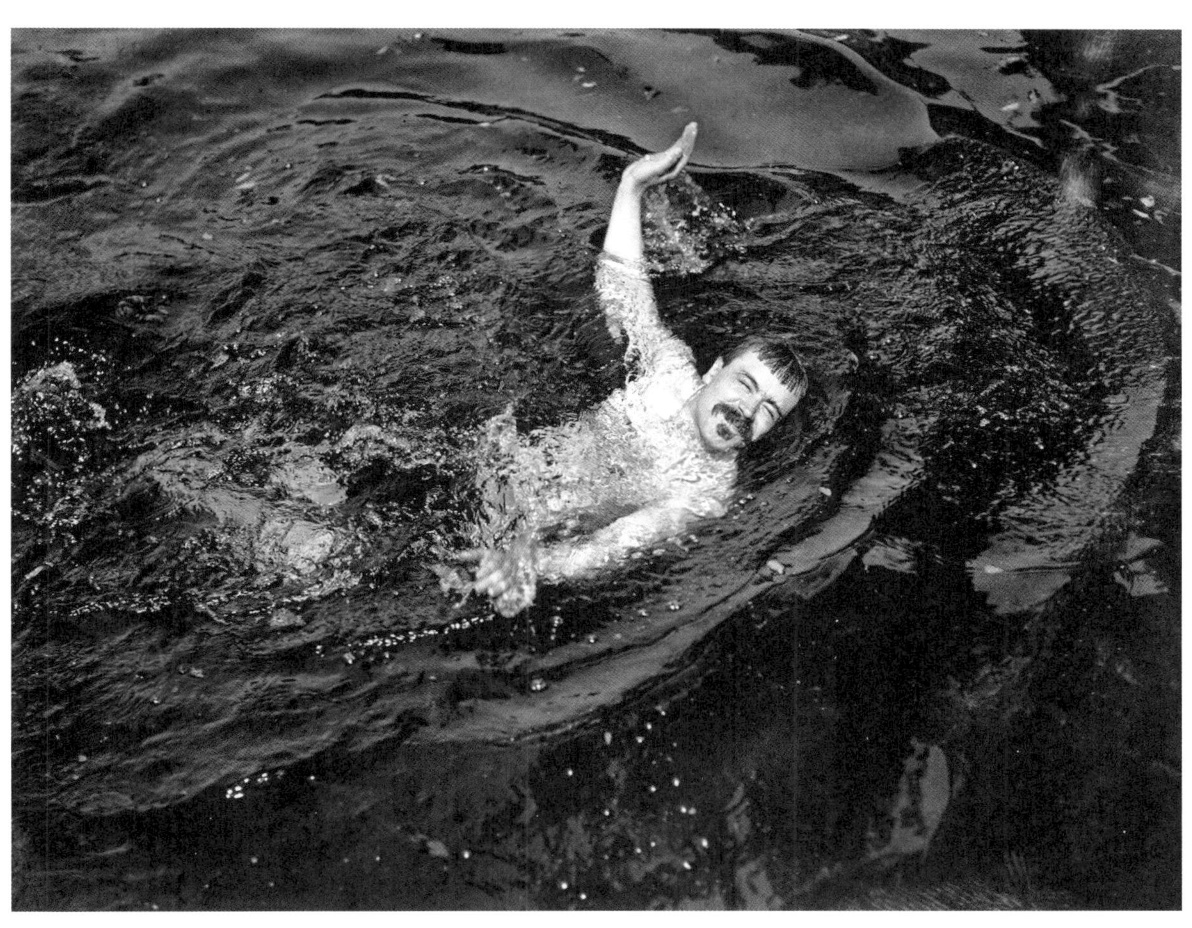

Lartigue's maths tutor Marius Aubert, Rouzat, 1911.

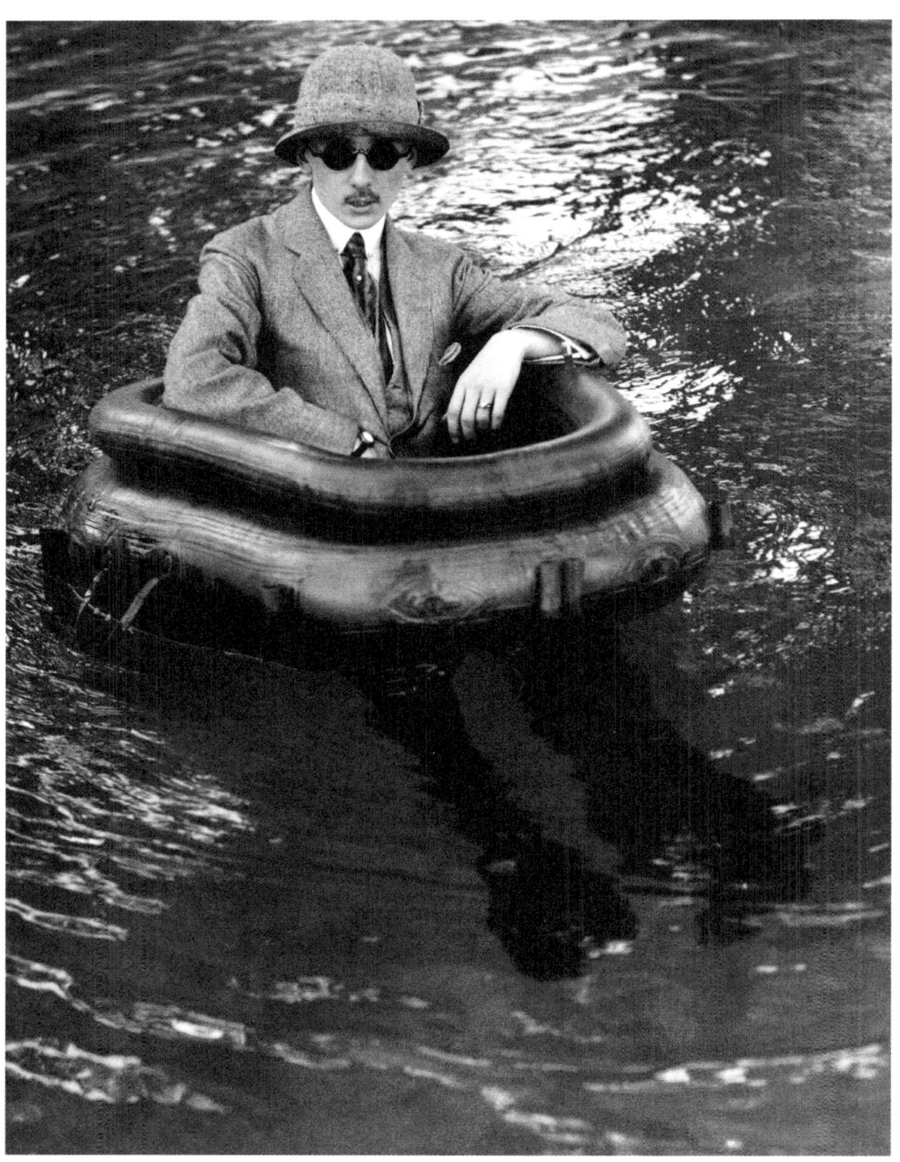

Zissou in the pool at Rouzat, 1911.

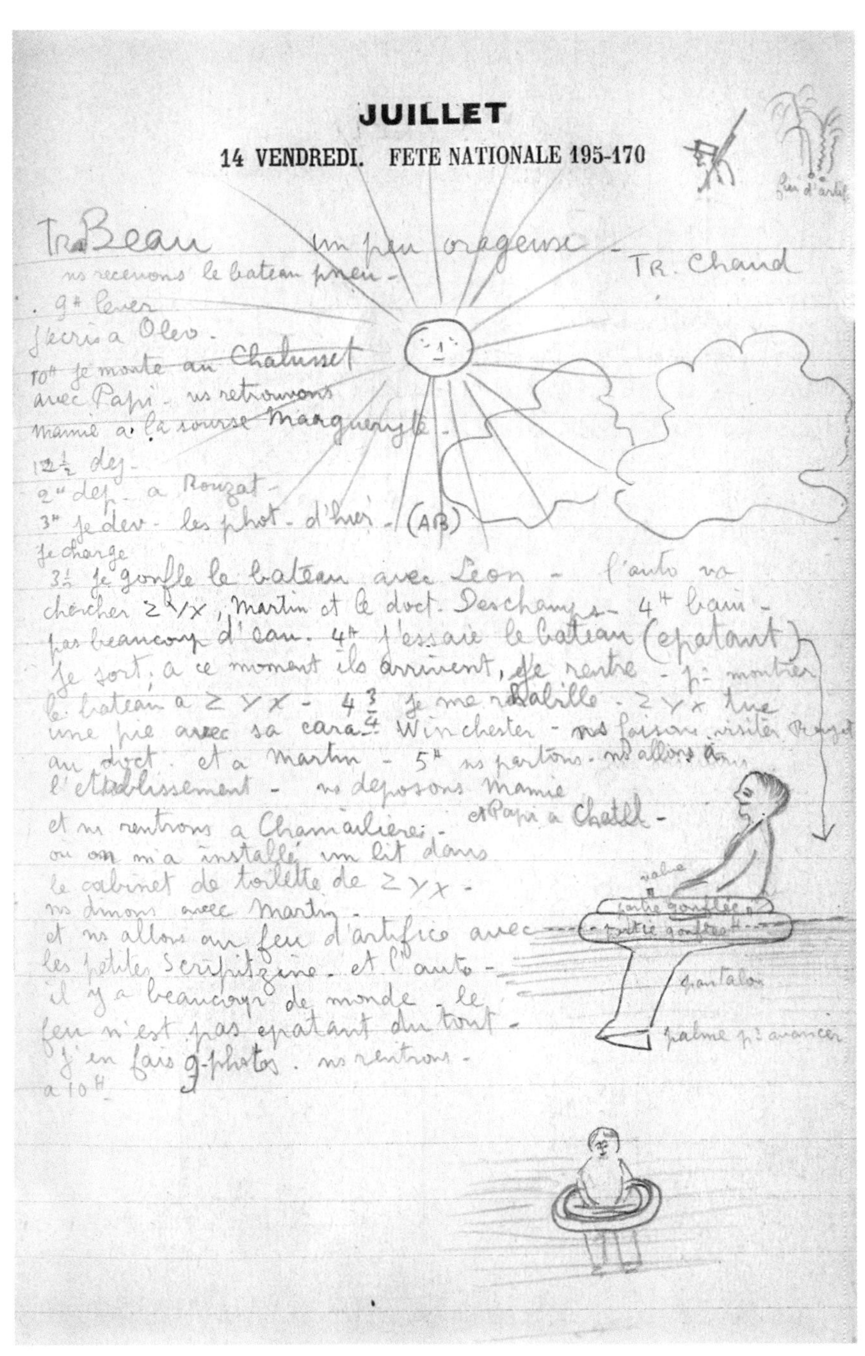

Page from Lartigue's diary, 14 July 1911.

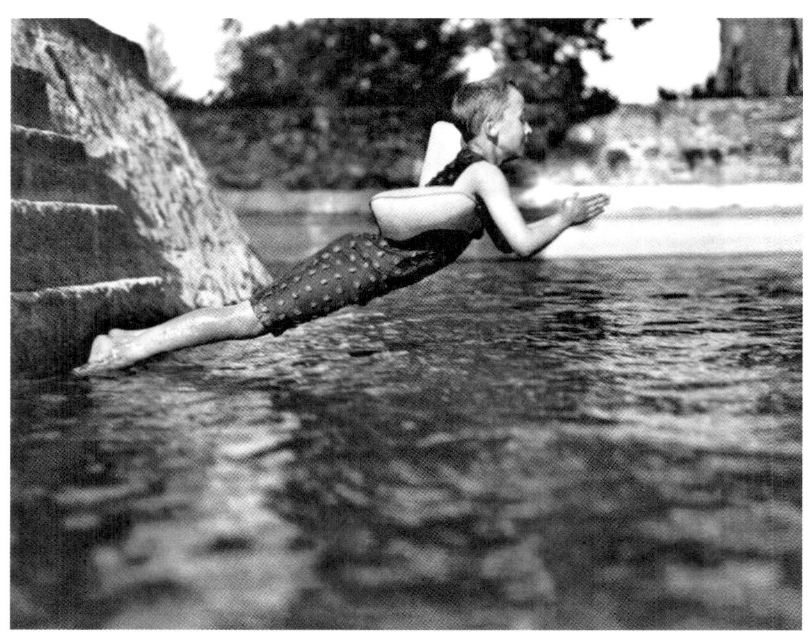

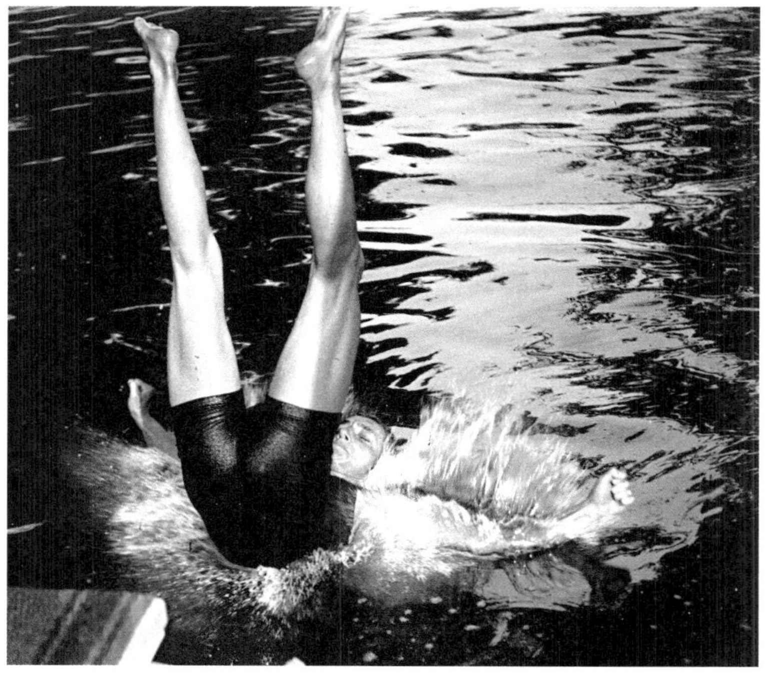

André Haguet (Dédé), Rouzat, 1911.
Lartigue's American friend Henry S. Broadwater (Rico), Rouzat, 1911.

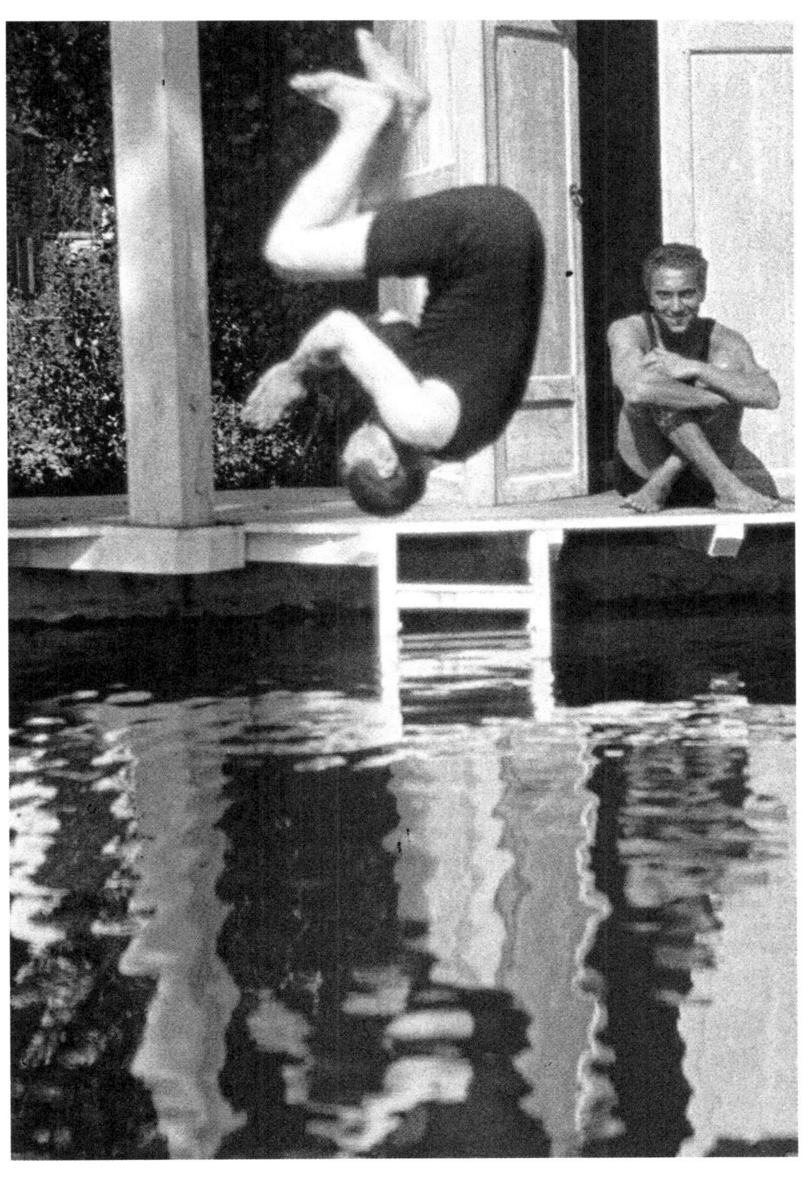

Charles Sabouret (Simone Roussel's husband), with Henry S. Broadwater (Rico), Rouzat, 1913.

Zissou's mania for innovation and experiment, inherited from his paternal forebears, found full expression at Rouzat. Both brothers' fascination with aeroplanes dated from April 1904, when Henri Lartigue took his sons (the nine-year-old Jacques weighed down with his camera) to watch pioneer Gabriel Voisin's attempts at flying with a modified Archdeacon glider on the dunes near Berck on the coast of northern France: 'All of a sudden, from afar, I see little black specks on the dune.... On approaching, I see that the black specks are people who've grouped together on a dune, surrounding a large, white, semi-transparent kite....'[9] Voisin flew up over twenty metres on a gust of wind for about twenty seconds, before falling back onto the sand. Jacques captured the scene from the bottom of the dune, borrowing his father's Gaumont Spido stereoscopic camera with 6 × 13 cm glass plates and a shutter release of 1/300 of a second (see p. 130), while his eccentric uncle, Raymond Lartigue, rushed about, pretending to be a Voisin bird-man.

Zissou's early attempts at Rouzat included jumping off the garden wall, his father's umbrella serving as a parachute. Then, in 1908, the American Wilbur Wright travelled to France, having shipped his engine-powered Wright aeroplane, and dispelled all doubts when he took to the air at Le Mans racecourse on 8 August. The Europe-wide euphoria spread to Rouzat: 'It's summer, we're at Rouzat, and almost every day now I rush towards the postman,' wrote Jacques. 'I have subscribed to *L'Auto*. Quickly, I tear off the magazine tape, so I can see what Wilbur [Wright] has done now.'[10] While Jacques dreamed of flying, Zissou, who later wrote articles for specialist magazines, put his ideas into practice, building a series of thirty-five gliders over successive summers, including the ZYX 22, 23 and 24. 'Often three weeks' effort is destroyed within five or six minutes.... But it's not the time that matters, it's the result, and sometimes the result is amazing because Zissou's feet lift a metre off the ground, and maybe more,' wrote Jacques in the summer of 1911.[11] Henri Lartigue, who believed in learning the laws of physics through experiment, financed the boys' projects. Jacques, following in his brother's footsteps, photographed each stage from model to test flight.

Assisted by Monsieur Pirou, a local carpenter, Zissou built his gliders in a disused *cuvage* (wine-fermenting cellar) in the park. When they were close to completion, the entire household, including the manservant, chauffeur, maids, even the local farmer, was pressed into service, helping assemble successive gliders on the lawn (see opposite). An image from 1909 stretches the

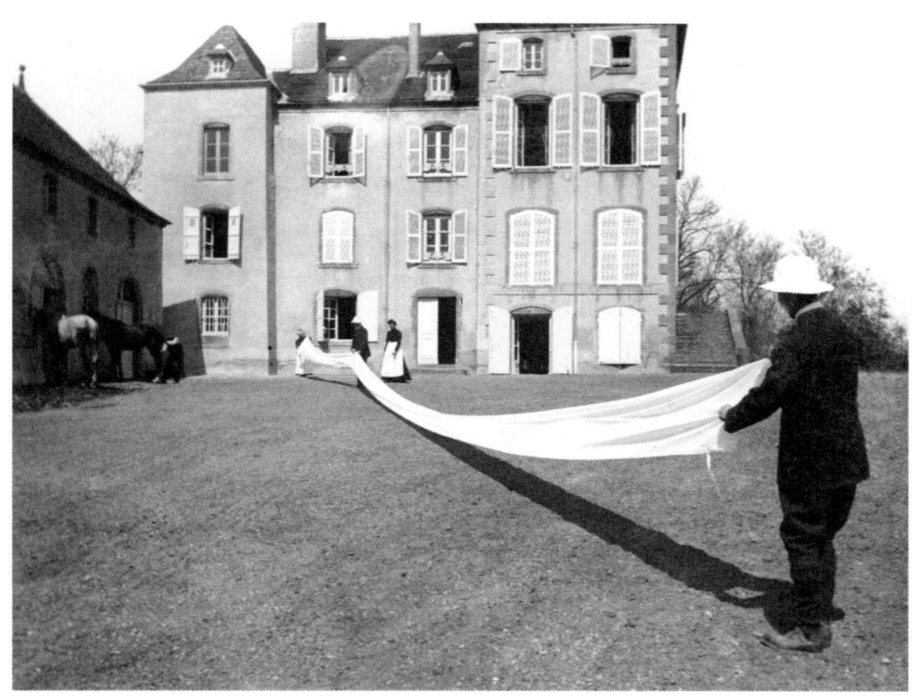

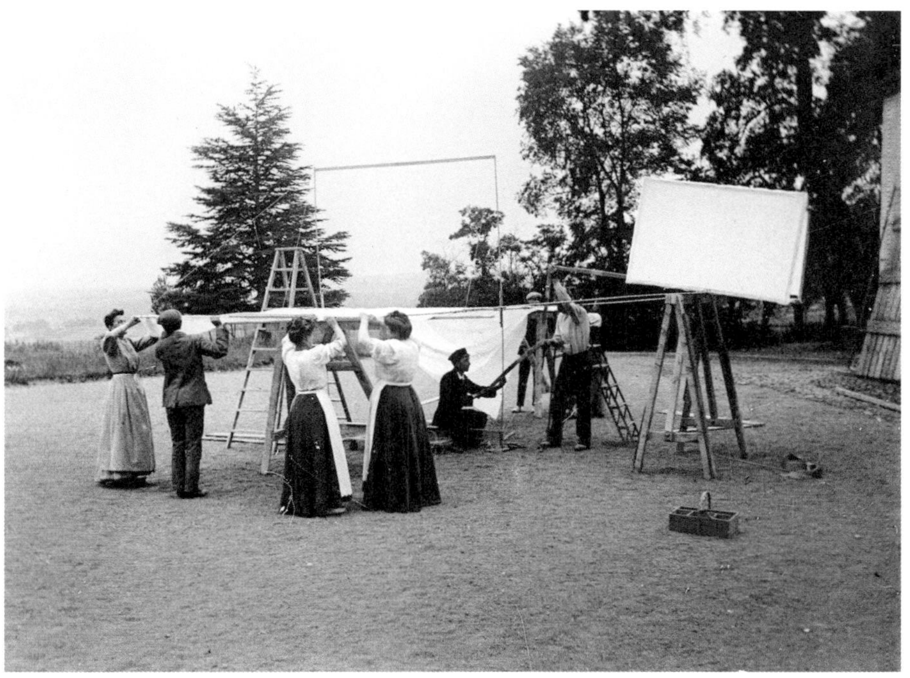

Preparations for Zissou's ZYX 22 glider, Rouzat, 1909.
Constructing the ZYX 21, Rouzat, 1908.

eye along a lengthy strip of bedsheet (purloined from Madame Lartigue's linen cupboard) shooting off into the distance. In another, staff help cut and stretch the material across the wooden framework of the wings. With his sure eye and sense of timing, Jacques photographs Zissou lifting off in his ZYX 24 from the hilltop at Rouzat (opposite). One figure holds the wings level, while a second tugs at the rope disappearing off the right-hand corner of the image. Kevin Moore shows how Lartigue drew inspiration for his compositional strategies from professional photographic reporters working for popular magazines like *La Vie au Grand Air*, the weekly illustrated sports periodical launched by Pierre Lafitte in 1898, as well as instruction manuals: for instance, Albert Reyner, the author of one such manual published in 1903, 'suggested keeping [the horizon line] low so that, in an image of a leaping horse, for example, the animal would appear to be much higher off the ground than it actually was'.[12] Lartigue in turn heightens the drama of the scene by photographing slightly downhill, Zissou's ZYX 24 glider silhouetted against the pale sky.

Another Zissou experiment arose after Docteur Variot forbade the brothers from attempting trick cycling on a brand-new loop-the-loop on the rue de Clichy in Paris. Zissou instead built his very own 'looping' at Rouzat to demonstrate centripetal force. The boys put a series of hapless chickens and rabbits to the test in an enclosed wooden 'carriage' that sped down to the loop from the second floor (see p. 82). 'Before the start and after the finish, we take a close look at the rabbit or chicken's eyes to see whether they are more dilated after looping the loop,' wrote Lartigue.[13] 'Zissou says this proves Docteur Variot doesn't know what he's talking about.' Indeed, a rabbit pulled out of the carriage resembling a stuffed toy rather than a live animal appears none the worse for its ordeal (p. 83).

Marius Aubert, the Sorbonne mathematics professor who tutored Jacques and Zissou, often supervised the boys' experiments (the brothers particularly enjoyed jumping competitions, testing whether the lesser gravity at high altitude at the summit of the Puy de Dôme enabled records to be broken). Like Monsieur Folletête, Aubert was a regular guest at Rouzat. Lartigue's snapshot of him disporting himself in the pool (p. 73), happy to be relieved of his academic duties, appears in John Szarkowski's 1963 catalogue. In common with many of their male contemporaries, both Folletête and Aubert were amateur photography enthusiasts, Lartigue sometimes

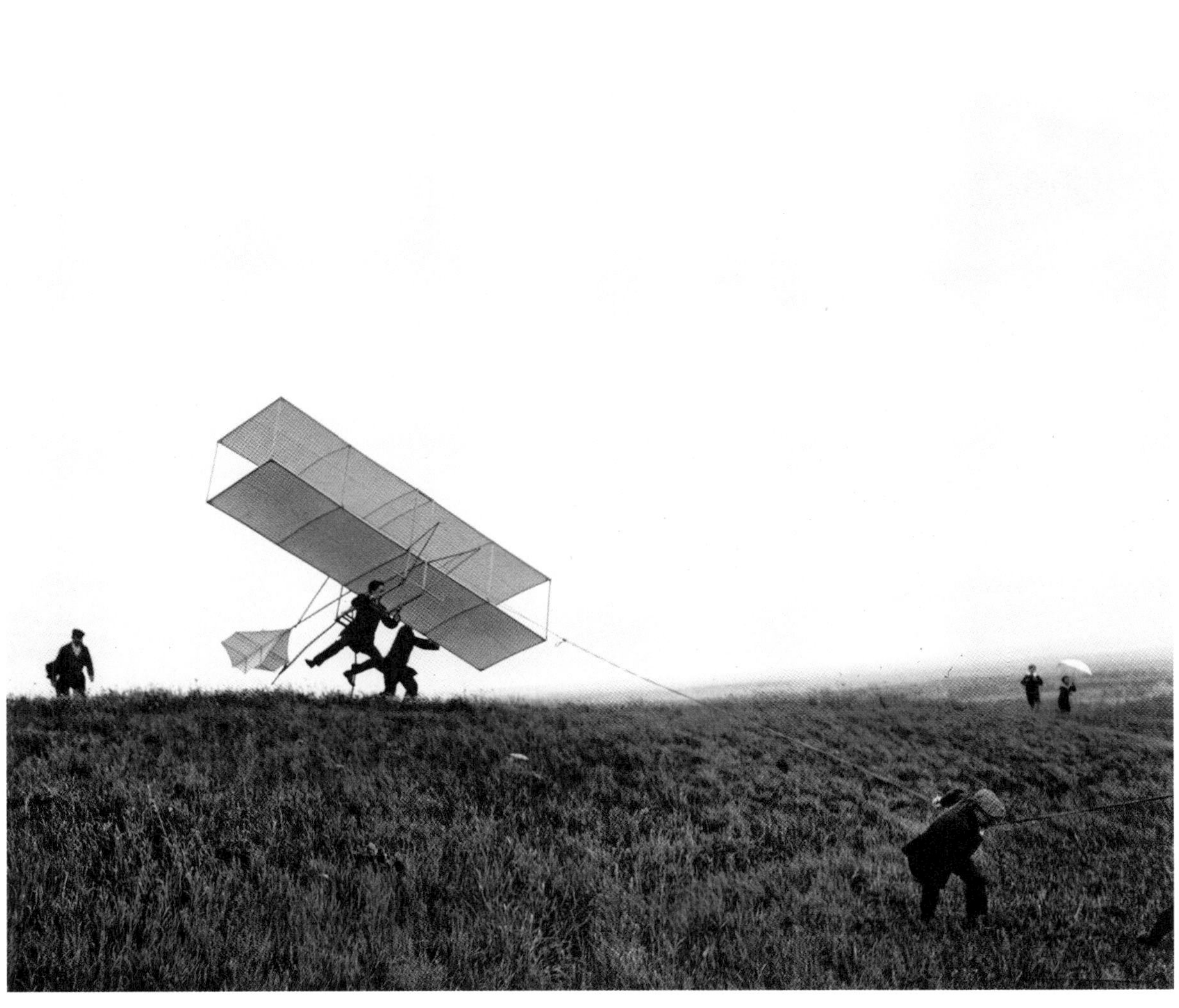

Attempting to fly the ZYX 24, Rouzat, 1910.

borrowing the former's Vérascope Richard. More importantly, Aubert prof-
ited from his position as assistant to Nobel prize-winning physicist Gabriel
Lippmann at the Sorbonne, where the young Lartigue attended his science
classes. Lippmann's early form of colour photography was based on the
interference phenomenon; the process, containing no dyes or pigments,
produced true and subtle colours.

'Aubert has shown me a colour photograph.... If only I could make them
like that,' wrote Lartigue.[14] The following year, in 1912, the eighteen-year-
old produced his first autochromes (an expensive early colour photography
process that the Lumière brothers patented, then marketed, in 1907), using
his new 6 × 13 Klapp Nettel stereoscopic camera. Accustomed only to black
and white, Lartigue found the combined colour and depth enthralling. But
the lengthy exposure time hampered his need to capture fleeting moments.

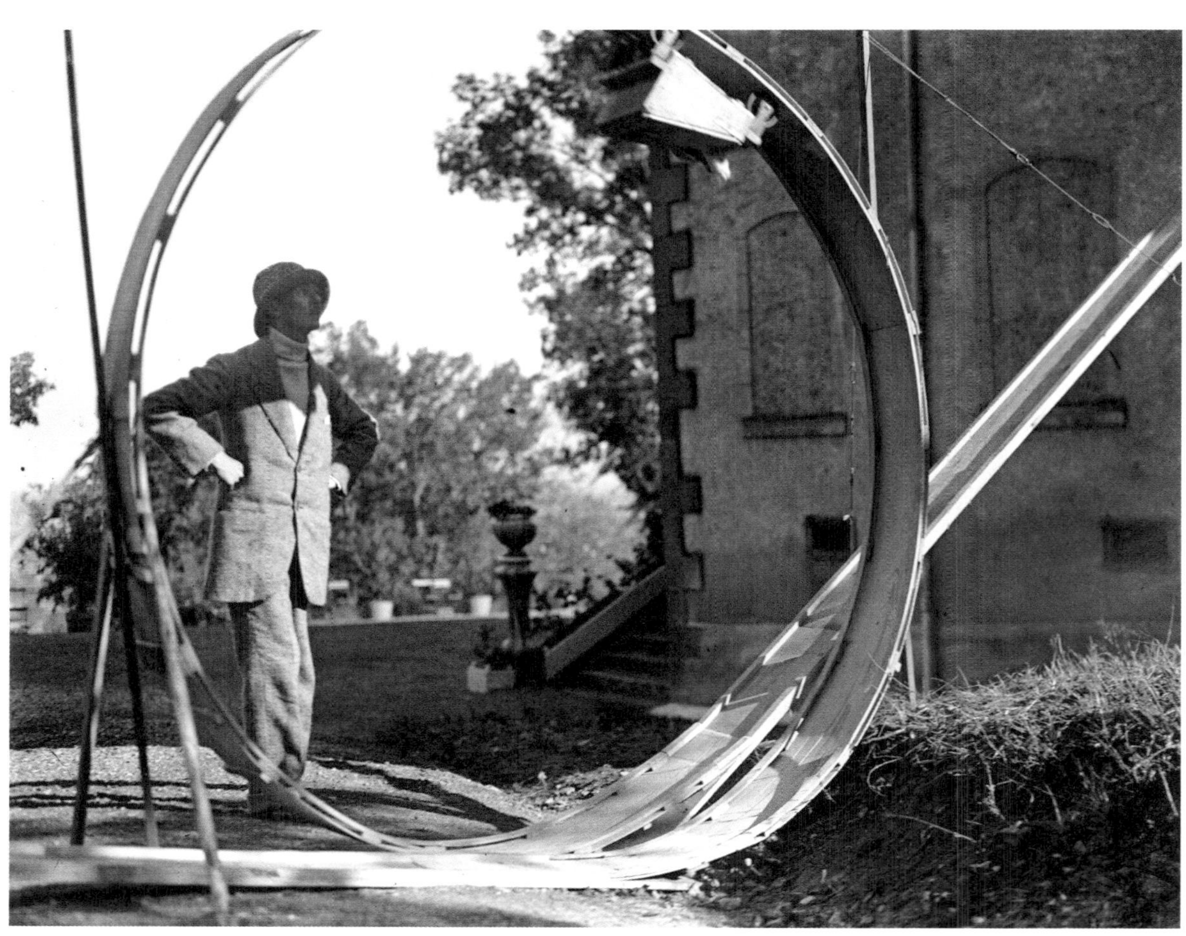

Zissou's 'looping' for rabbits and chickens, Rouzat, 1911.

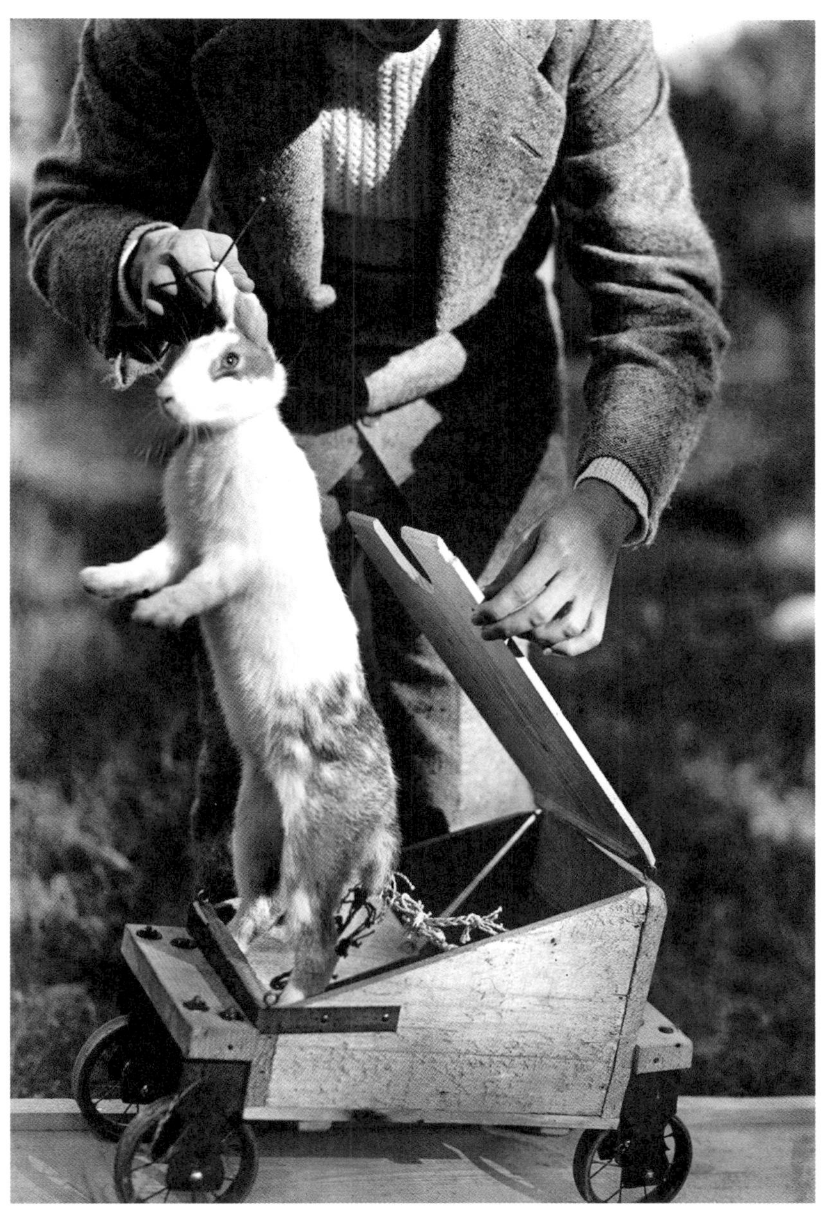

Rabbit 'looping', Rouzat, 1911.

His colour photograph of a row of friends fishing from a wooden bridge at Rouzat in 1913 appears static, while a sedate Simone Roussel in a green hat and cardigan posing on a two-wheeled bobsleigh (one of Lartigue's own designs) was a far cry from his black and white snapshot seizing the moment as a laughing Simone tumbles off her scooter, legs sprawling (see p. 67). His diary for that day (16 August 1913) even states that he filmed her with his Pathé Professionnel. Lartigue enjoyed capturing his cousin's crumbling composure at a time when the bourgeoisie schooled their daughters in the art of decorum. Away from prying eyes, Bichonnade plays tag with Louis Ferrand, tearing across the courtyard at Rouzat in long skirts and feather-trimmed straw hat. Even the family maid Kätchen crosses the swimming pool clinging onto the fir tree trunk, the skirts of her summer dress trailing in the water (opposite).

'It's fun developing [photographs] in darkness when you've just been running in the sun.... Above all, what's marvellous is being able to see straight away the photos you've just taken,' wrote Lartigue.[15] Late in the afternoon he would bound up to the top of the château to kneel before the wooden crucifix affixed to his bedroom wall, asking God to help improve his photographs, thus at times approaching his hobby with an almost religious fervour. He also wrote that he loved God, adding, with apparent conviction, that he would always be happy, thanks to Him. Once revolutionaries, the French bourgeoisie had embraced Catholicism as a mark of respectability by the end of the nineteenth century. The Lartigues were no exception. Jacques received his first Holy Communion in Paris on 2 May 1907, describing the experience in a notebook. 'He often spoke of the ceremony, which made a deep impression on him,' recalled his wife Florette.[16] 'His lifelong faith never wavered either.' Marie Lartigue nevertheless allowed her son to bring his camera to Mass, so he could rush off afterwards in pursuit of his subjects.

Before returning to Paris at the end of September each year, staff helped Zissou store his inventions (go-karts, kites, scale models, the ZYX series of gliders, the 'looping', rafts, hydroplanes, etc.), as well as Jacques' own efforts, in the *cuvage* ready for the following summer. Jacques even photographed these creations carefully positioned in place. When he took apart and reconfigured his albums sixty years later, the elderly photographer ordered an enlargement to paste on a single album page. Eager to preserve every detail, he meticulously numbered and identified each invention with a key in the margin.

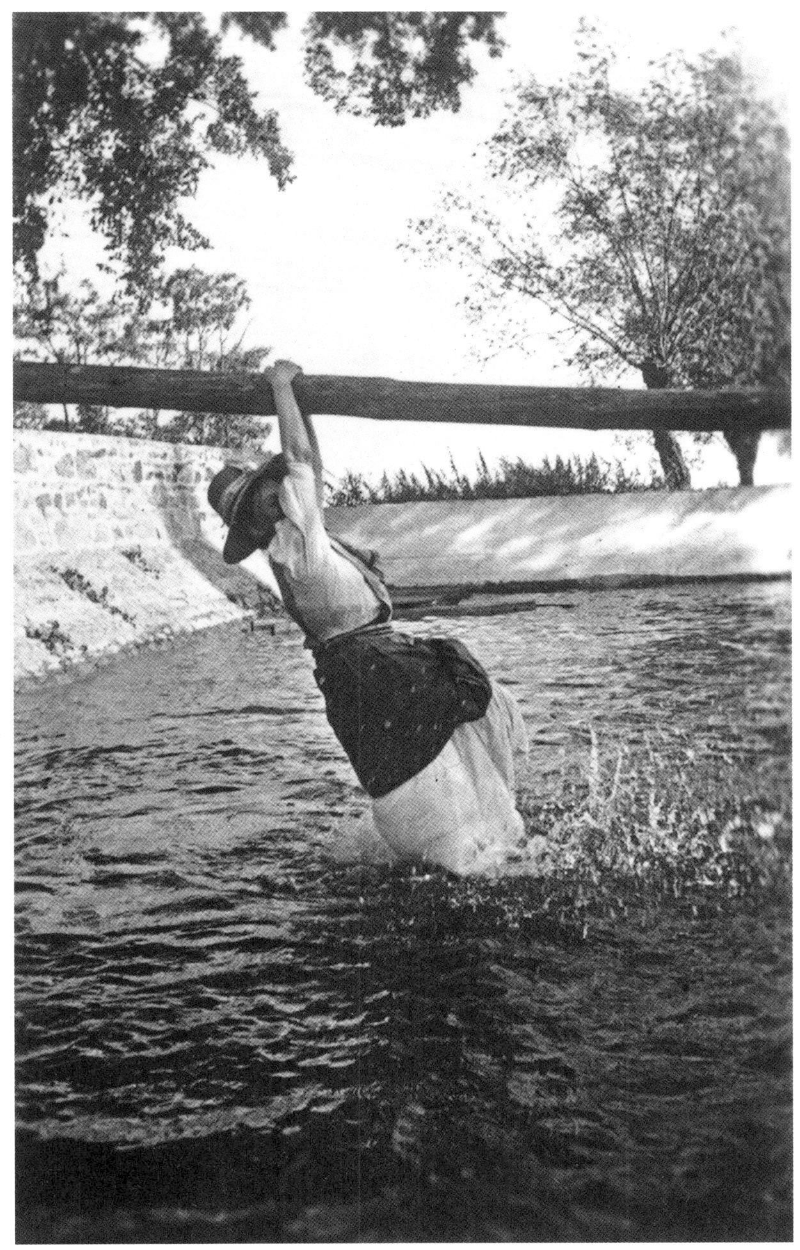

Kätchen, Rouzat, 1909.

The First World War and the Russian Revolution dented Henri Lartigue's fortune. A series of bad loans, combined with inflation, obliged him to sell Rouzat in the autumn of 1923. Unaware of his father's financial affairs, Jacques was shocked by the sale. 'I don't want tomorrow to come when I won't see "my things" anymore,' he wrote at Rouzat in August that year.[17] 'Saying that gives a little twinge that makes me want to cry.... Through a tiny hole, I think I have seen a great emptiness in my heart that gives me vertigo. Before me are memories that I've been used to rediscovering every year, which, I suddenly realize, will never return.'

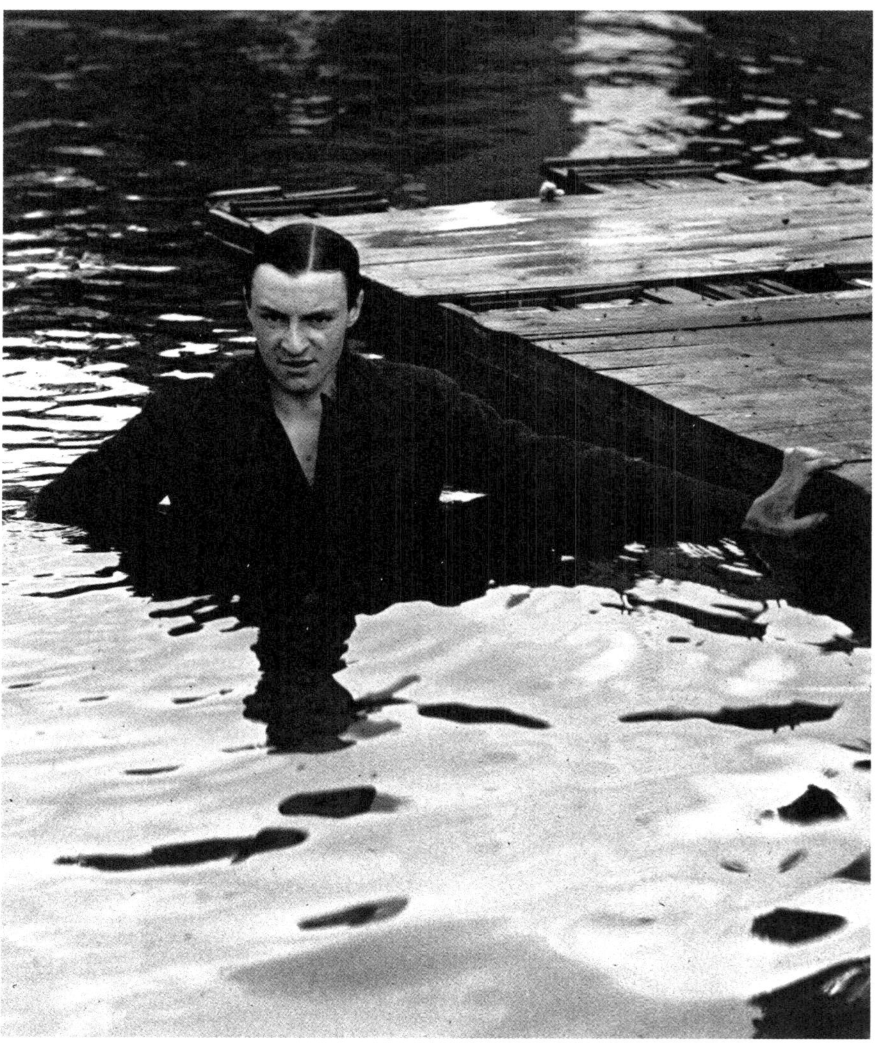

Raymond van Weers (Oléo), Rouzat, 1910.

On the afternoon of 29 May 1910, the fifteen-year-old Lartigue set off from his family's *hôtel particulier* at 40 rue Cortambert down the Avenue du Bois de Boulogne towards the Allée des Acacias, his hefty Klapp camera pulling on his arm. 'Suppose I go to the park to photograph the ladies in the most outrageous and beautiful hats.'[1] Lartigue had already begun making detailed fashion drawings from 1907 (see p. 90). One even appears in his maths exercise book: a sketch of a veiled woman's head, her hat decorated with quill feathers (below). 'Instead of drawing lions, palm trees or racing cars, I've had the idea of drawing women with hats and rings…. I've got a little piece of furniture for the purpose, and it has two drawers: my coloured pencils are in the top one, my drawings are in the bottom one.'[2]

The Bois de Boulogne offered rich pickings: from mid-April until Bastille Day on 14 July, the former royal hunting forest became Paris's open-air *salon*. From four until six in the afternoon, motor cars and horse-drawn

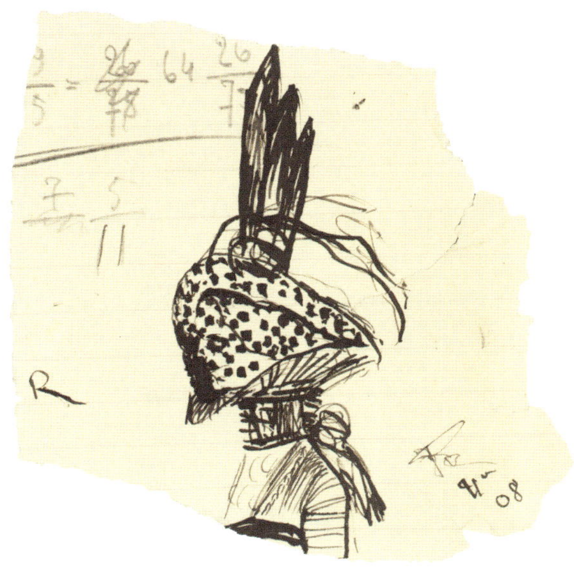

Sketch in Lartigue's
maths notebook, 1908.

open carriages circled the tree-lined drives, stopping at the Pavillon d'Armenonville, a seventeenth-century hunting lodge re-built as a restaurant, for '*le five o'clock*'. Earlier in the day, before lunch, high society and the demi-monde collided on the Allée des Acacias (the setting for several encounters in Marcel Proust's *Swann's Way*, published in 1913) or the Sentier de la Vertu (Path of Virtue) reserved for strollers, the women leaving their vehicles to display the latest fashions. A rush to the races or ritual social visits followed, with the theatre, dinners, balls or galas in the evening (including several changes of dress), the smart set leading what the novelist Colette described as 'the bustling lives of people with nothing to do'.[3]

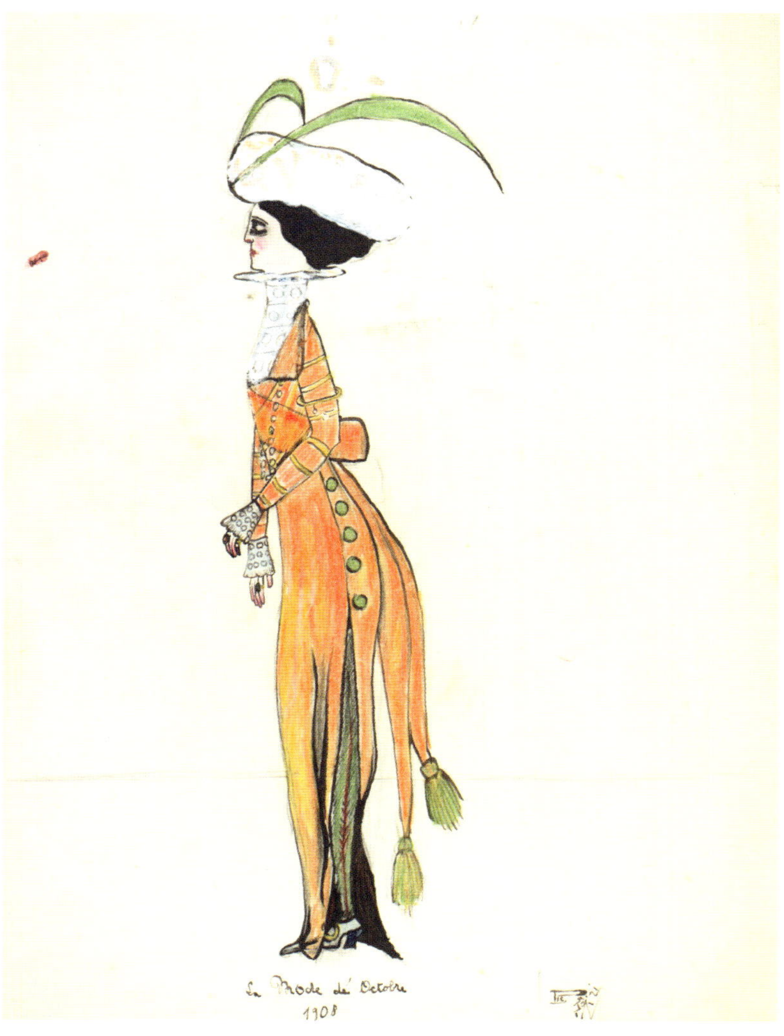

Lartigue fashion drawing, 1908.

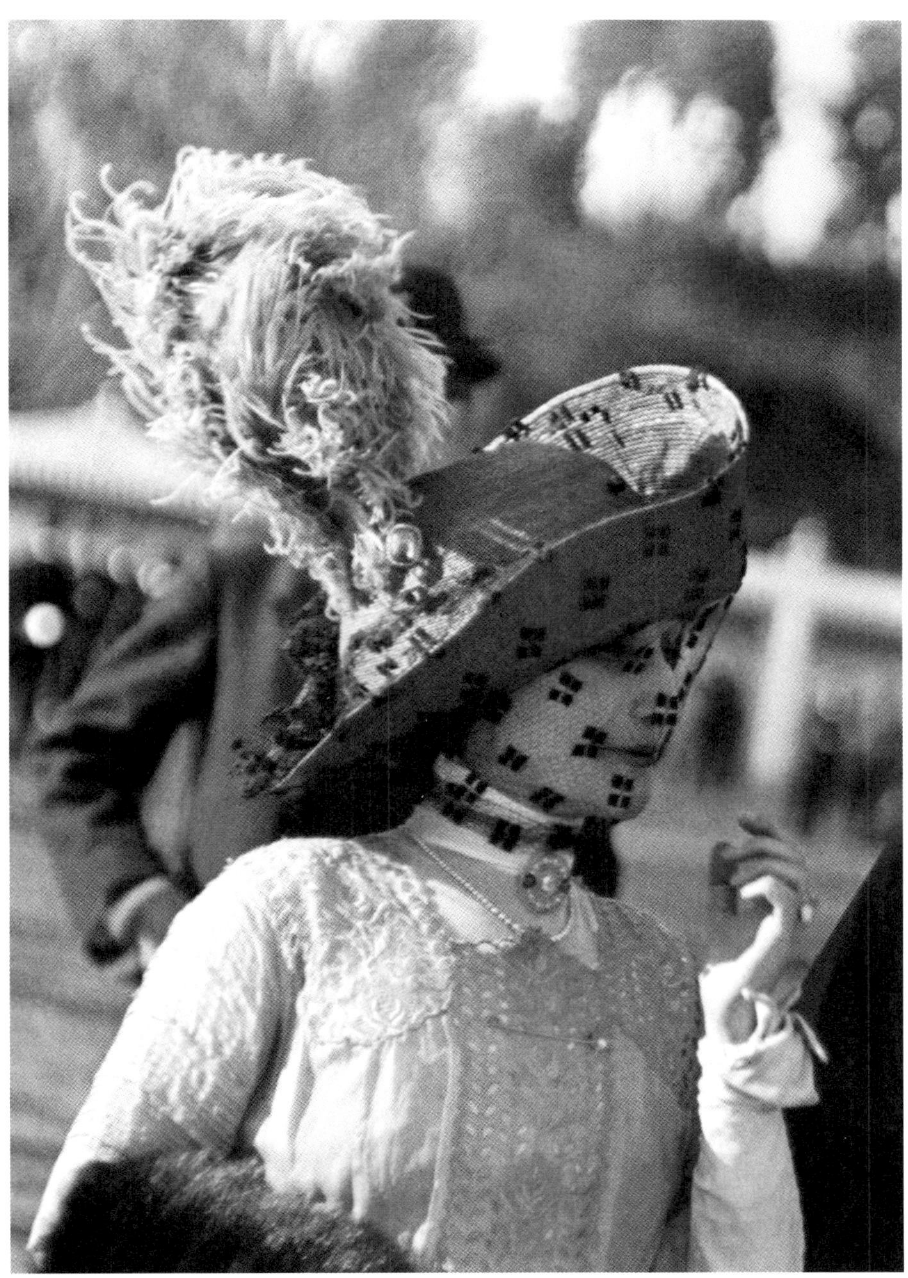

Bois de Boulogne (detail), 1912.

In 1911, Jacques set to work in earnest. In early February, Henri Lartigue moved the family from rue Cortambert to another *hôtel particulier* at 17 rue Leroux, even closer to the Bois de Boulogne. There, with characteristic dedication, Jacques arranged and rearranged his darkroom, with its multi-tiered storage cabinets, in a space next to the stables (recently converted to a garage) in the inner courtyard. He hurried to the Bois on the first night, before the family sat down to eat in their new dining room: 'One hundred metres on foot to go and take my fashion photographs!'⁴ His photograph albums reveal how he devoted about one-third of his images over the next three years to his new series.

'Sitting on a wrought-iron chair, I'd watch the ladies coming,' he recalled in a television interview over seventy years later. 'I'd think, "This one is pretty", so I'd jump up and take the photograph.'⁵ His new 9 × 12 cm Klapp Takyr (a gift from his father), with its larger-format negatives, captured

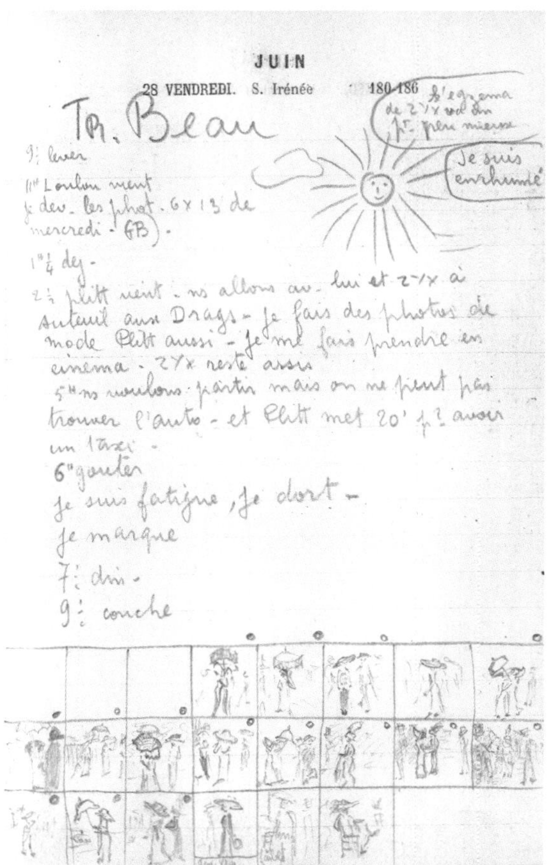

Page from Lartigue's diary,
28 June 1911.

greater detail. Its faster shutter speed of 1/1000 of a second offered him greater compositional flexibility. The teenager no longer needed perfect lighting conditions, nor to remain stock still. He estimated distance, as well as calculating light and depth of field, with the precision of a surveyor: 'Distance: four or five metres; speed: shutter screen slit 4 mm; diaphragm: that depends on what side she comes from…', he noted. 'I know very well how to judge distance…. What's not so easy is to get the correct focus, just as she has one foot ahead (but that's the most amusing thing to calculate).'[6]

'*She*', as Lartigue famously explained, was 'the lady who is very decked out, very fashionable, very ridiculous…or very pretty…. From afar she stands out among the strollers like a golden pheasant in a hen coop. She approaches…. I'm shy, trembling a little…. Twenty metres…ten metres… eight…six…Clack! My camera shutter makes so much noise that the lady jumps almost as much as I do.'[7] If alone, she would smile. Otherwise her

Page from Lartigue's diary, 12 June 1912 (compare drawing with photograph on p. 99).

male companion, infuriated by the growing band of amateur 'snapshot pests' in the Bois, would protest. 'But I was young. All that mattered to me was I had my photograph....'[8] If an attempt failed (say, people got in the way, or there was insufficient time to focus), Lartigue remained happy in the knowledge that the woman would return for her ritual walk (known as '*le footing*') along the same pre-determined route, if not that afternoon, then the following day. On an earlier occasion on the street near his home, he found himself unprepared: 'It is already getting quite dark and I don't have my camera.... Suddenly, on the pavement, I glimpse the prettiest woman I have ever seen coming towards me.... She advances, she approaches, and the closer she gets the more pretty she is. She's carrying a large muff and has such a pretty face under her big hat that regret for the missed photo is beginning to haunt me. Something different from regret, even...like a kind of inconsolable sorrow,' Jacques recalled, revealing the extent of his personal investment in his work.[9]

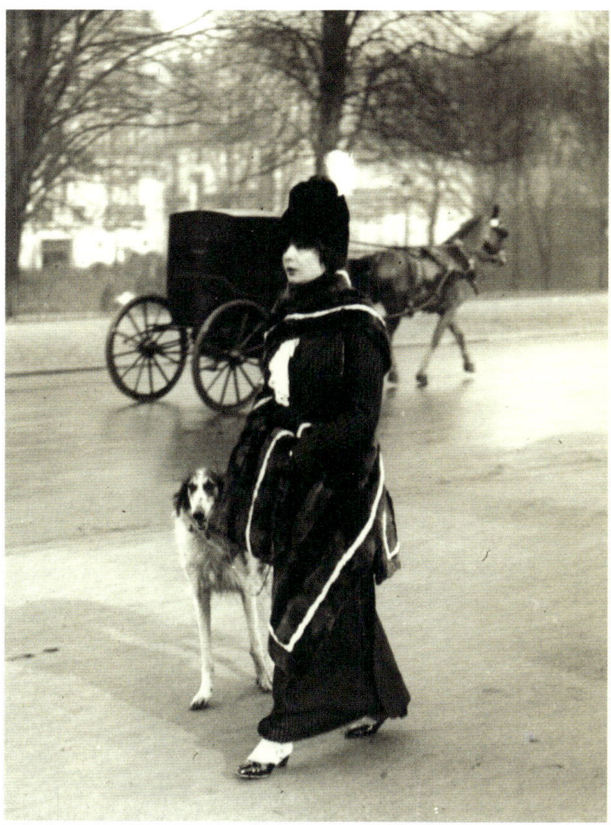

Avenue du Bois de Boulogne, 1912.

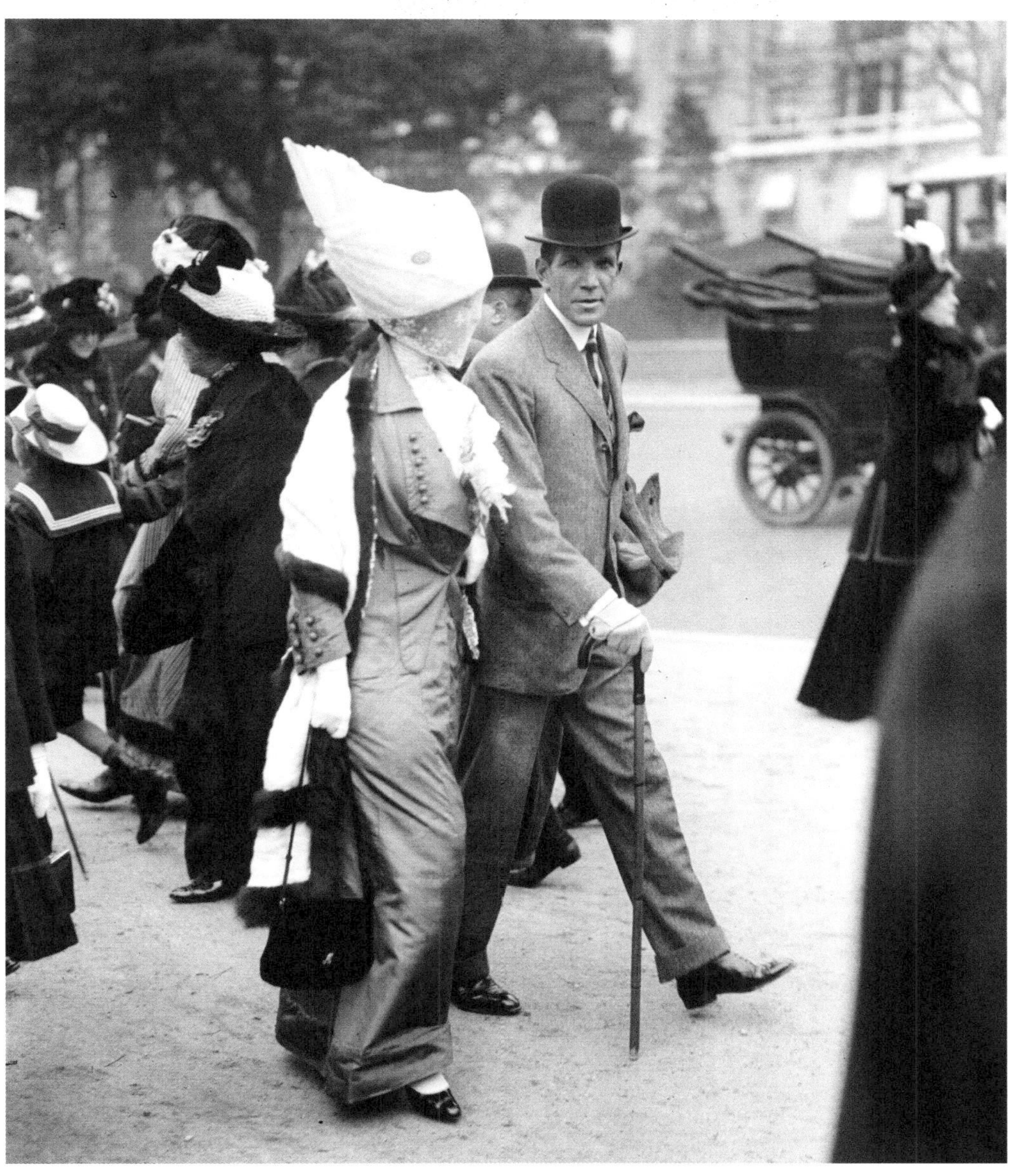

Tennis player and man about town Léon Freeborg, Avenue du Bois de Boulogne, 1911.

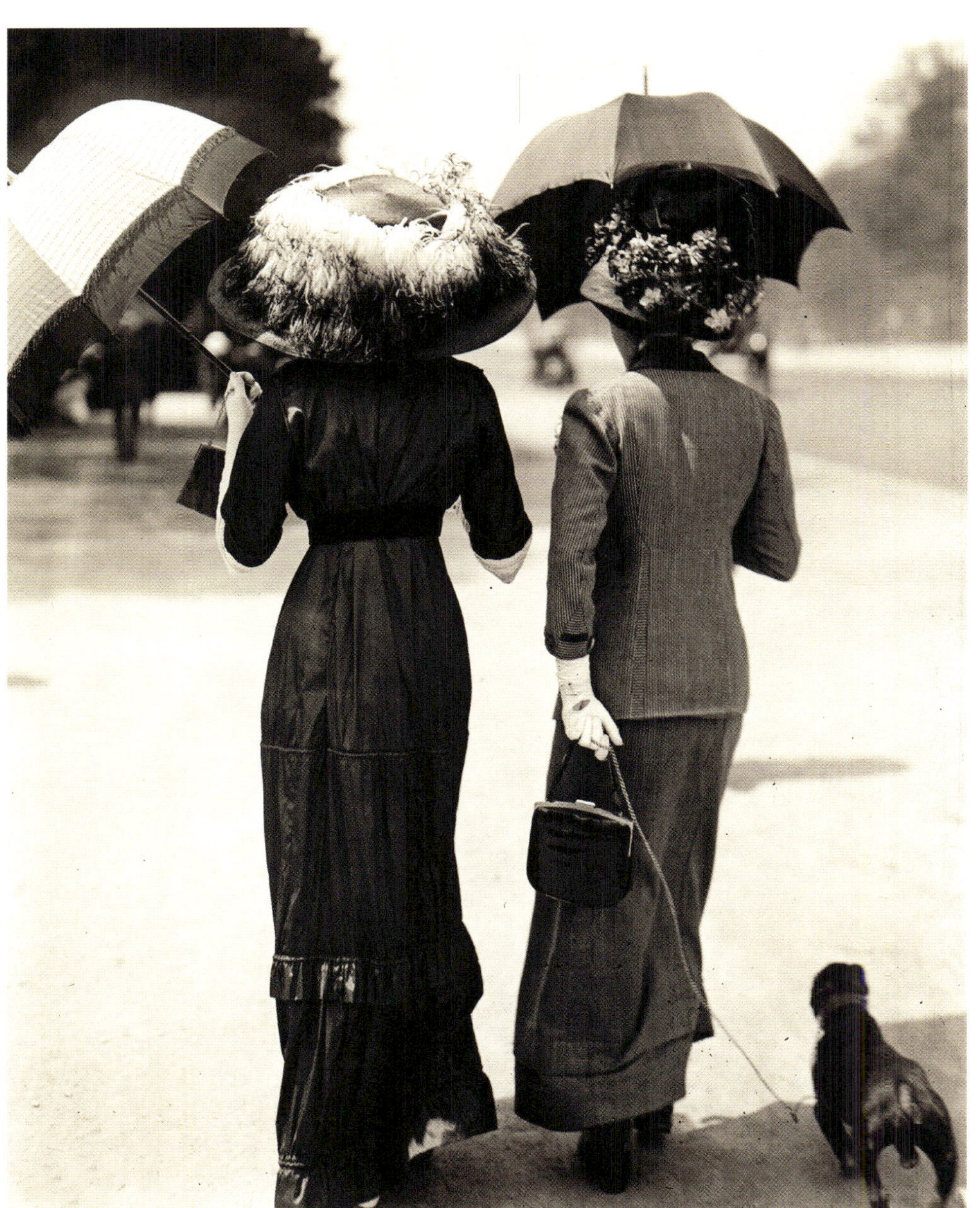

The Paris beau-monde enjoyed elaborate social rituals, greeting one another in the Bois de Boulogne whenever their paths crossed: 'Every time you saw an acquaintance, you raised your hat…. This went on every day of the week. It made for the most enormous number of greetings,' Lartigue recalled.[10] In one image, he captures a man accompanied by his over-dressed wife, tipping his homburg hat at a passer-by, while a figure walking in the opposite direction lifts his top hat to a lady (below). An elegant woman also graced the inside cover of John Szarkowski's catalogue for his 1963 Lartigue exhibition at MoMA, her intricate white lace veil pulled tight against her face to protect against the dust and sun, a lorgnette in her white-gloved hand ready to spot members of her tight-knit social set with its myriad hierarchies (p. 98).

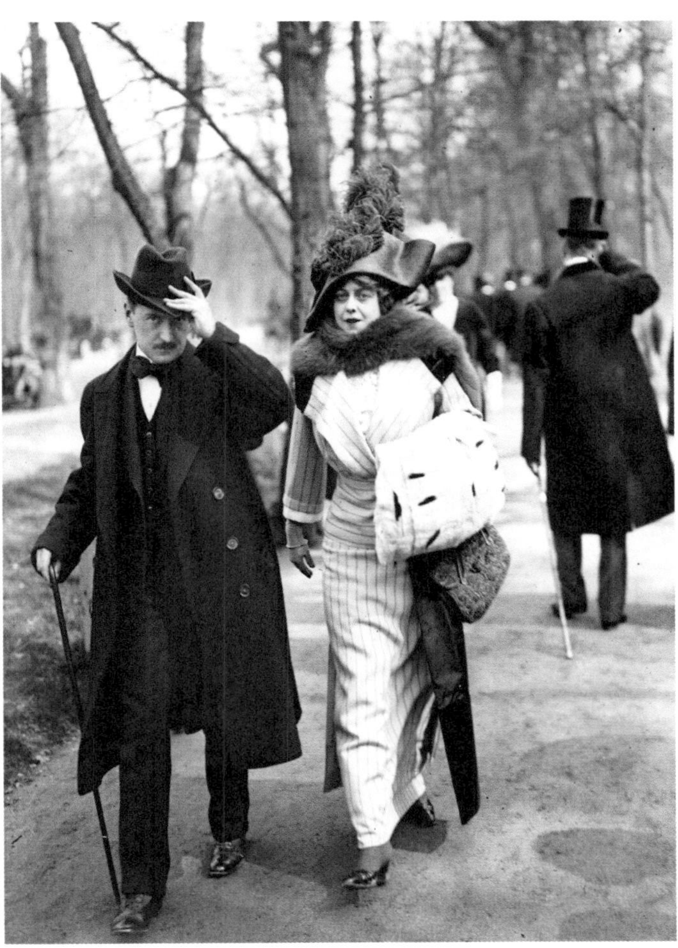

Le Sentier de la Vertu,
Bois de Boulogne, 1911.

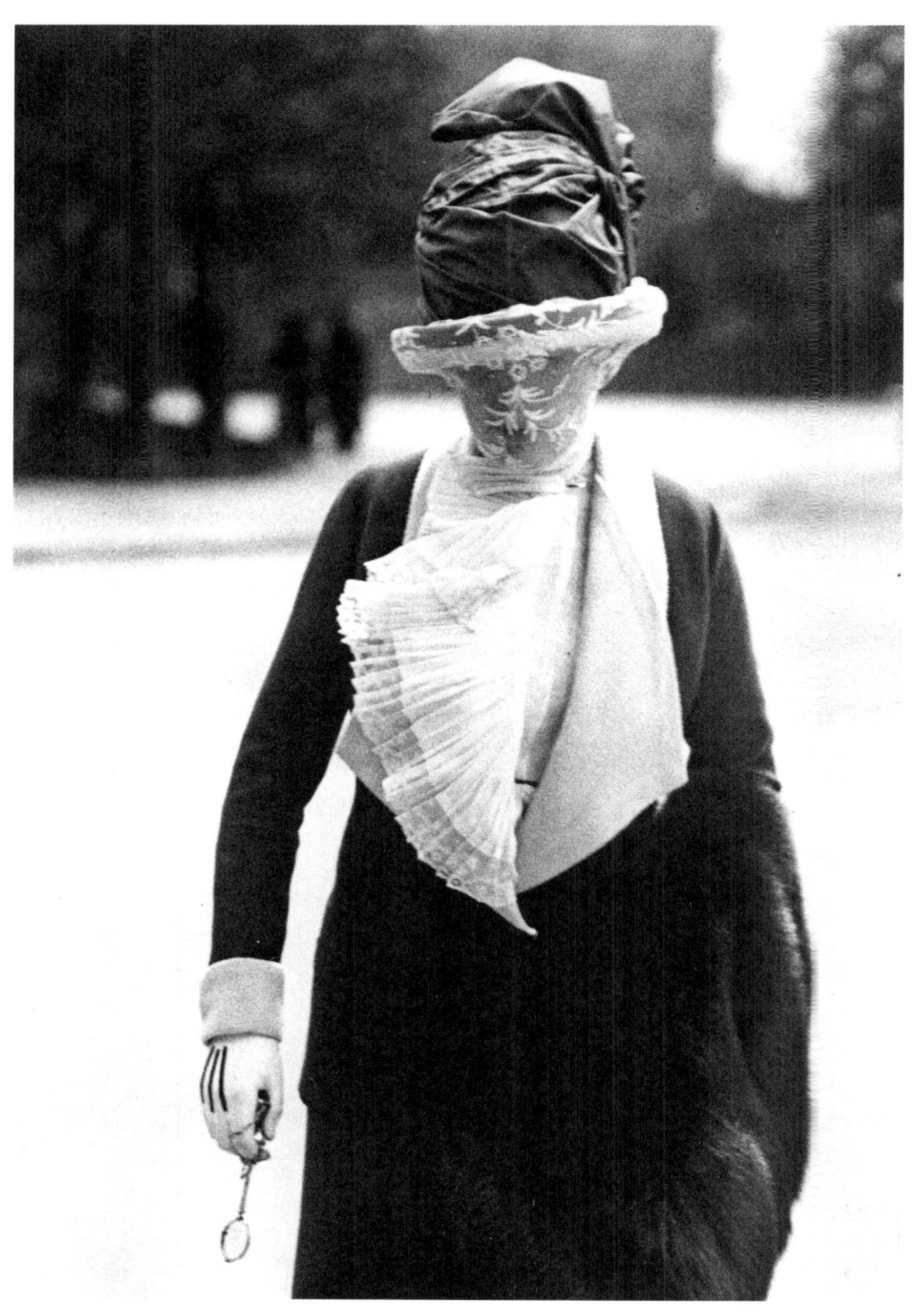

Porte Dauphine (detail),
Bois de Boulogne, 1911.

An actress or demi-mondaine, on the other hand, was cold-shouldered in public. Mary Lancret, a well-known courtesan, cuts a solitary figure as she walks diagonally into the frame with her small dog (an essential accessory), her slender figure encased in a silk dress with a striped skirt, her hat topped with an ostrich plume (below). Another young woman strolling along the Allée des Acacias, with a chinchilla wrap, muff and kohl-rimmed eyes, attracts a covetous glance from a male passer-by (pp. 100–1). A third woman, her Pomeranian leading the way, walks past Lartigue at a brisk pace, oblivious to the camera, her youthful profile barely visible (p. 102). 'Further away, on the more secluded paths, sometimes a fur-coated woman with a rouged mouth strolls, on high heels that make her walk like a strange bird, leaving a trail of perfume in the warm wafts of the spring air…'[11] Sundays at the Bois de Boulogne were reserved for parents with young daughters or young people on their own. 'No actresses or *cocottes*,' Jacques added regretfully.[12]

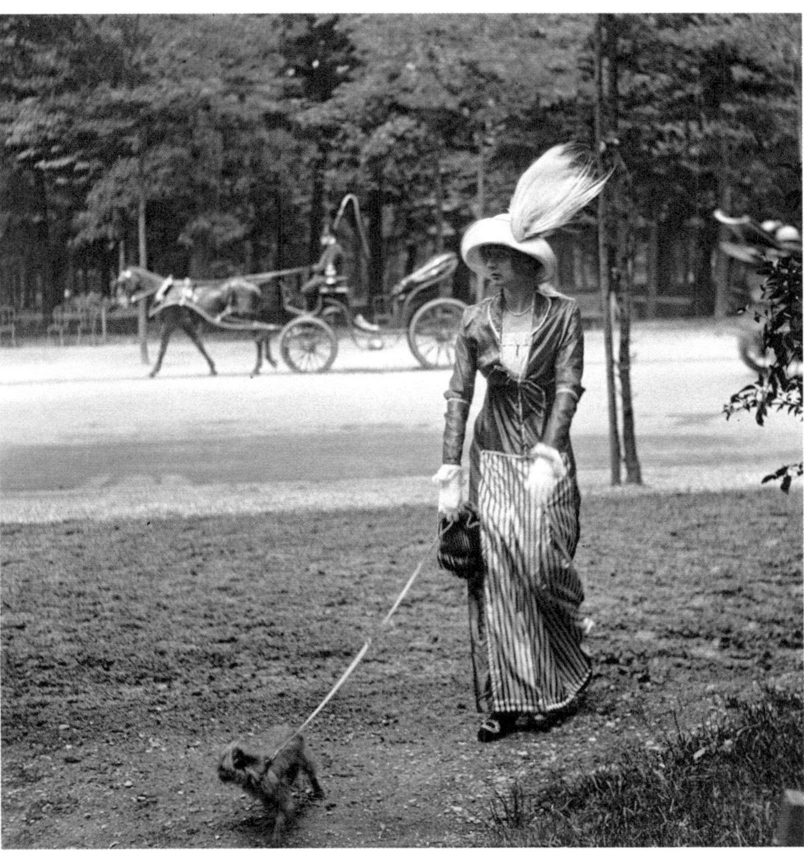

Demi-mondaine Mary
Lancret, Allée des Acacias,
Bois de Boulogne, 1912.

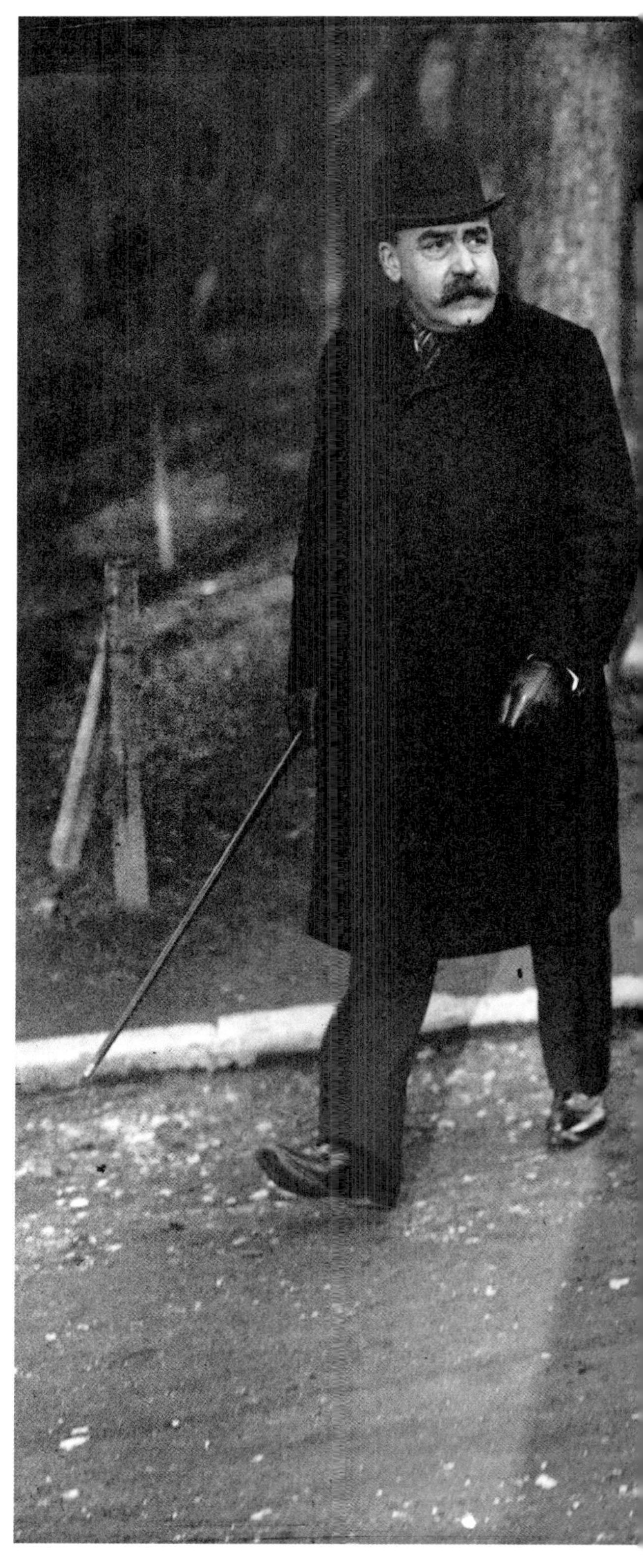

Allée des Acacias, Bois de Boulogne, 1911.

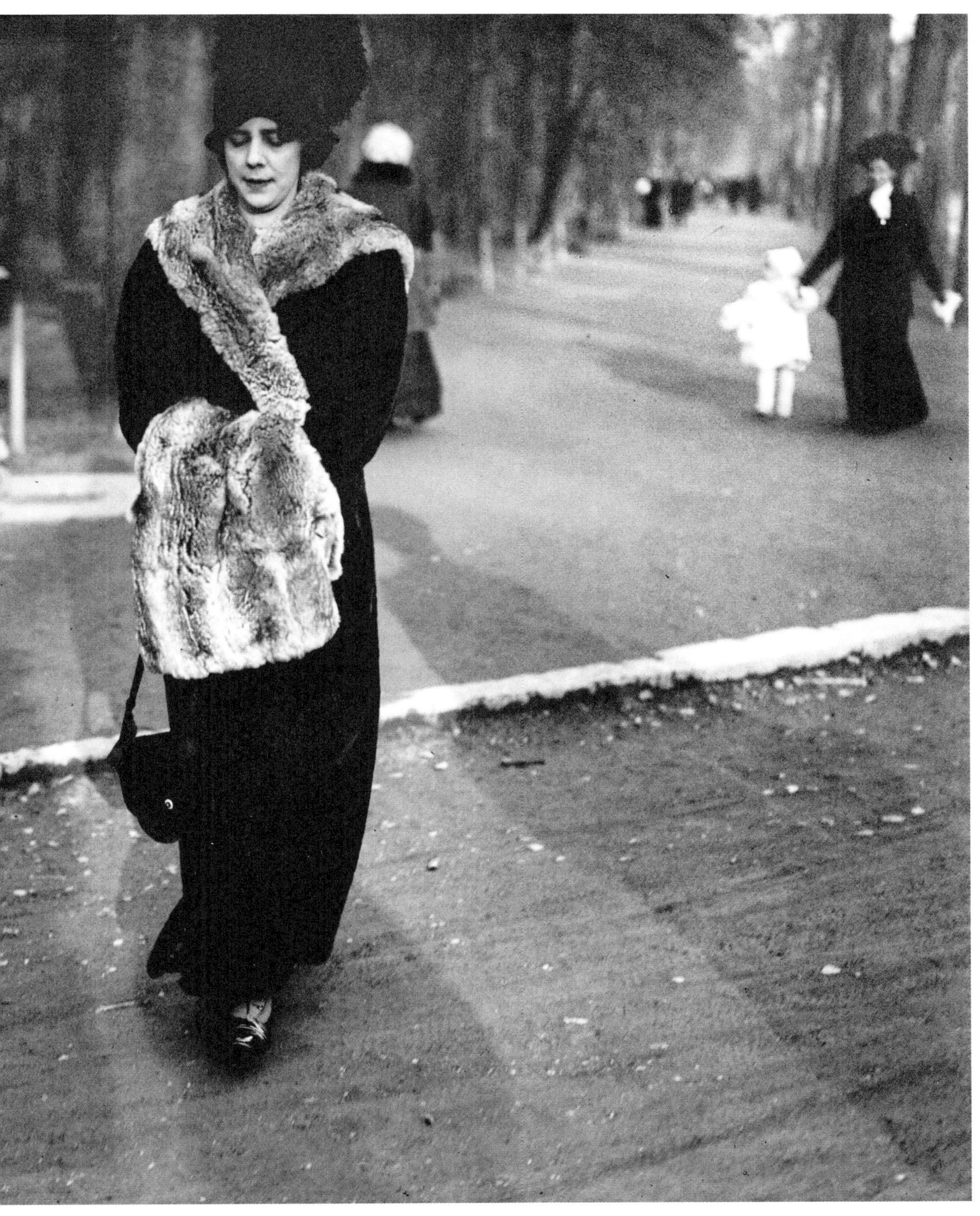

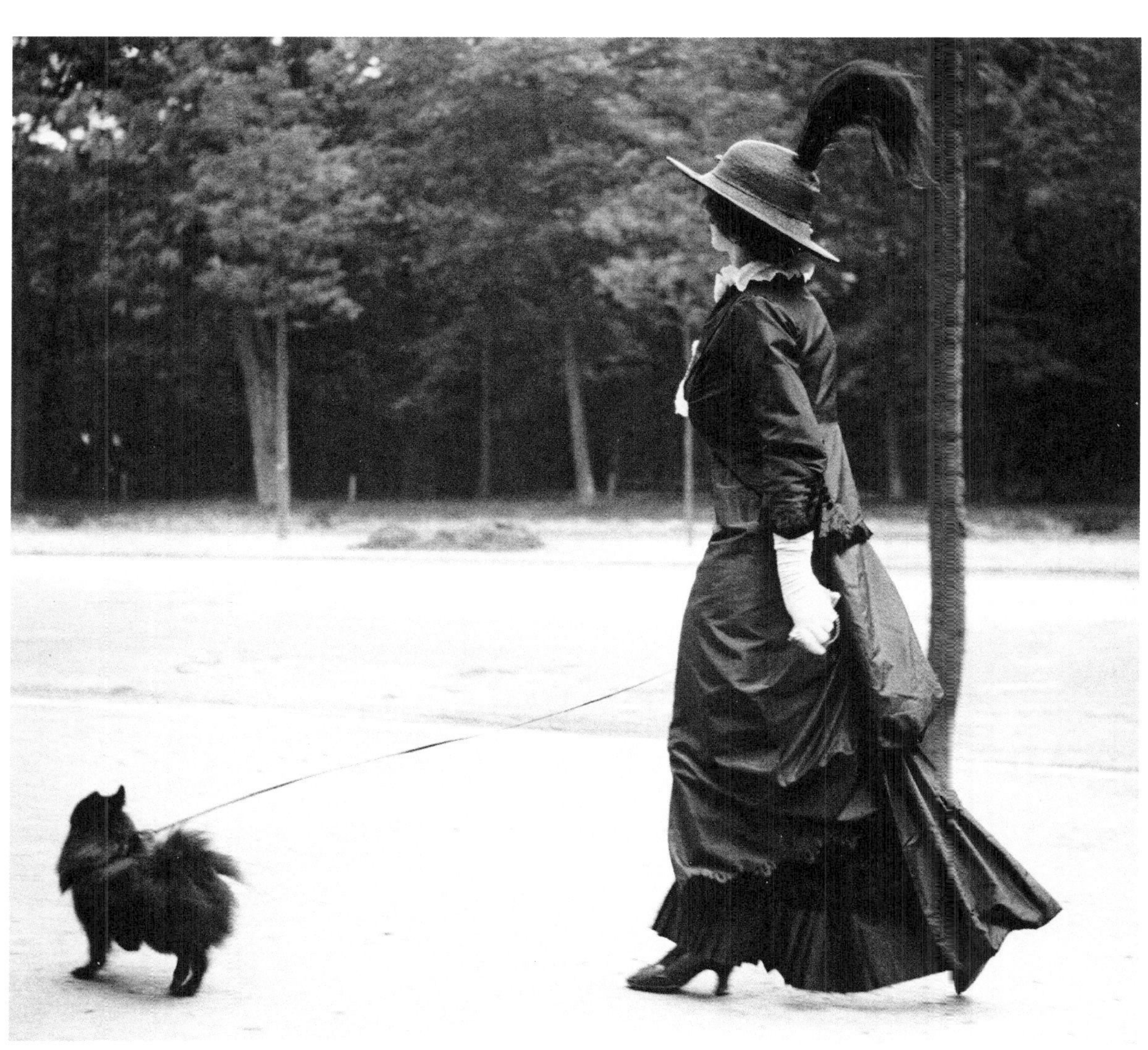

One morning in early 1911, the teenager captured Régina Badet, an actress and dancer at the Opéra Comique (below). Realizing she had been photographed, Badet asked Lartigue to bring his snapshot to her, writing down her address on a scrap of paper. 'I return to my wrought-iron chair on the Sentier de la Vertu. I feel a strange kind of excitement which makes me happy.... I take several more photos before going home for lunch, my appetite gone.'[13] The star-struck teenager (he had watched Badet perform at the Opéra Comique a few days before) sent Zissou in his place. But the encounter appears to have emboldened him. In his classic photograph from that spring, actress Anna la Pradvina walks her two Jack Russell terriers, Coco and Chichi, down the Avenue du Bois de Boulogne, her majestic figure, swathed in dark furs, silhouetted against the pale background (pp. 104–5). 'The automobile was just in the right place, not behind her...', recalled the elderly photographer in a television documentary. 'You have to anticipate the moment, recognize it in a hundredth of a second. It's like a tennis match.'[14]

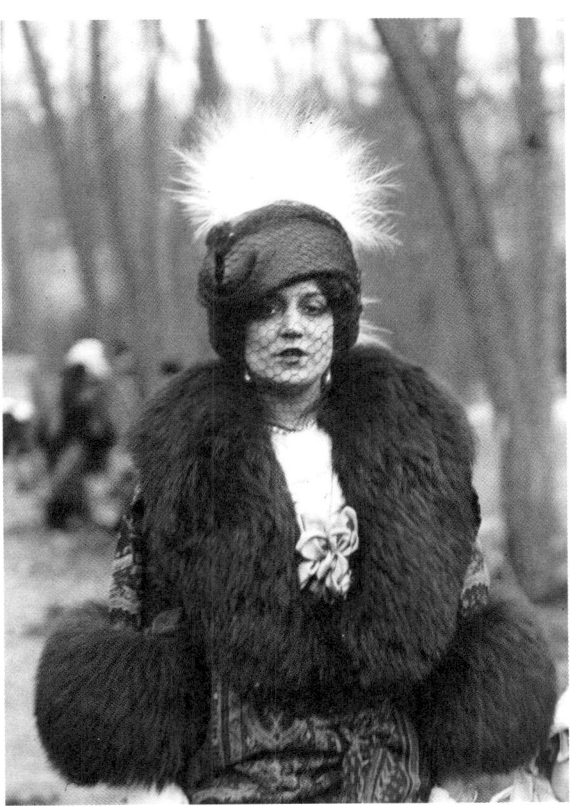

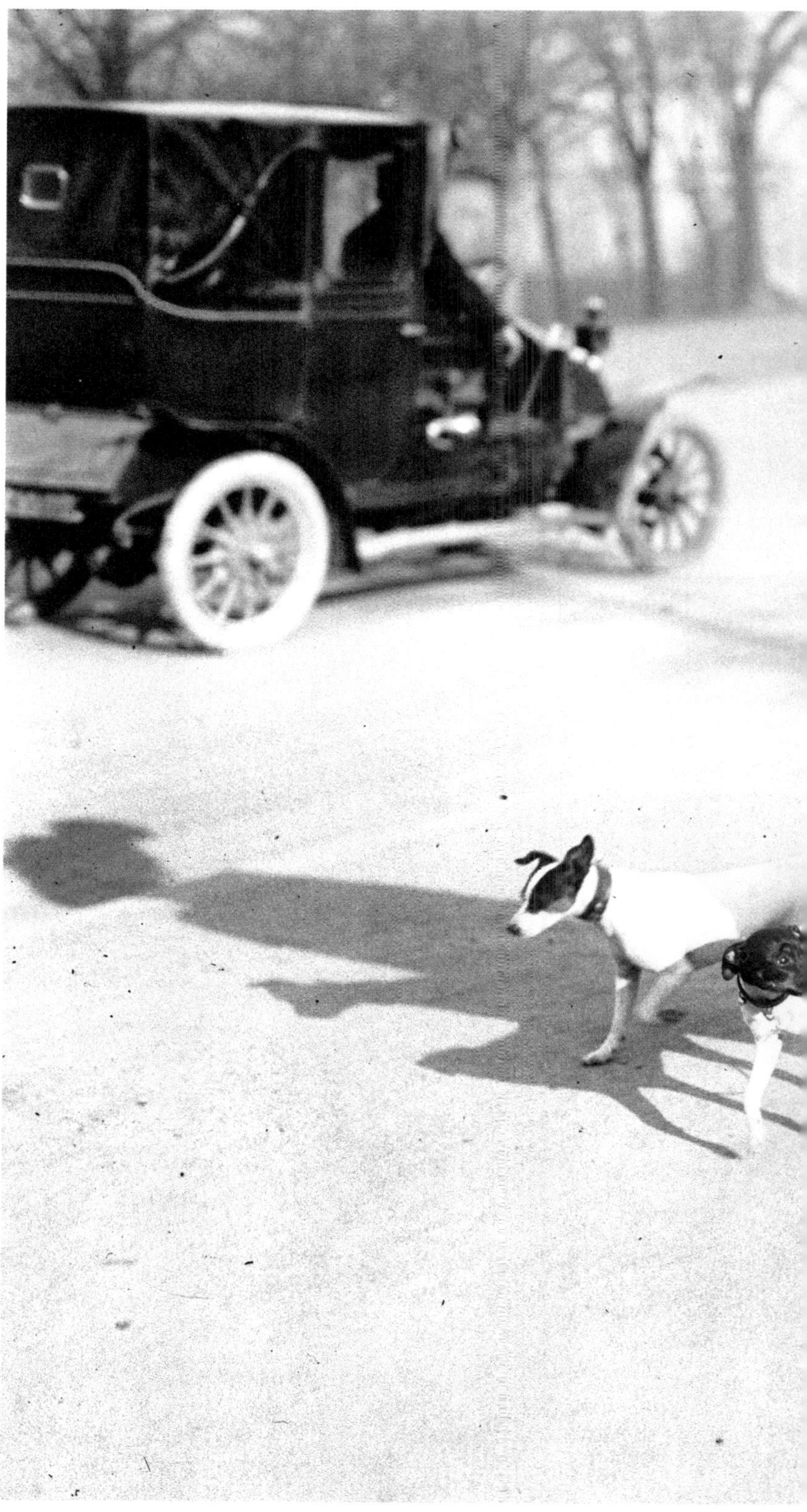

Anna la Pradvina, Bois de Boulogne, 1911.

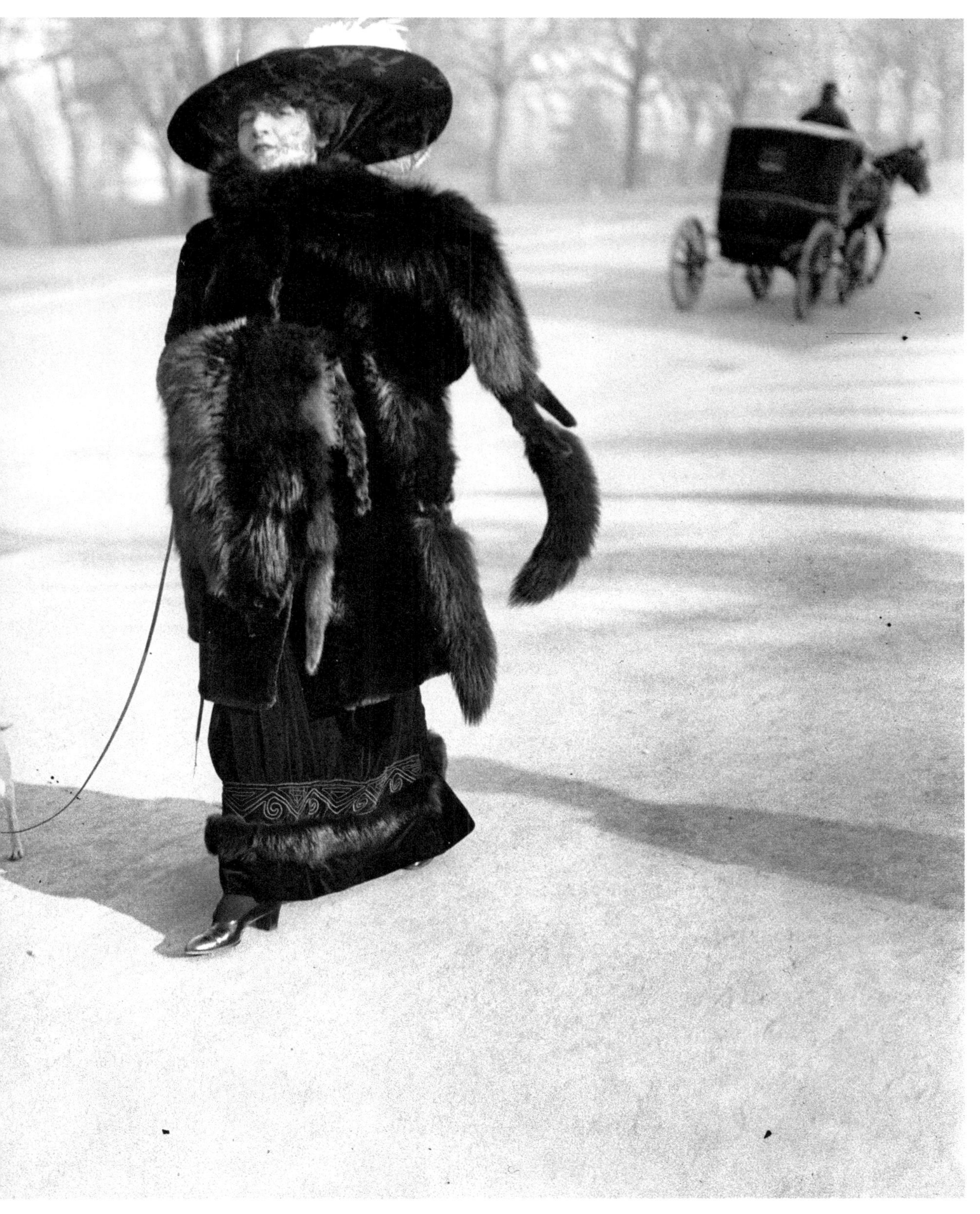

Lartigue was not, as already noted, the only photographer in the Bois de Boulogne. From 1909, a trio of postcard photographers, the Séeberger brothers (Jules, Louis and Henri), focused their lenses on Paris socialites and actresses in all their finery at the Bois, the races, and resorts like Deauville and Monte-Carlo. The brothers followed in the footsteps of other professional photographers, like the Marquis de Givenchy, an upper-class insider, whom Lartigue described as a 'real photographer who uses a [Klapp] Nettel 13 × 18 cm'[15] (Givenchy even captured Lartigue as a young man about town), Carle de Mazibourg, Albert Flament and Edmond Cordonnier, all of whom had begun photographing fashionable women in public places in the early 1900s. These '*instantanés de haute-mode*' (high-fashion snapshots), as the Séebergers called their work, were published in illustrated magazines like *La Mode Pratique* (edited by a Mme de Broutelles), *Femina* (the periodical favoured by Marie Lartigue) and *L'Illustration*, as well as national daily newspapers like *Le Figaro*. Editors like Mme de Broutelles required their photographers both to flatter their subjects' vanity and to satisfy readers eager for a glimpse of the latest fashions. 'You will never encounter elsewhere a woman with the same allure as those [you see] in the Bois,' wrote a Madame Carette in *Femina*.[16] 'She has a style that...enchants.' Magazine photographers delivered static images, complete with a brief description of the ladies' finery. One copy of *Femina* shows how images were sometimes created by gluing cut-up fashion snapshots onto a photograph of the Bois de Boulogne. The montage was then re-photographed to create the final print. These images (by 1910, a majority of illustrations in such publications were photographs) played a key role in disseminating the latest styles from Paris on both sides of the Atlantic.

The young Lartigue suffered no such editorial constraints. Despite his love of elegance, he had a satirical eye: 'Whenever Mme Linol comes to dine at our house, nothing amuses me more than...watching her talk,' he wrote of one of his mother's dinner guests.[17] 'She is pale and ugly, with bony cheeks and skin like tissue paper, and she has what is called "rice powder" on her face.... She finds it extraordinary that I remember the colour of the dress she was wearing last time. What would she say if I told her everything I had noticed about her: her hat with big ostrich feathers, her wrinkled neck tightly squeezed into the big band of lace around it, her bag as gleaming as her jewels....' As Kevin Moore observes, the young Lartigue's

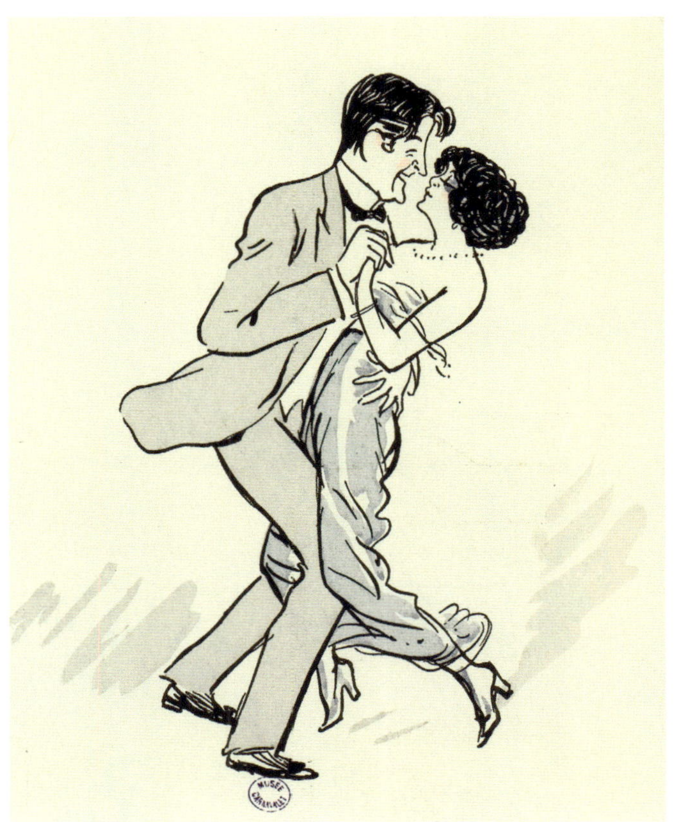

fashion photographs are closer in spirit to the illustrations of Georges Goursat, known as Sem, an *haut-bourgeois* insider who enjoyed instant success with his caricatures of prominent Belle Époque men and women, whether Rothschild bankers or figures like Régina Badet (above), the writer Colette, the comic playwright Georges Feydeau, or the aviation pioneer Louis Blériot.

Lartigue met Sem only in 1915, but a detail from a group photograph he took at the Stade de Saint-Cloud two years earlier (p. 108), reveals his admiration. A number of Lartigue's own subjects (had they seen the results) may not have appreciated his adaptation of a Sem-like humour to the more revealing photographic medium. Unlike the sensuous beauty of his later photographs of women, the teenager liked to capture his prey unawares: on the Sentier de la Vertu he photographs a middle-aged woman from behind, her high-waisted silk jacket emphasizing her bulk, while her miniature dog looks up askance at his mistress (p. 109). A fellow stroller's plain face is at odds with the elegance of her shot-taffeta gown and marabou boa; socialite Max de Cazavent is caught striding in gleeful pursuit of two women on the Avenue du Bois de Boulogne; while Gaby Boissy, a soprano at the Opéra Comique, and her sister Alice Clairville sport identical white fox pelts slung over their arms and around their necks, their black Pomeranian decorated with a matching white bow (p. 110). Another dedicated follower of fashion wears a giant sugarloaf hat, her vision so obscured that a friend guides her by the elbow (p. 111).

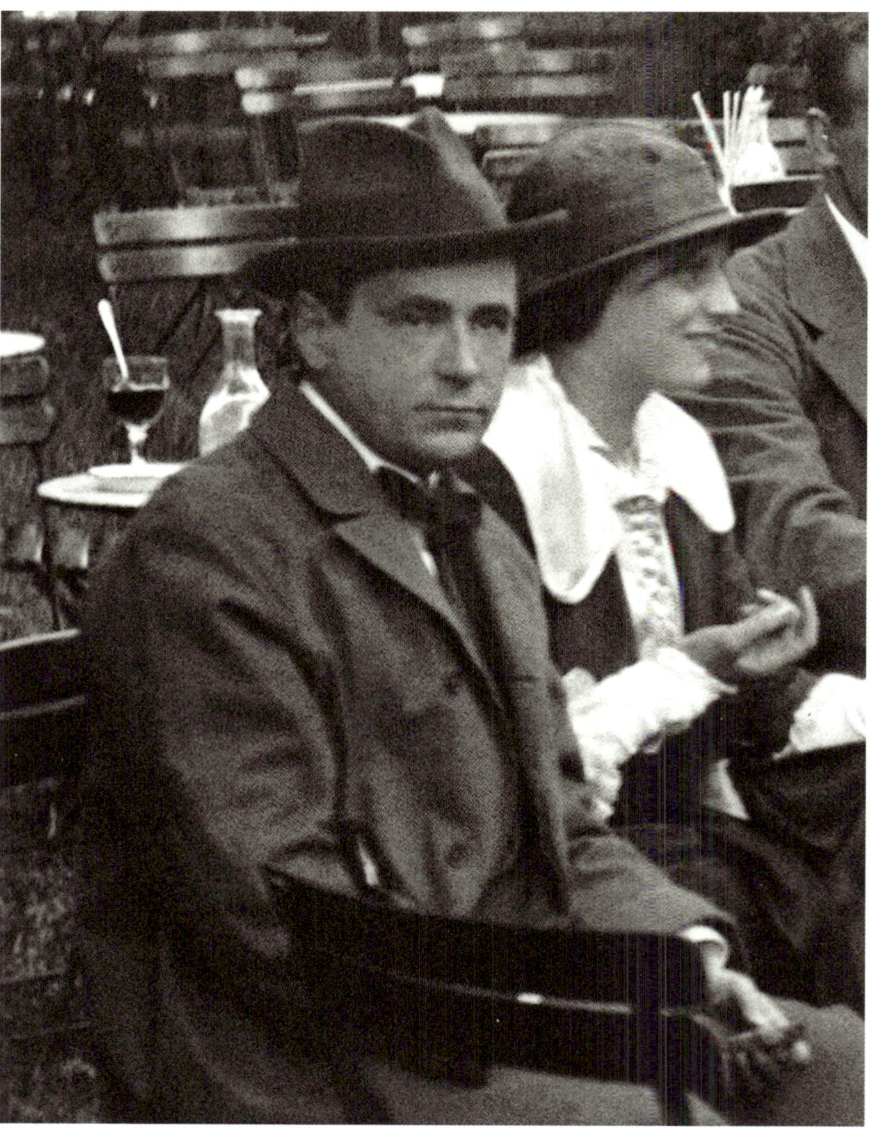

Sem (detail), Stade de Saint-Cloud, Paris, 1913.

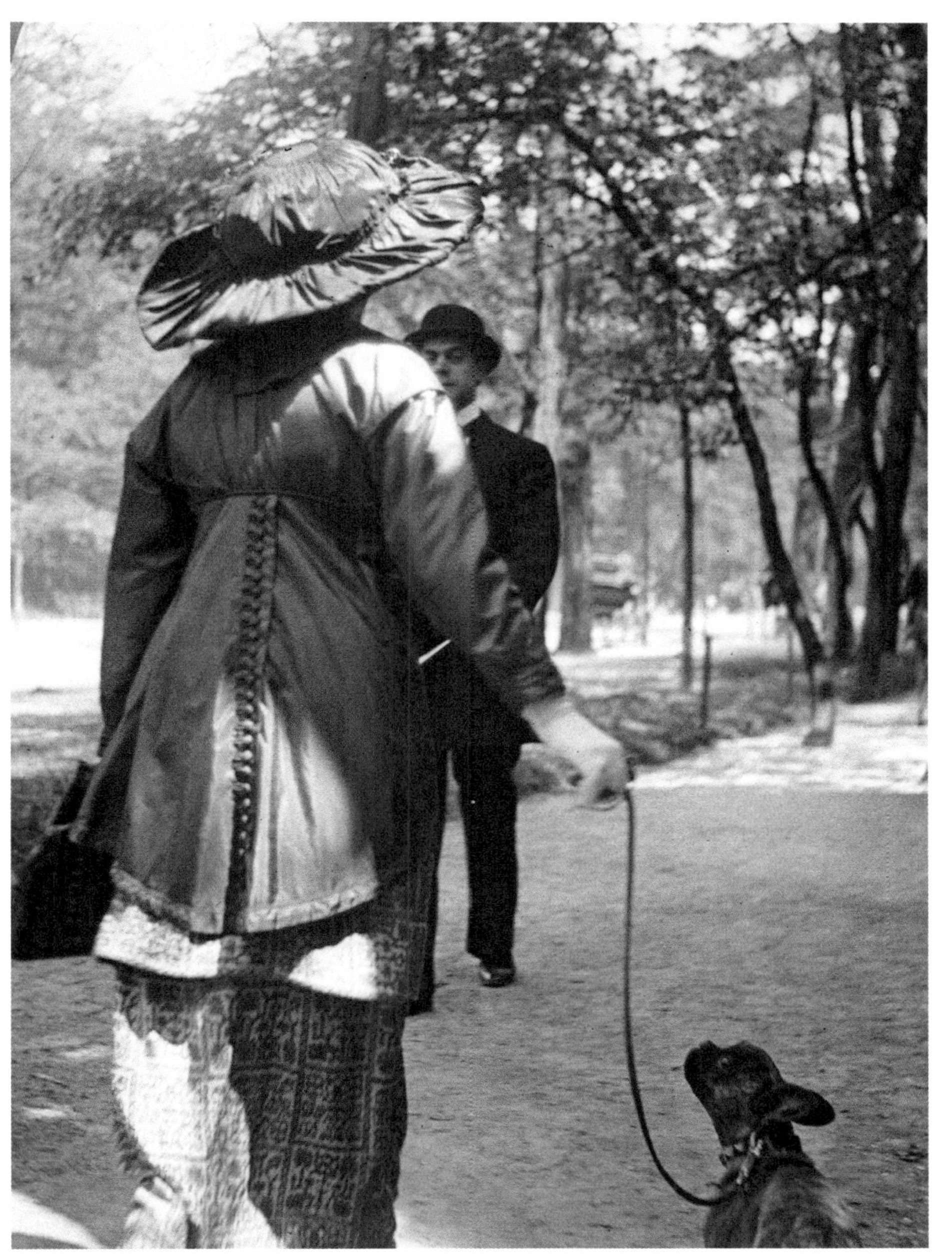

Le Sentier de la Vertu, Bois de Boulogne, 1912.

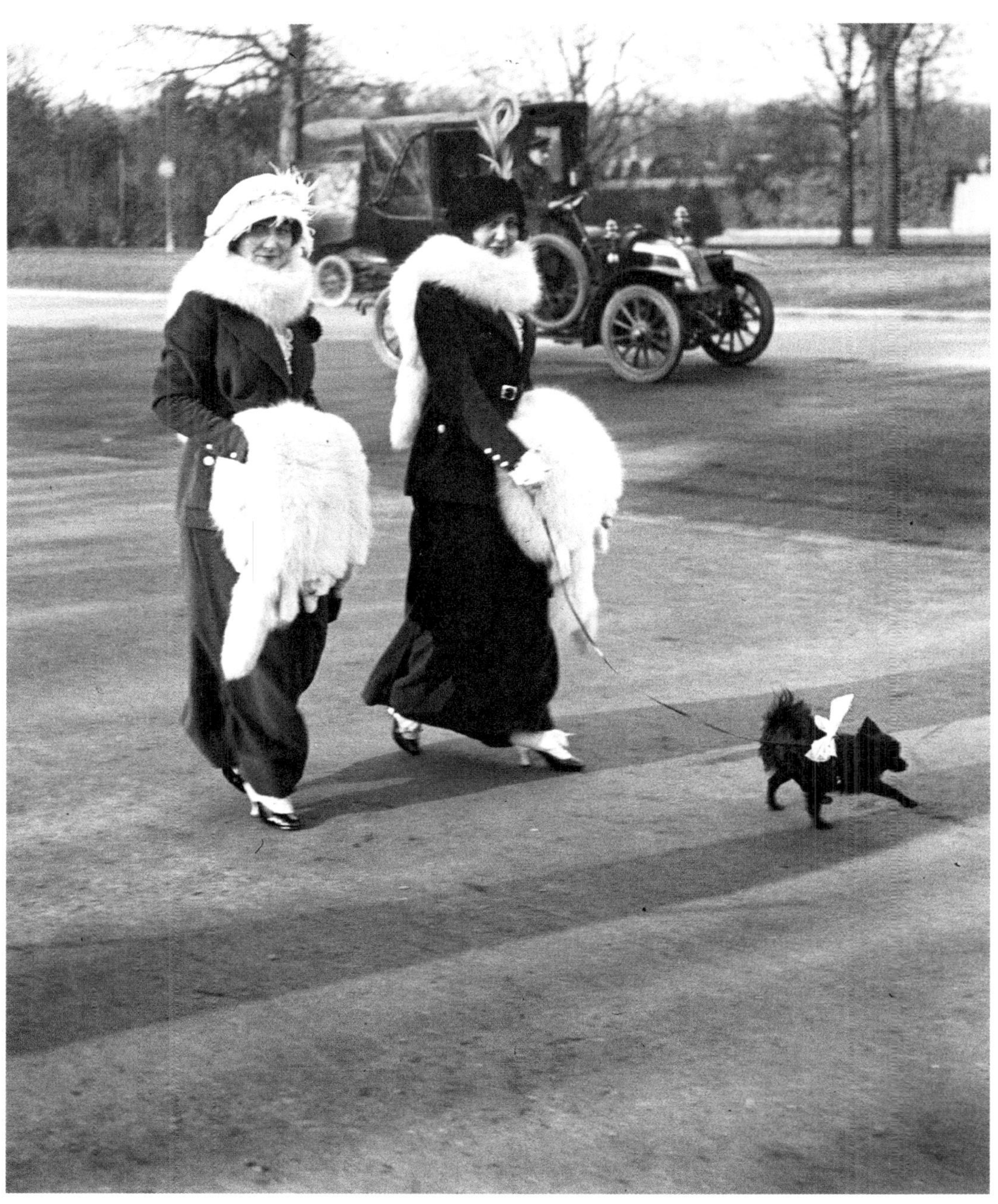

Gaby Boissy with her sister Alice Clairville, Avenue du Bois de Boulogne, 1913.

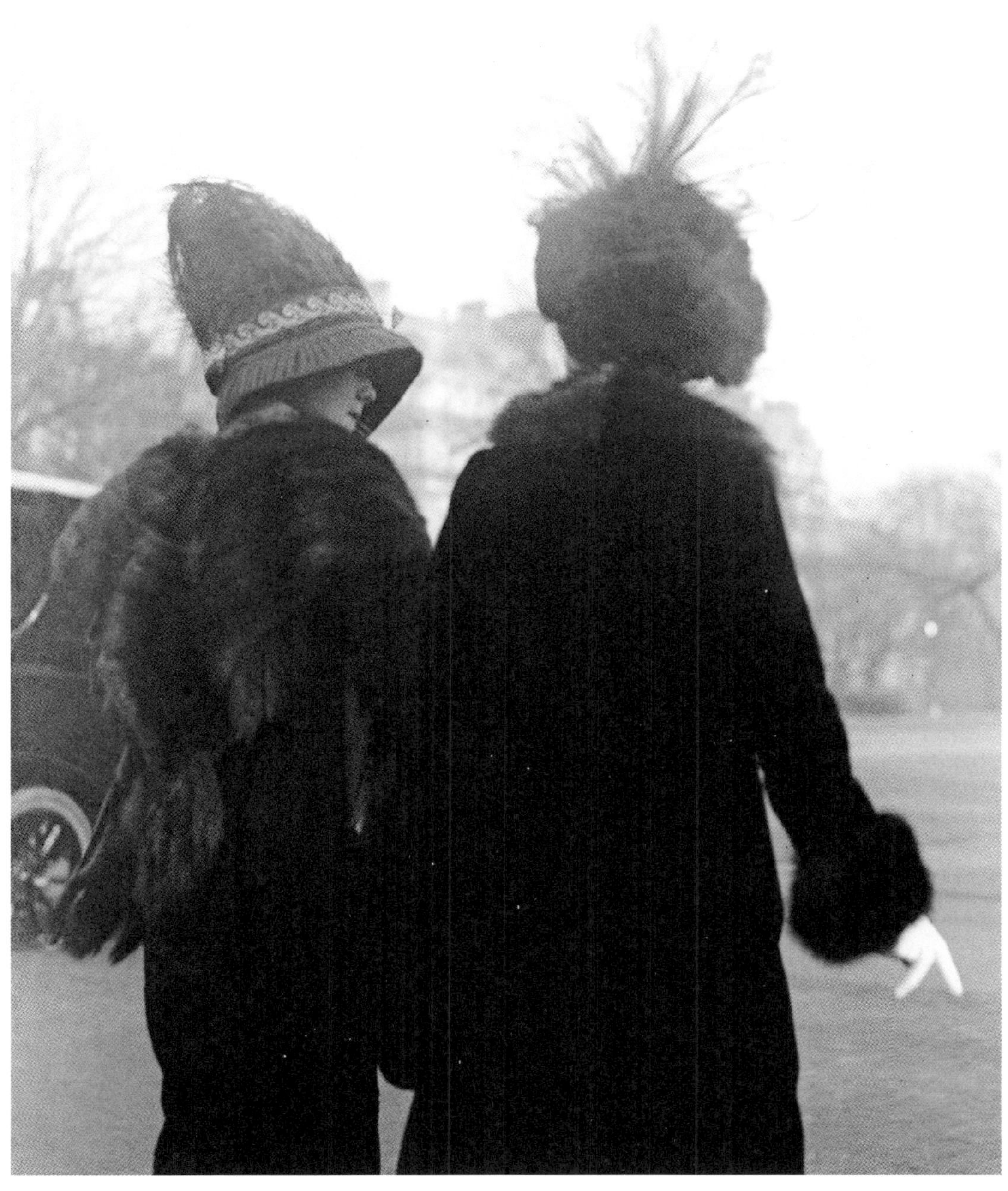

Bois de Boulogne, 1911 (from album page).

By the mid-1900s, hats had grown to vast proportions (see, for example, opposite and p. 114), much to the irritation of Monsieur Galbrun, a Lartigue family friend who complained that such confections blocked theatregoers' views of the stage. Even motor cars were built with a slightly higher body and wider top to accommodate them. Lartigue soon widened his search for women in 'amusing, enormous or ridiculous hats',[18] following in the footsteps of the Séeberger brothers to the races: Thursdays at Auteuil and Sundays at Longchamp, culminating in the Grand Prix de Paris at the end of June. There, models and fashionable women – rather than the horses – provided the ultimate spectacle. Unlike at the Bois, 'the prettiest and most outlandishly dressed women are often what are called "mannequins",' wrote Lartigue. '[They model] especially beautiful dresses or fantastic hats made by the great *couturiers* or designers…[and] they smile nicely instead of getting angry when I point my camera at them, and they walk around everywhere without even looking at the horses.'[19]

Like the courtesan Nana in Émile Zola's eponymous Second Empire novel, whose arrival at Longchamp racecourse causes a sensation 'as with the passing of a queen', the demi-mondaines set the style, deciding which couture creations would rise or fall in the coming season, blurring the boundaries with the haut-monde. Respectable women followed, copying their dresses, or hurrying to the same fashion houses: Doucet and Paquin on the rue de la Paix next to the Place Vendôme, or Poiret on the Avenue d'Antin. Dressing was arduous but essential work in the pursuit of status. *Grandes cocottes* like Liane de Pougy (who owned a *hôtel particulier* in the 8th *arrondissement*) and Cléo de Mérode spent vast sums on clothes, courtesy of their rich lovers – whether nouveau-riche industrialists, Indian rajahs, Eastern European royalty or kings of Spain. Periodicals like *Gil Blas* detailed their escapades: a stolen diamond necklace, a court case, quarrels, reconciliations, a 'suicide' attempt, or a *cadeau de rupture* (a farewell gift, like Liane de Pougy's seven-strand pearl necklace). Emblematic of the twilight of the Belle Époque, these women lived by their own set of moral values. 'Marriage is not forbidden to us. Instead of marrying "at once", it sometimes happens that we marry "at last",' explains Alicia, a retired *cocotte* in *Gigi*, Colette's novella about the demi-monde, who teaches her fifteen-year-old great-niece how to eat asparagus or *homard à l'Américaine* in 'faultless style', as well as the meaning of the word 'carat'.[20]

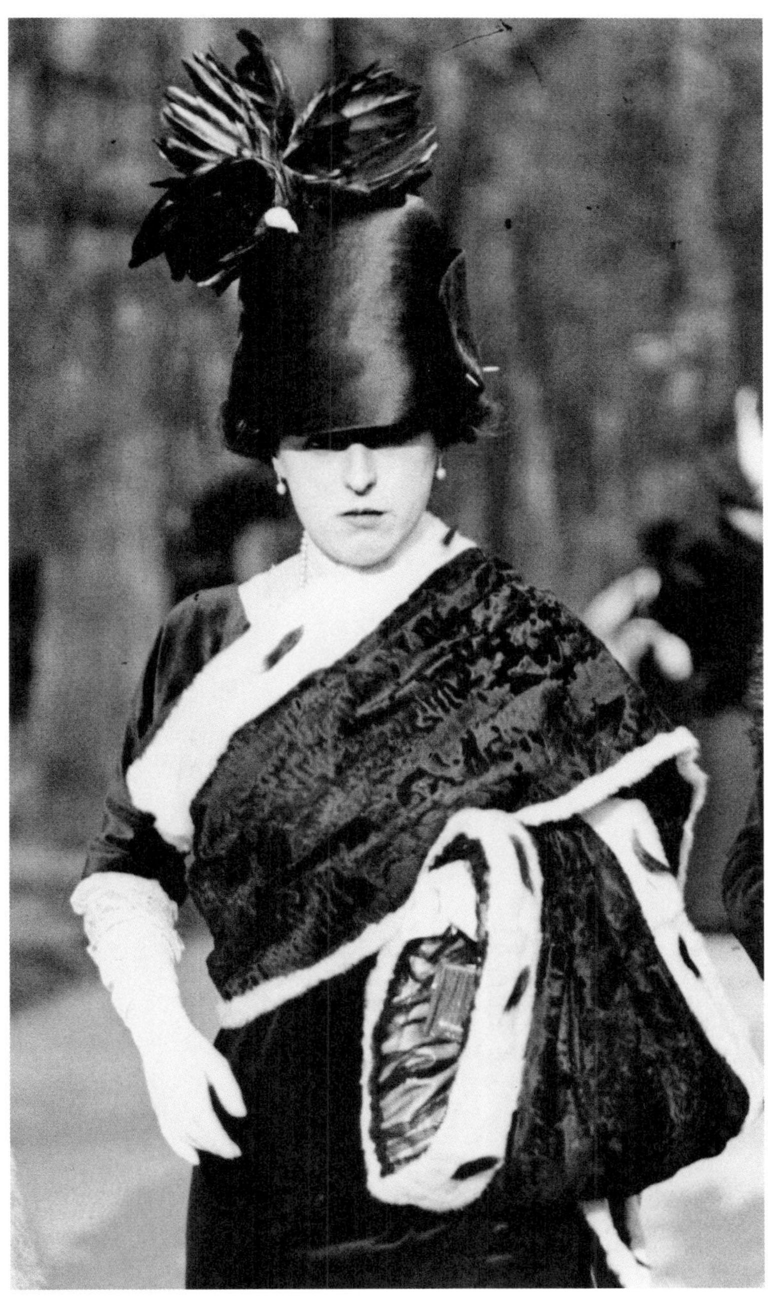

Bois de Boulogne (detail), 1911.

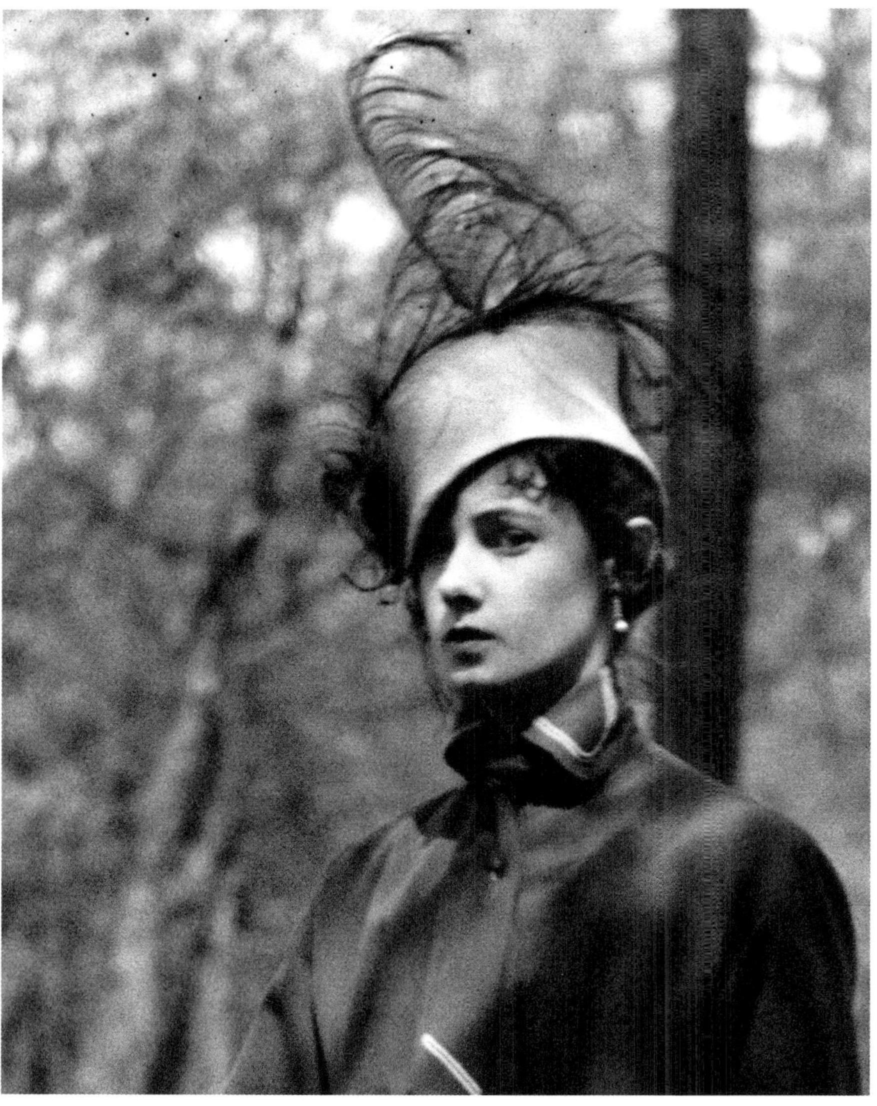

Circulating bare-headed among the bowlers and top hats, Lartigue sought out these *grandes cocottes*, whom his worldly cousin Oléo van Weers had already identified for him in the Bois de Boulogne: 'Liane de Pougy, Cléo de Mérode, Émilienne d'Alençon, Madame de Grandval…. I recognize them easily…', he wrote.[21] 'But I wouldn't want to speak to them,' he added, excitedly aware that such women, for all their fascination, were barred from polite society. His photographs of Cléo de Mérode, a great beauty, proved unsuccessful. Though he had already drawn a miniature ink sketch of her in 1908, she does not feature in his albums. But he captured Émilienne d'Alençon at Auteuil. Born the daughter of a Paris concierge, at a time when a career choice outside marriage was limited (forty per cent of all working women in 1900 were in service), d'Alençon started out presenting performing rabbits at the Cirque d'Été. Within months, a young aristocrat, Jacques d'Uzès, had set her up on the Champs-Élysées with servants, a carriage and a clothes allowance. 'If you sleep with a bourgeois, you're a prostitute, but if you sleep with a prince, you're a favourite,' d'Alençon once argued.[22] Her later lovers included Edward VII, as well as the elderly Leopold II of Belgium. 'A courtesan must never cry, must never suffer. She must stifle any sort of sentimentality, and play her part in a heroic comedy, and carry on,' explained her rival, Liane de Pougy, a friend of Colette.[23]

These '*princesses d'amour*', as Oléo called them, often licensed their photographic portraits to be sold as postcards in shops. Émilienne d'Alençon was no exception. She even had her studio portrait taken by Nadar, who had photographed Lartigue's maternal grandfather, Auguste Haguet. A late 1880s postcard photograph by a Professeur E. Stebbing shows the scantily clad young courtesan, crowned with an ostrich feather hat (below).

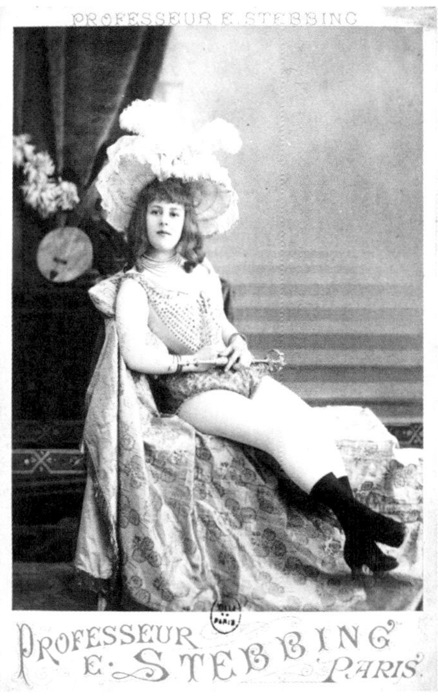

Postcard of Émilienne d'Alençon, by Professeur E. Stebbing, late 1880s.

Lartigue photographed the forty-one-year-old d'Alençon (below), her best years behind her, one hand drawing across her silk summer coat, as if concealing herself from the young man's merciless lens. In fact, the *cocotte* alarmed him so much, he later wrote, that his photographs of her were out of focus. A surprisingly modern second snapshot reveals d'Alençon's retreating figure as she evades his frame, with blurry, overexposed shadows in the background.

Lartigue catches a lascivious man at Auteuil ogling a demi-mondaine (a recurrent theme in his series), his companion joining in the fun. In another unforgettable image, a determined young woman bites her lip, unaware she is being photographed, while her swarthy companion appears uneasy, as if anticipating trouble ahead (opposite). Less satirical is his composition of a trio of women standing on chairs, all looking in the same direction at the approaching horses (pp. 118–19), which inspired Cecil Beaton's costume

Émilienne d'Alençon, the races at Auteuil, 1911 (album page).

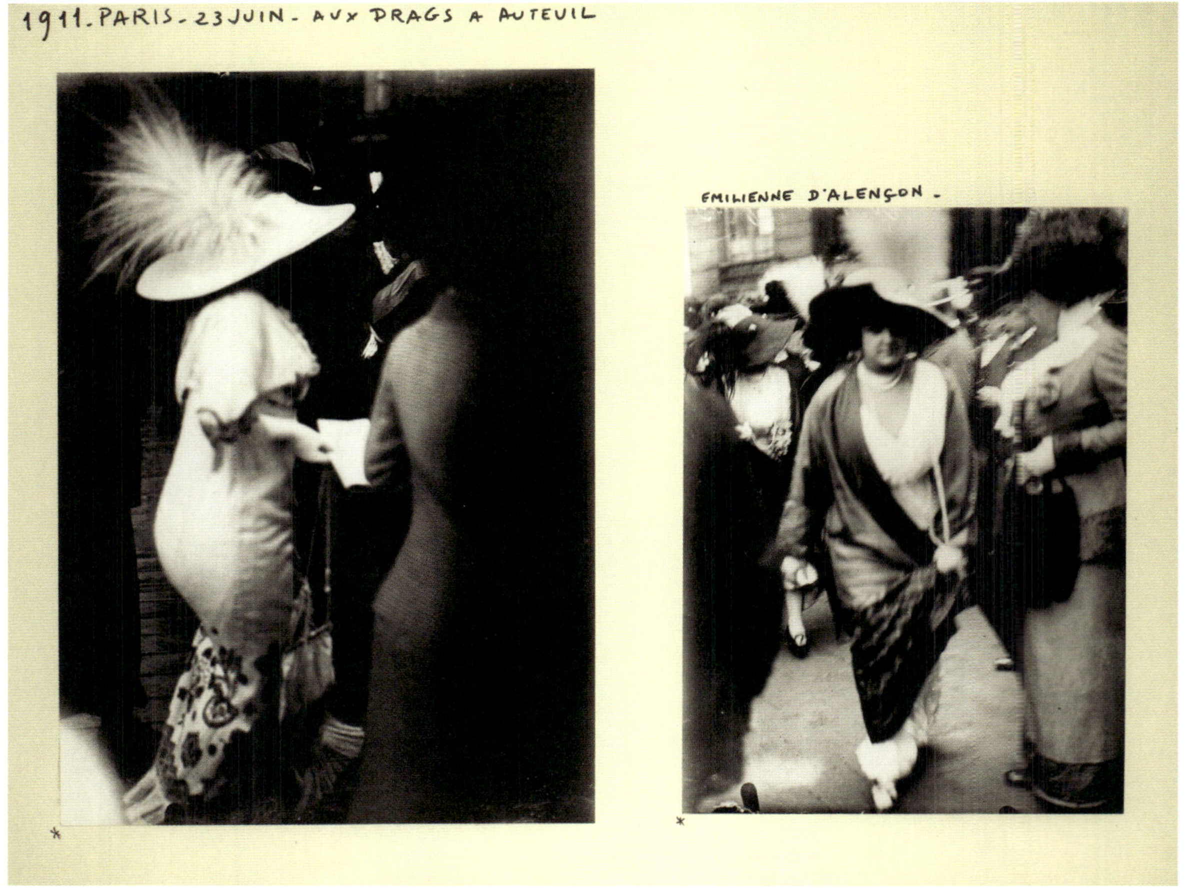

designs for the 1964 film adaptation of Lerner and Loewe's *My Fair Lady* – as Lartigue discovered when he met Beaton at an exhibition of his work at the Photographers' Gallery in London in 1971. Black and white stripes were all the rage in 1911, the vertical stripes of the women's gowns echoing the fence posts. The photograph reveals how a softer, more fluid silhouette had replaced the tightly corseted fashions of the early 1900s. The Ballets Russes' production of Rimsky-Korsakov's *Scheherazade*, meanwhile, inspired Paul Poiret's *jupe-culotte* (trouser skirt), then deemed an affront to western values. Lartigue first spotted the new fashion on a Paris street, but the light proved too dark. He fared better in Monte-Carlo in April 1911 (p. 120): 'All of a sudden I spot a "*jupe-culotte*"! She's walking over by the casino. A pretty woman, all in white. I hurry, and before she arrives at the casino steps I've been able to take two photos of her. For the second photo, she turned her head (furiously) to the other side.'[24]

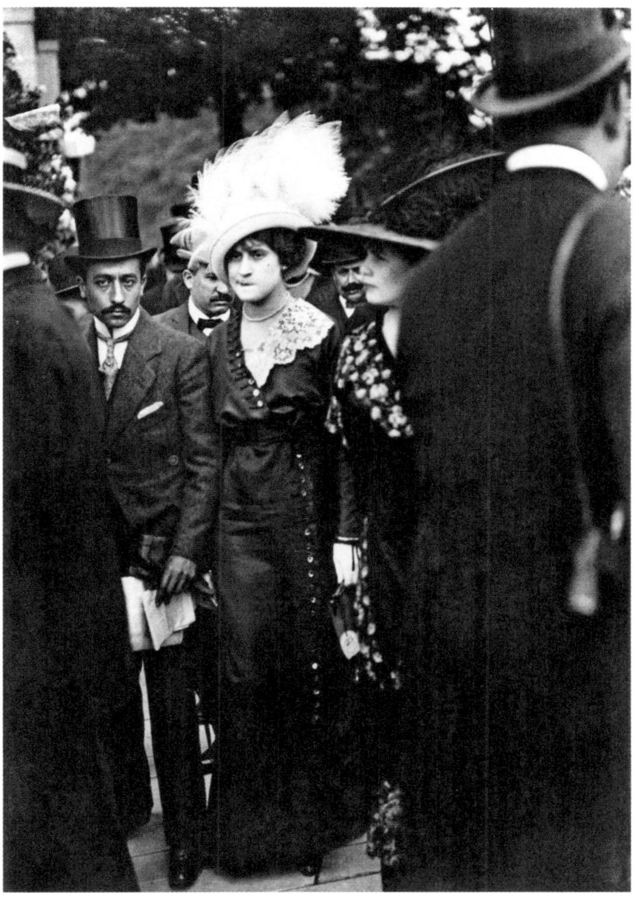

The races at Auteuil, 1911.

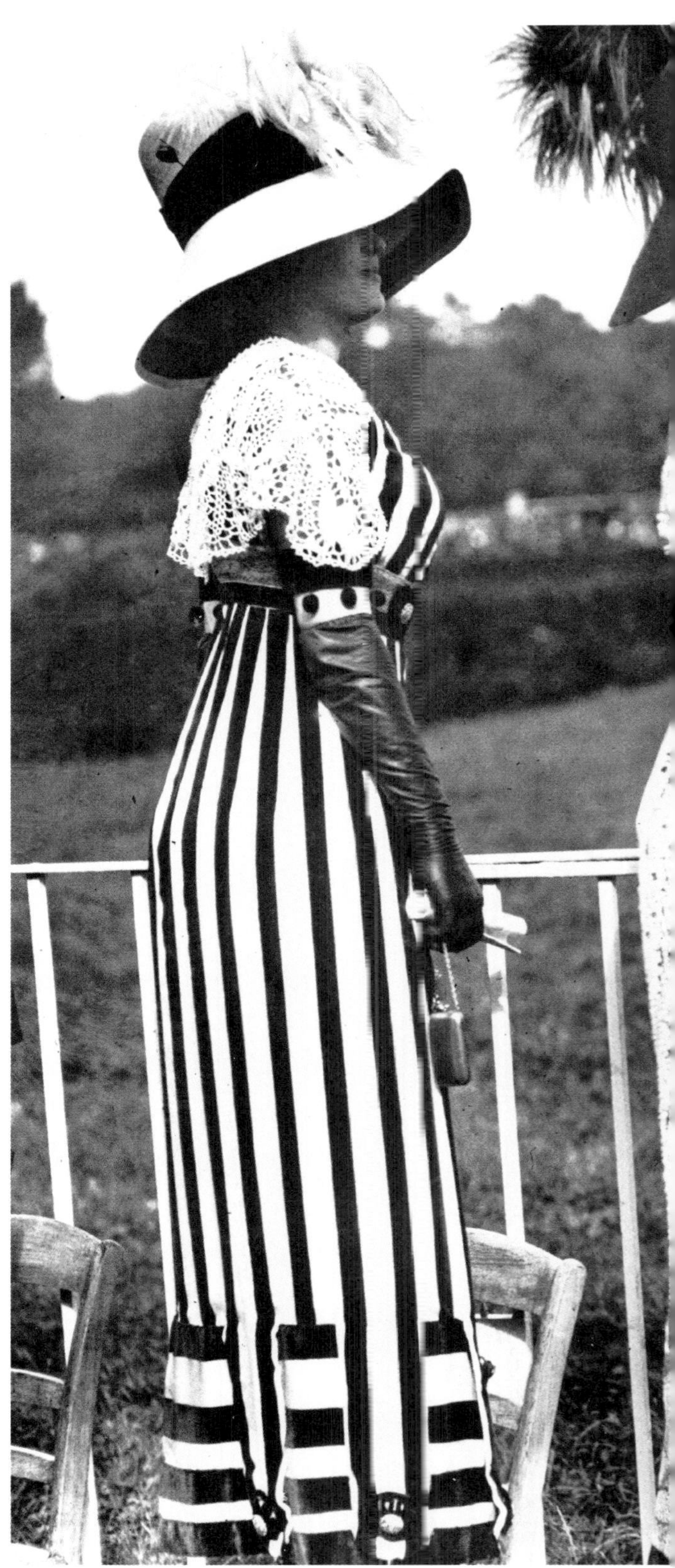

Carriage day, the races at Auteuil, 1911.

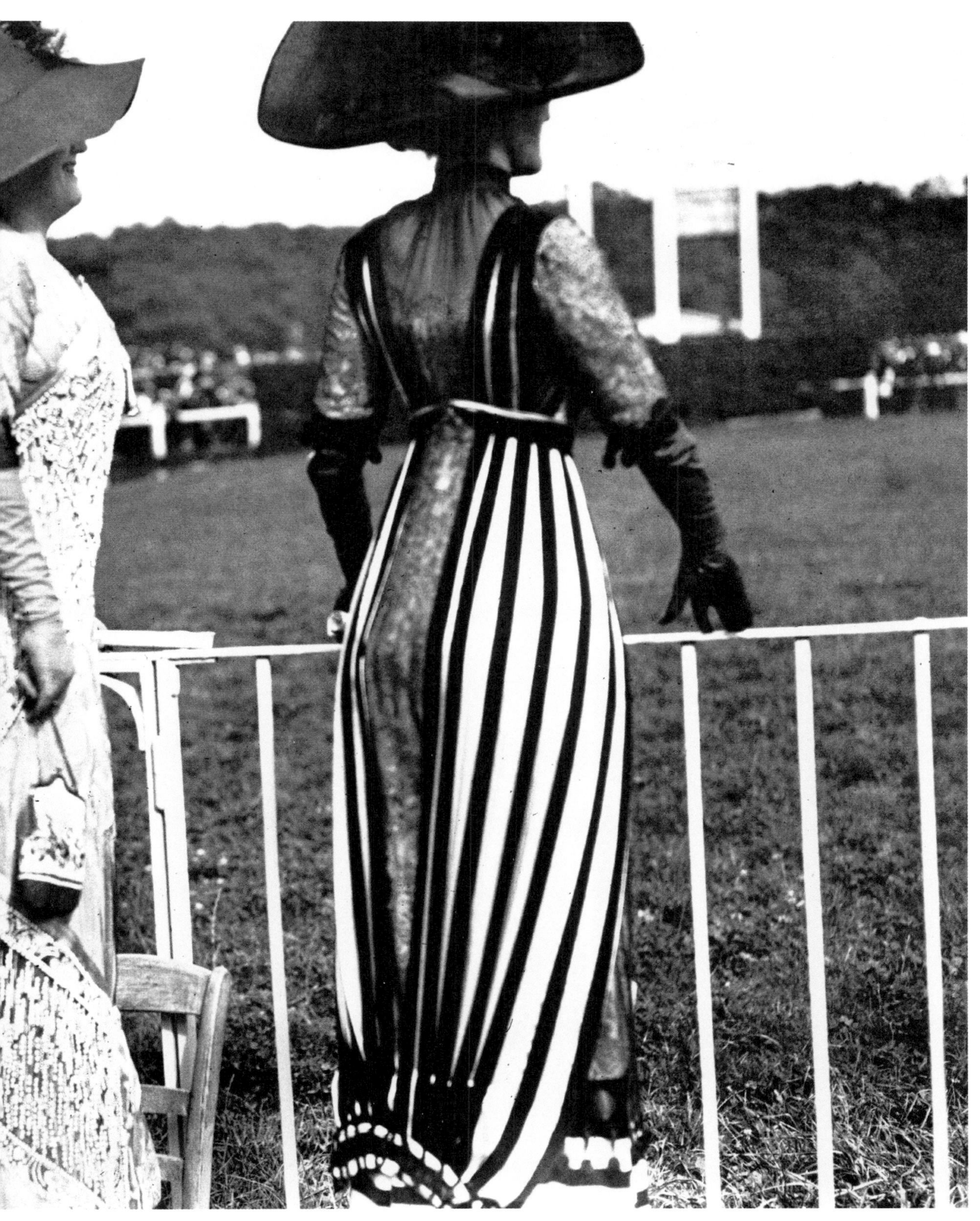

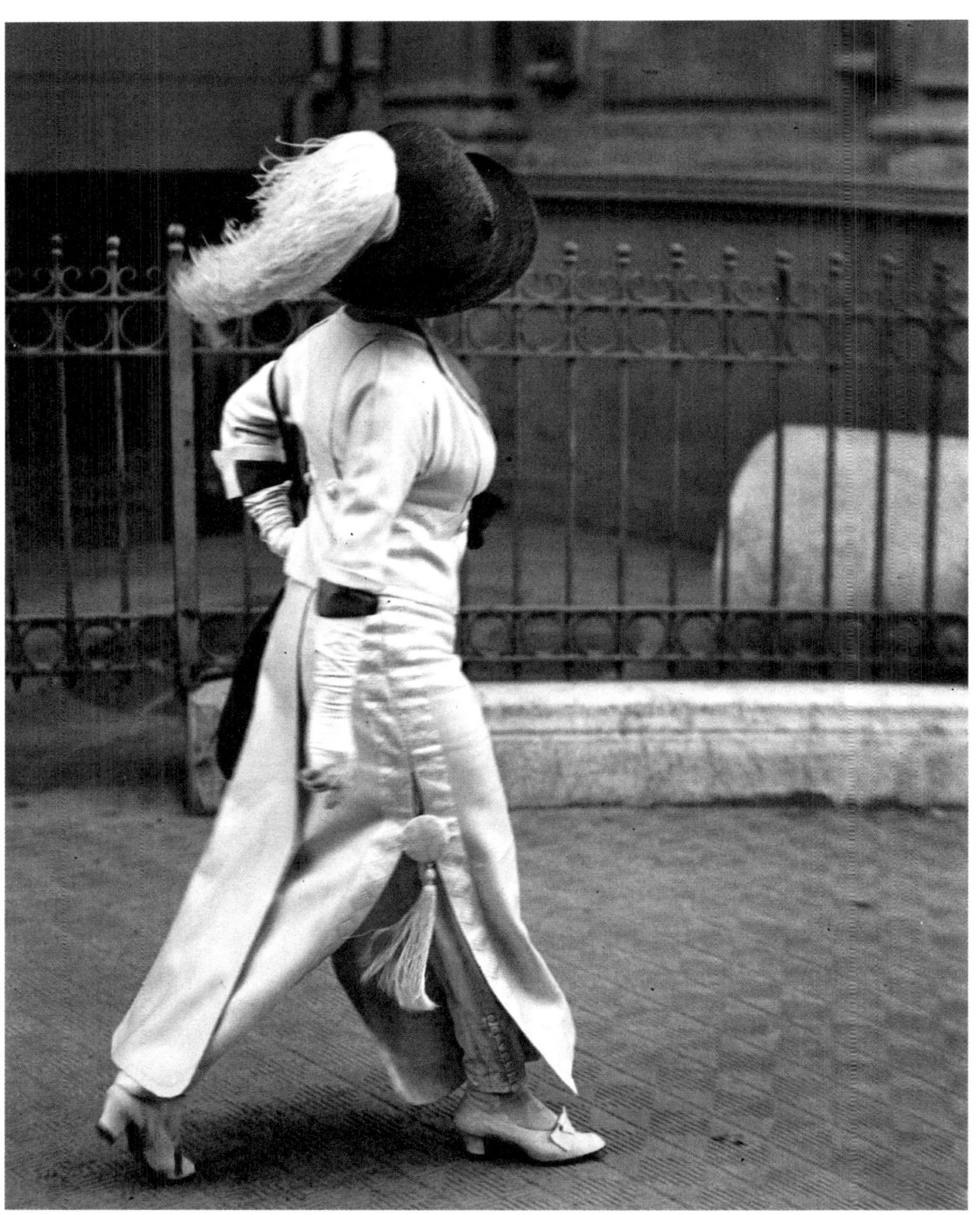

Unlike at the Bois de Boulogne or Monte-Carlo, few women objected to Lartigue with his camera at the races. One *cocotte*, Liane de Lancy (below and p. 122), even offered to pose for him – though Lartigue disliked photographing women rooted to the spot. While both Liane de Pougy and Émilienne d'Alençon dressed as great ladies, Liane de Lancy favoured a more exaggerated style. Crowds would await her arrival in her coupé upholstered in yellow silk, whether at the races or the Palais de Glace, a mirrored indoor skating rink on the Champs-Élysées, complete with a fifty-piece orchestra, where she was a star skater. Open from October until the beginning of March, the rink attracted *le tout Paris*: 'Oh what a gracious, exquisite, shimmering mix! Statesmen and diplomats, politicians and financiers, men of letters and artists, poets and intellectuals, scholars and pleasure-seekers, members of clubs and members of societies – sense the nuance – sportsmen and sportswomen, beautiful women of great and easy virtue, every level of *noblesse*, of distinction, of elegance...in a word, the flower of all these Parisian sets...', wrote *Le Figaro* when the Palais de Glace first opened in 1893.[25]

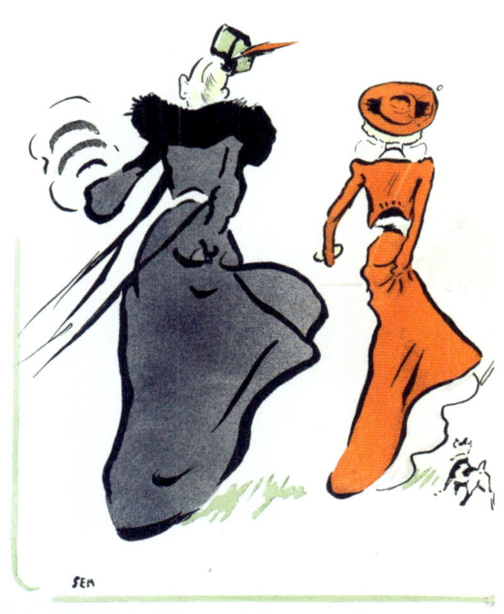

Marthe Helly and Liane de Lancy (detail), by Sem, 1913.

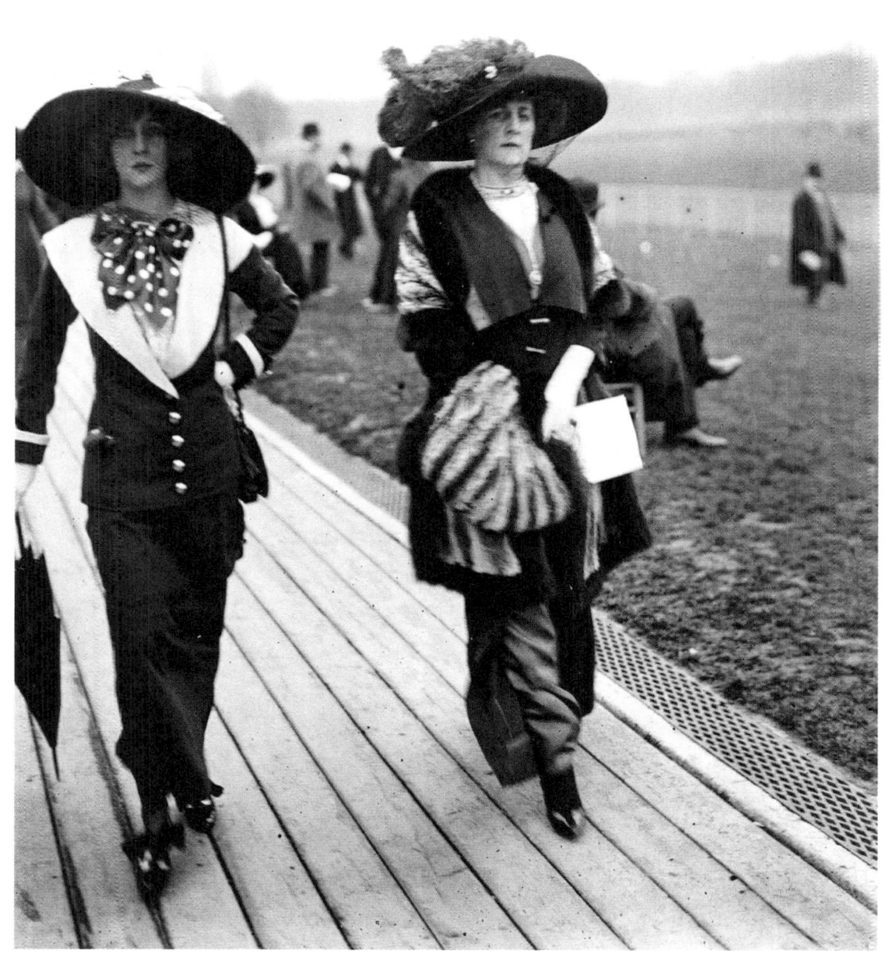

Patrons segregated themselves by the hour. At 4.45 p.m., respectable women or young girls with their mothers quickly finished their hot chocolate and left. After 5 p.m. a racier crowd took over: 'The *cocottes* arrive, many of whom I recognize from mornings at the Bois de Boulogne or the races. They aren't as dressed up as usual, but still wear a lot of embellishments, necklaces, rings, large hats and, as always, enormous muffs.'[26] Accompanied by their skating instructors dressed in dark green, they glided off, their followers watching from one of several bars, or from the fresco-decorated gallery above. Madame Lartigue did not care for Polaire, a music-hall singer, actress and skilful skater (Toulouse-Lautrec once portrayed her on a magazine cover), though Jacques admired her tiny figure with a wasp waist, so slim that it seemed her upper half might snap off. The young Jean Cocteau, meanwhile, described Polaire's friend, the diminutive Colette, as being as thin as 'a little fox in a skating outfit'.[27] Though never a courtesan herself, Colette enjoyed their company, a fascination reflected in her sympathetic portrayals of their world and what she described as 'the honourable habits of women who have lost their honour'.[28]

Men like Gaston Lachaille, a sugar baron in Colette's *Gigi*, kept their *cocottes* as an overt status symbol. Lachaille is weary of high society and the demi-monde (his own mistress, Liane d'Exelmans, based on Liane de Pougy, runs off with Sandomir, a skating instructor at the Palais de Glace), yet social custom compels him to remain within that world: '[His] luxuries were cut and dried: motor cars, a dreary mansion on the Parc Monceau, Liane's monthly allowance and jewels, champagne and baccarat at Deauville in the summer, at Monte-Carlo in the winter…yet from none of this did he get any fun.'[29] Contemporary social observers Edmond Benjamin and Paul Desachy, the authors of a book entitled *Le Boulevard: Croquis parisiens* (The Boulevard: Parisian Sketches), described such men and women as 'prisoners of pleasure'.[30] Likewise, with a few triumphant exceptions (including the fictional Gigi), the demi-mondaines remained trapped within their own sub-culture, most leading a life of only fitful opulence.

Though he captured skaters on a frozen lake in the Bois de Boulogne and at the Vélodrome Buffalo in Neuilly, Lartigue was not permitted to take photographs at the Palais de Glace. Nor, of course, was photography allowed at the public swimming baths at 26 rue de Chazelles, near the Parc Monceau. Sharp-eyed as ever, however, the teenager observed the

Demi-mondaine Liane de Lancy with Berthe de Fontane, the races at Auteuil, 1911.

cocottes' attempts at swimming, then a novel form of exercise for women. '[Émilienne d'Alençon,] supported by her skating instructor at the Palais de Glace, can look quite chic showing off her marvellous dresses and giving out gracious smiles.... In the water, [the *cocottes*] look like big celluloid dolls that are too white.... As they don't know how to swim, they make a lot of little uncoordinated movements that are very rapid and completely useless....'[31]

Grandes cocottes, artists and society revellers alike flocked of an evening to Maxim's on the rue Royal – one of over a dozen Belle Époque restaurants and cafés in Paris that attracted a *'clientèle de luxe'*. There Eugène Cornuché, Maxim's urbane proprietor, created an Art Nouveau interior replete with elaborate woodwork, stained glass, bevelled mirrors and racy murals. He welcomed Polaire, Liane de Pougy, Liane de Lancy and Émilienne d'Alençon, along with a mix of Russian Grand Dukes, Rothschild bankers, members of the beau-monde like Boni de Castellane, Marcel Proust, the painters Giovanni Boldini and Édouard Vuillard, as well as Feydeau (who entitled one of his farces *La Dame de chez Maxim*) and Lartigue's hero Sem, who drew caricatures of many of the guests. 'Don't think we allowed in that many [*cocottes*]. Absolutely not!' wrote Hugo, Maxim's maître d'hôtel for twenty years until he retired in 1917.[32] His detailed green notebook, however, served as an aide-memoire: 'Twins who share the rigours of the job', he wrote of Liane de Lancy and her sister, also describing Émilienne d'Alençon in the early 1900s as a 'notorious sportswoman always accompanied by a swarm of admirers', adding the initials 'RAF', standing for *rien à faire* (nothing to be done). Cornuché, meanwhile, entertained diners, seated amid rose-shaded lights, with pianists, orchestras or acts hired from the Folies Bergère, the evenings stretching until dawn.

Lartigue's mother, who ate in restaurants only on occasion, would doubtless have found the clientele at Maxim's too risqué. She gave big dinners at rue Leroux or invited her friends to an 'at home' once a fortnight. 'Few are worth photographing,' Jacques observed of the assembled women, all of whom addressed his mother as *'chère madame'*.[33] After dinner, he would escape to his darkroom to examine his photographs that had dried overnight, or to develop those from that day.

'I call this one Proust,' said the elderly Lartigue in a television interview,[34] pointing to a large print from February 1911 of a retreating male figure complete with a top hat and cane (opposite), walking along the Sentier de la

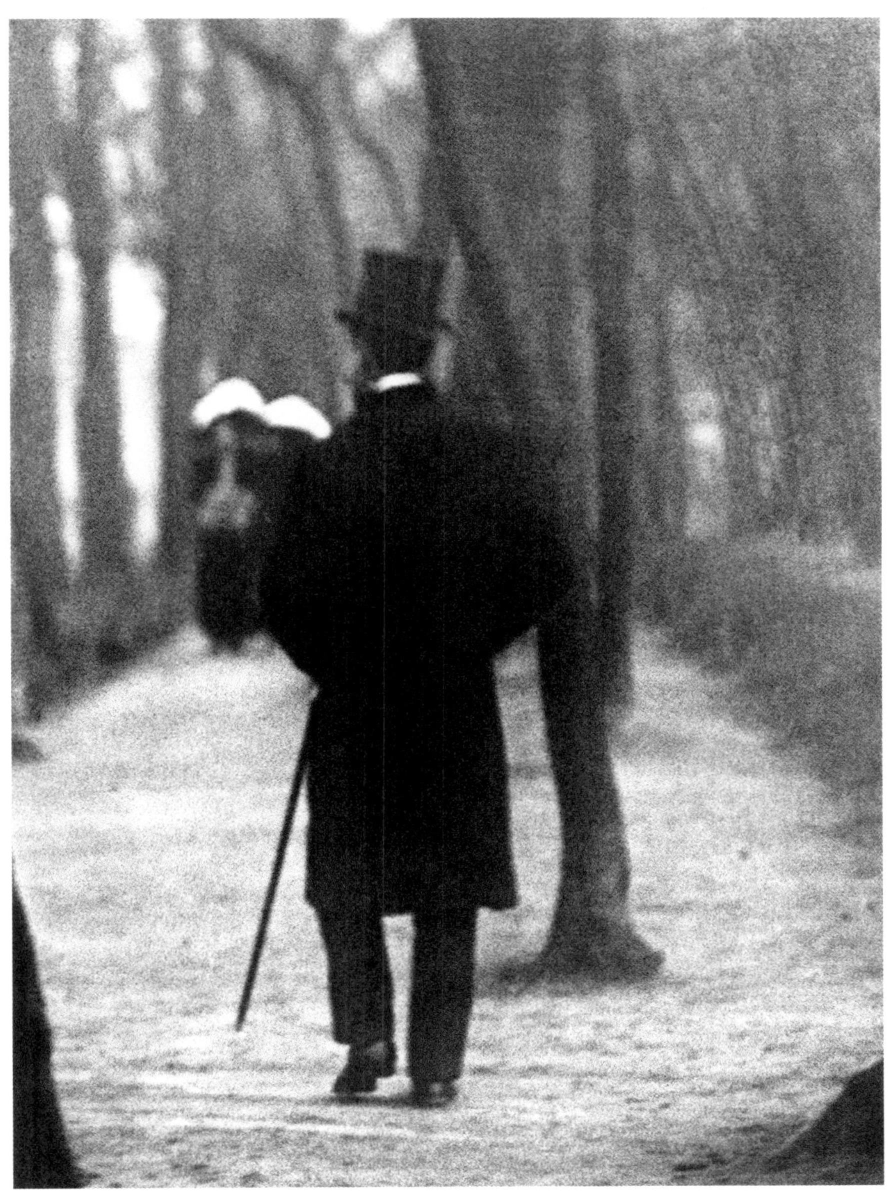

Le Sentier de la Vertu, Bois de Boulogne, 1911.

Vertu. The atmosphere is solitary and mysterious. Yet Lartigue's album from early that year reveals the original photograph with two middle-aged women dominating the foreground, the elegant man only in the distance. As with other examples, Lartigue often drastically cropped and reframed an image down to the most compelling part of the picture, and then reprinted it.

Marcel Proust, who described the Bois de Boulogne in *Swann's Way* as a garden of women in their 'varied, enclosed little worlds',[35] may have crossed paths with Lartigue on the Allée des Acacias or the Sentier de la Vertu, but they did not meet. Never a great reader, Lartigue came to Proust only late in life, when his third wife Florette read out loud to him pages from *Swann in Love*.

'I would, of course, have been delighted to meet Proust,' he told Hervé Guibert in an interview for *Le Monde* in 1985, 'though I'm not sure a rabbit can talk to a cat.'[36] Indeed, their work has little in common. Yet Proust was an avid collector of photography, appreciating, as he did, novel ways of seeing the world: 'Photographs, once they cease to be a reproduction of reality, and show things that no longer exist, acquire a certain dignity,' observes the Baron de Charlus in *Within a Budding Grove*.[37] In *Swann's Way*, the protagonist returns to a photograph of the *cocotte* Odette de Crécy to 'remember how exquisite she had been',[38] revealing how both men shared a powerful sense of the way in which everything one experiences disappears, and yet remains.

Chapter Five
The Beauty of Speed

'Yesterday, an aeroplane flew above me,' wrote Lartigue. 'Right above me! From below, I saw the real live man, sitting on his seat, legs apart… And suddenly something mysterious came into my head…as though I had vertigo upside down! It was as though I'd seen this man go by with eyes other than mine; perhaps his!? I watched him go off into the distance, still in the air…. One sometimes experiences unique emotions that one chases after but can never bring back…. I wonder what one should call the "opposite of fear", that "joyful fear" that suddenly entered my head.'[1]

An aeroplane craze swept France in 1908. In August of that year, Wilbur Wright took off in his engine-powered flying machine at Le Mans racecourse. Though the public demonstration lasted only one minute and forty-five seconds, Wright's ability to perform banking turns and fly a circle silenced sceptics. The euphoric Jacques began photographing model aeroplanes on the floor or on bare ground in the park. As already seen, Zissou also started building his own designs, Jacques documenting each stage, from model to test flight. Even the sports magazine *La Vie au Grand Air* published an article entitled 'How to Construct an Aeroplane', complete with diagrams. In December that year, the Grand Palais held the first Salon de l'Aéronautique (p. 132, above). Louis Blériot then made the first flight across the English Channel in his own plane, the Blériot XI, on 25 July 1909. Flushed with success, the engineer inventor moved his company, Blériot Aéronautique, to Buc, near Versailles, where he set up a private airport and flying school. It was at Buc that Lartigue took his photograph of Zissou at a diagonal, caught in the blast of Italian aviator Stefano Amerigo's propeller (p. 131), capturing a magic the photographer described seventy years later: 'What was marvellous was the air, the wind, the cold, the noise of the propellers – all gave you an extraordinary feeling.'[2]

Lartigue caught a glimpse of Wilbur Wright at Pau, near the Pyrenees, where the latter continued his flight demonstrations in early 1909: 'Wilbur,

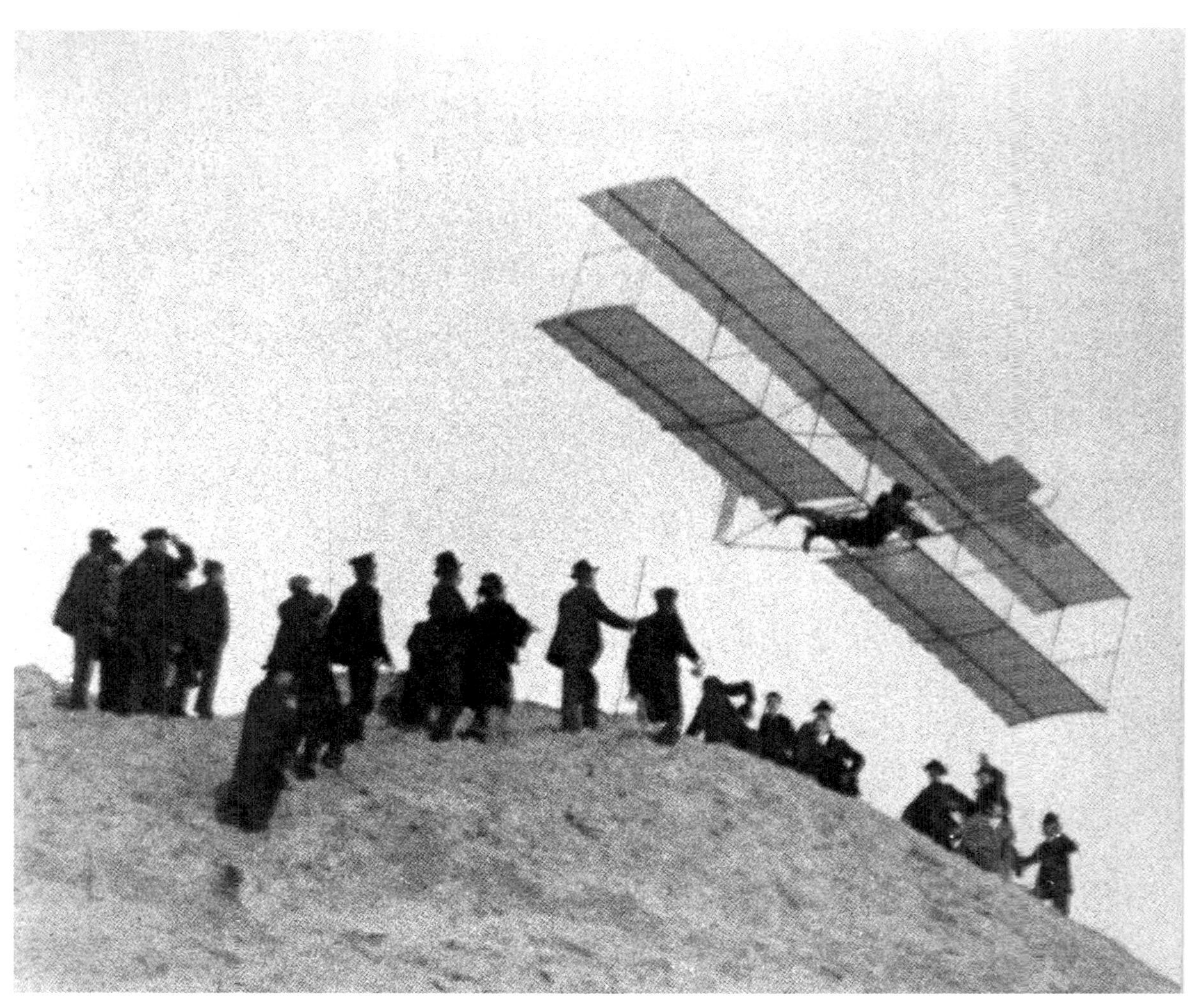

my famous Wilbur! I recognize him very well…. I approach him, my little
Gaumont Block-Notes hidden in my hand…. I take a photo from afar….
I come closer…. Wilbur looks at me, then suddenly turns his back!…Perhaps
he's furious, but the photo has been taken. This consoles me a little for the
bad weather that prevents us from being able to see him fly.'[3]

An aerodrome at Issy-les-Moulineaux, just outside Paris, meanwhile,
became the site of countless flight experiments. Aviation pioneers like
Blériot (p. 133, above), Henry Farman (p. 134, above), René Simon (p. 139) and
the Brazilian-born Alberto Santos-Dumont (p. 132, below; his obsession
with flight extended to suspending his dining-room table and chairs in
the air, obliging dinner guests to climb a stepladder to reach their seats)
built their own hangars. In one photograph, a solitary young couple out
for a stroll with their baby in a pram are interrupted by a Blériot aeroplane
hovering nearby, another like a giant bird in the sky above.

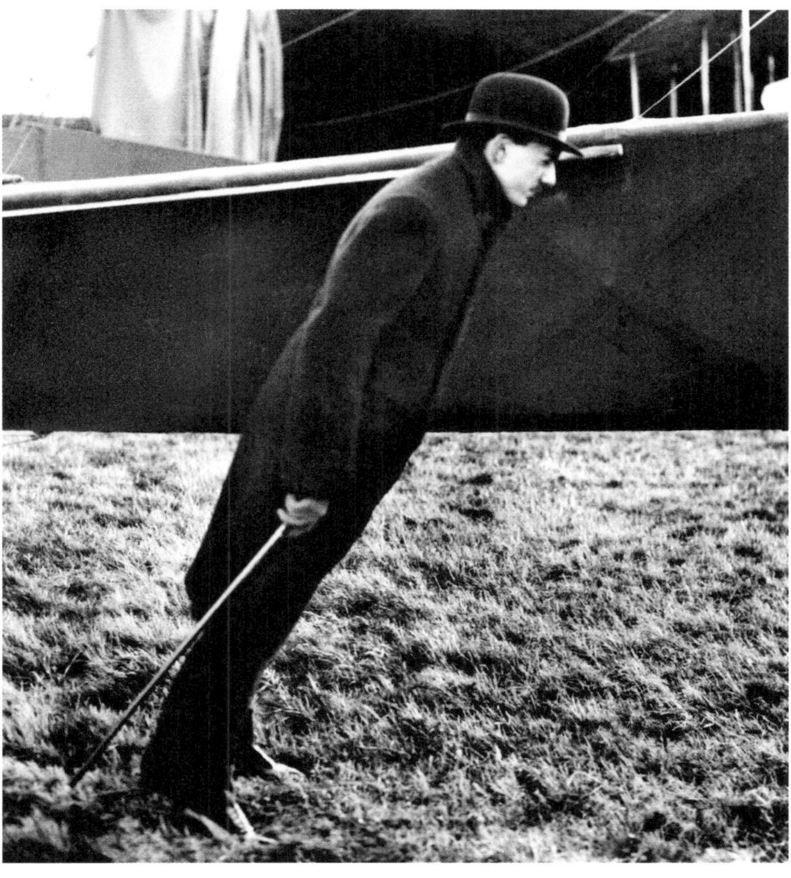

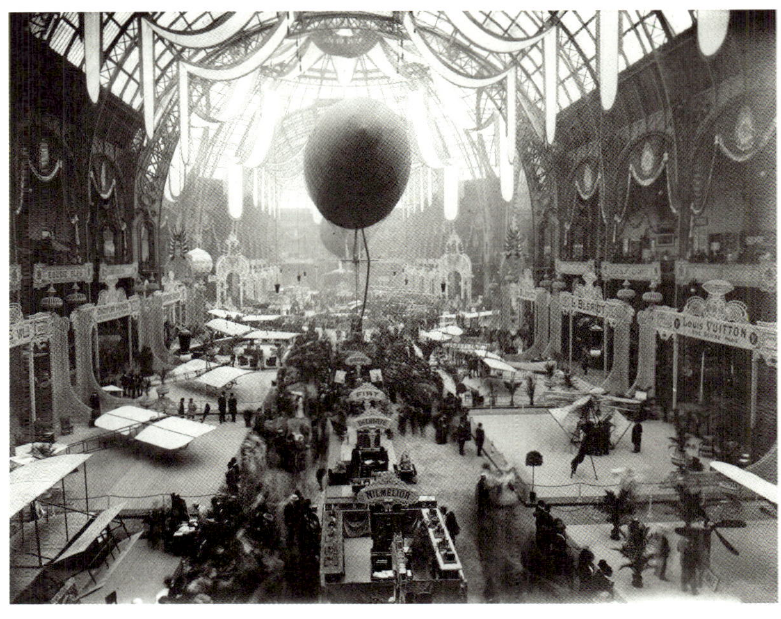

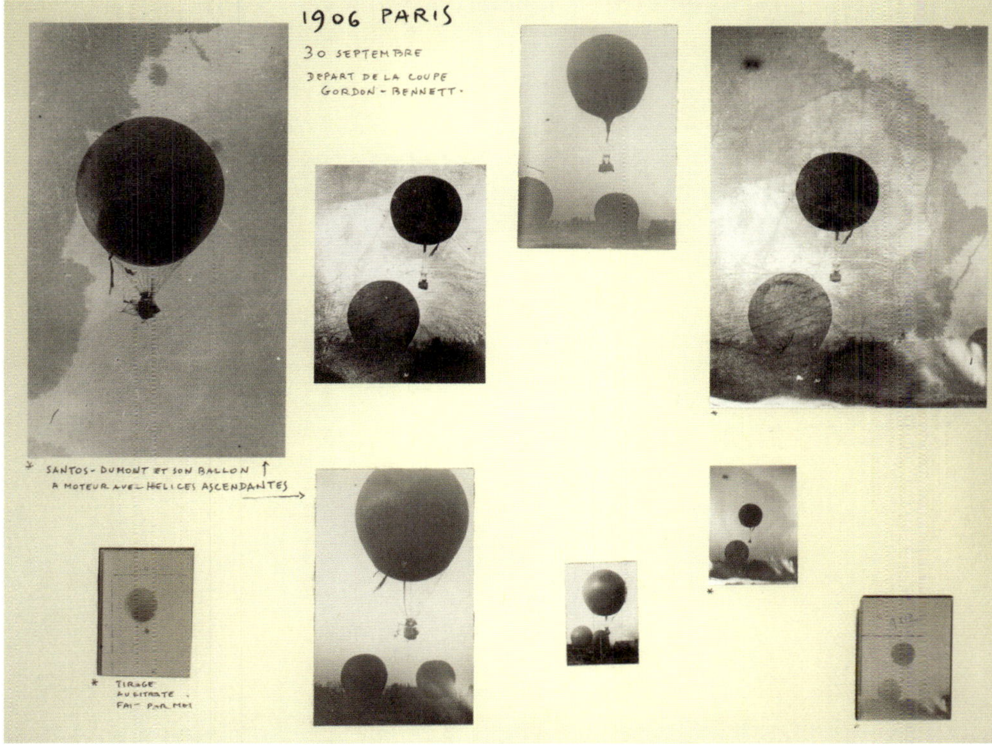

Opening day of the first air show, 'Exposition internationale de locomotion aérienne', Grand Palais, Paris, 1909. Contemporary photo.
The first Coupe Gordon Bennett for balloon racing, featuring Alberto Santos-Dumont (album page), 30 September 1906.

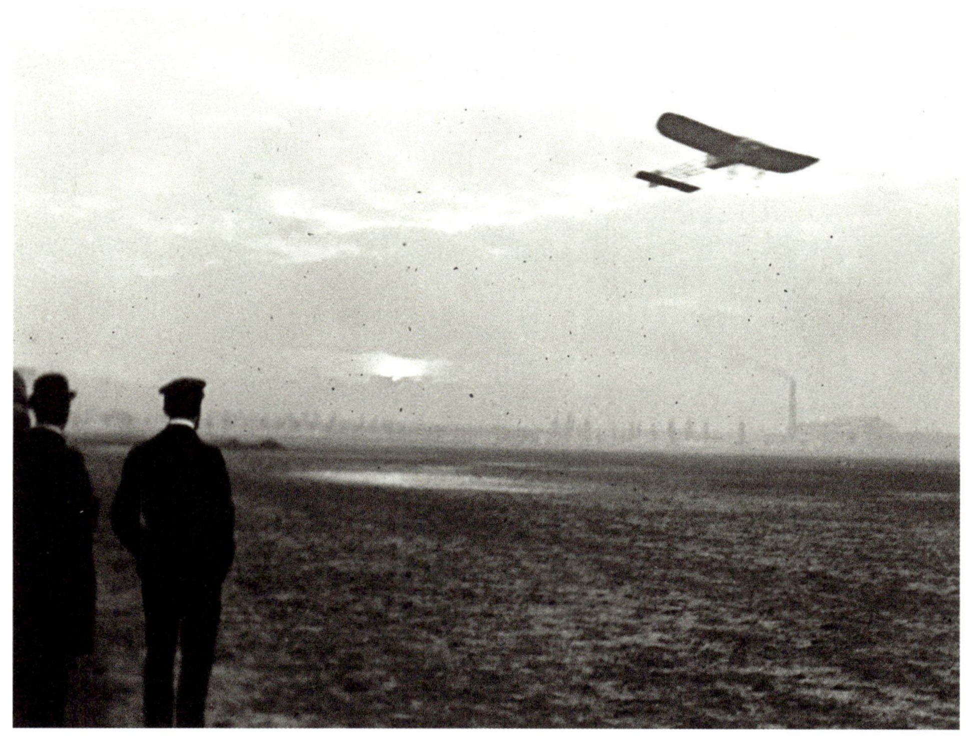

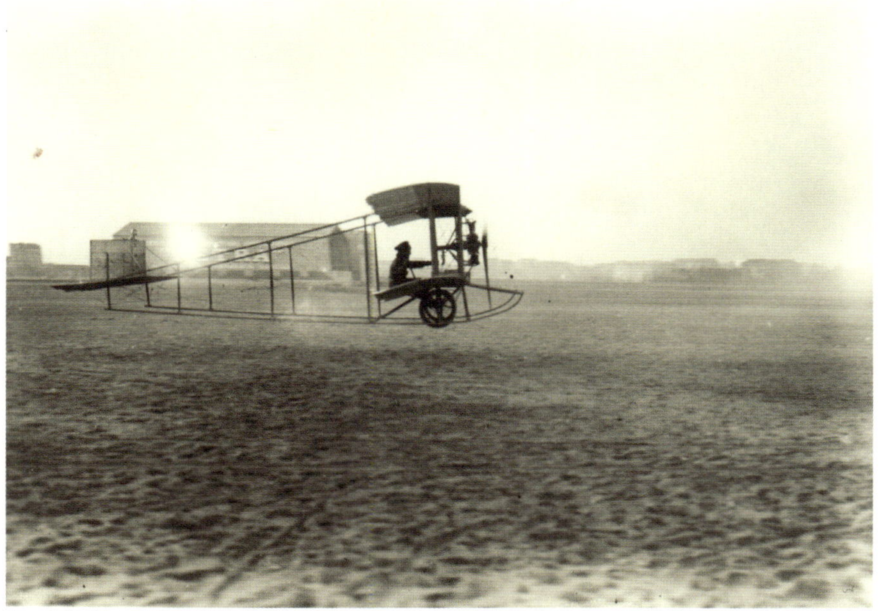

Louis Blériot flying the Blériot XI, Issy-les-Moulineaux, 1909.
Issy-les-Moulineaux aerodrome, 1910.

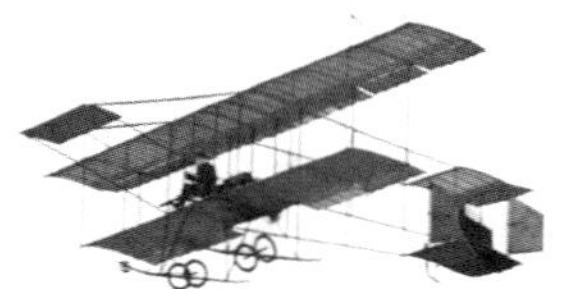

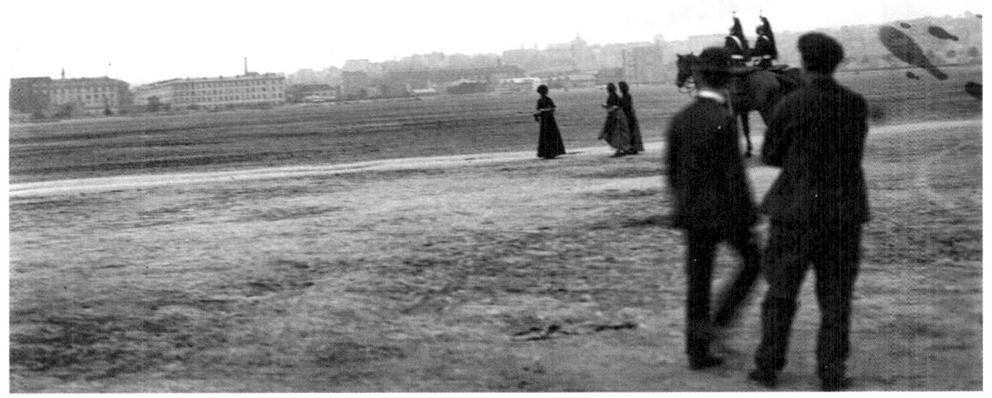

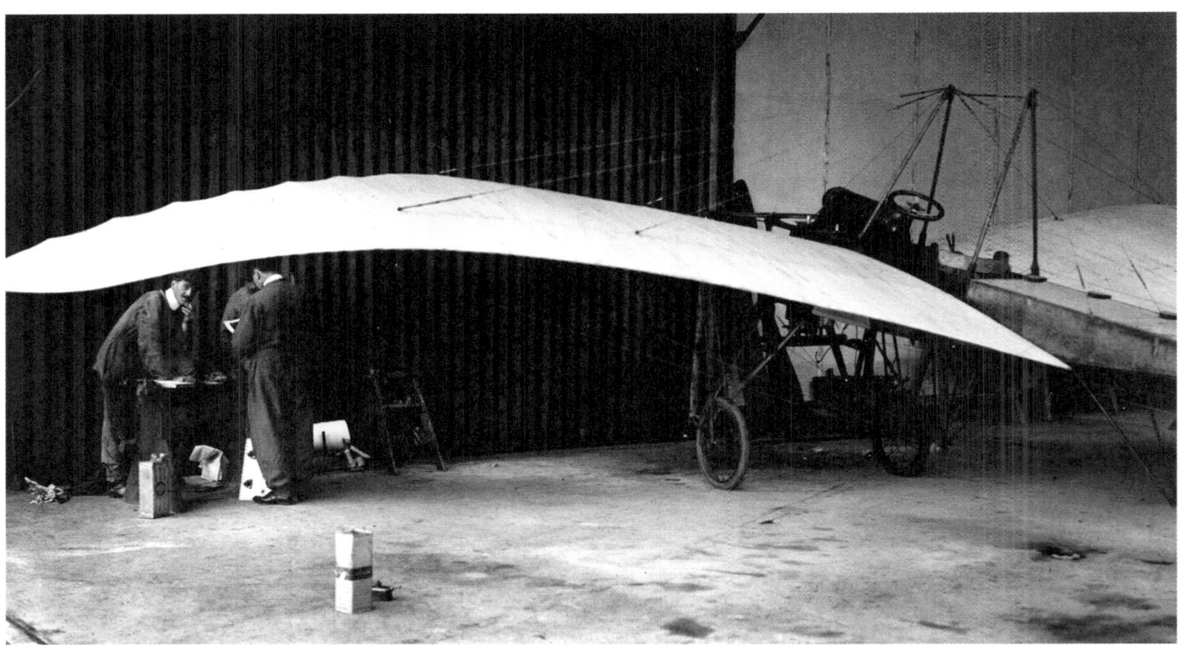

But the aerodrome soon attracted hundreds of spectators each day. In early 1911, a government minister closed it to the general public. Only members of the press, the Aéro-Club de France or the Ligue Aérienne could enter the area. Too young to join any club, Lartigue sought advice from the Simons brothers, star sports photographers at *La Vie au Grand Air*. Much to his excitement, one of the brothers (it is unclear which) obtained a press pass for Lartigue: 'Simons, the best of all the [photo] reporters for La Vie au Grand Air is my friend. He has made me a press card with a red, white and blue flag and my photograph glued on top. Thanks to this, policemen let me enter everywhere…even at Issy-les-Moulineaux.'[4]

Aviators sometimes even landed next to him. In one example, Lartigue photographed Giuseppe Cei, a twenty-two-year-old Italian aviator, who began flying planes at Issy-les-Moulineaux while studying engineering in Paris. Lartigue captures him in a tweed coat and flat cap, in profile like a Renaissance portrait, seated on his Caudron bi-plane (p. 136). In his diary that evening, Lartigue drew meticulous storyboard-style sketches of his photographs of the Italian, including his take-off (p. 137). Cei died only seven weeks later, in March 1911, when his plane crashed on the outskirts of Paris; his funeral attracted hundreds of mourners. Then, at the start of the 1911 Paris to Madrid air race at Issy-les-Moulineaux on 21 May, Louis Émil Train made a forced landing in his monoplane, killing Henri Maurice Berteaux, the French Minister of War. 'I was having a lesson at the time,' wrote Lartigue, adding with characteristic detachment, 'At 11.30, in the street, newspaper criers started to run everywhere, announcing the accident (and to think, without that grammar lesson, I could have taken a photo!).'[5] Not that such early disasters hindered innovation. On 19 December that same year, Lartigue hurried to the Salon d'Aviation at the Grand Palais crammed with the latest technological developments: 'The aeroplanes are displayed on stands like motor cars at the Salon d'Autos. They need more space…. I know and recognize them all. They look as if they're asking themselves what they're doing there, immobile and polished, like ladies on a social call'.[6]

The Simons brothers offered Lartigue technical advice, recommending the Klapp Nettel camera he acquired in 1912, as well as allowing him to examine their photographs at *La Vie au Grand Air*'s offices on the Champs-Élysées. An opportunity presented itself at Issy-les-Moulineaux on 25

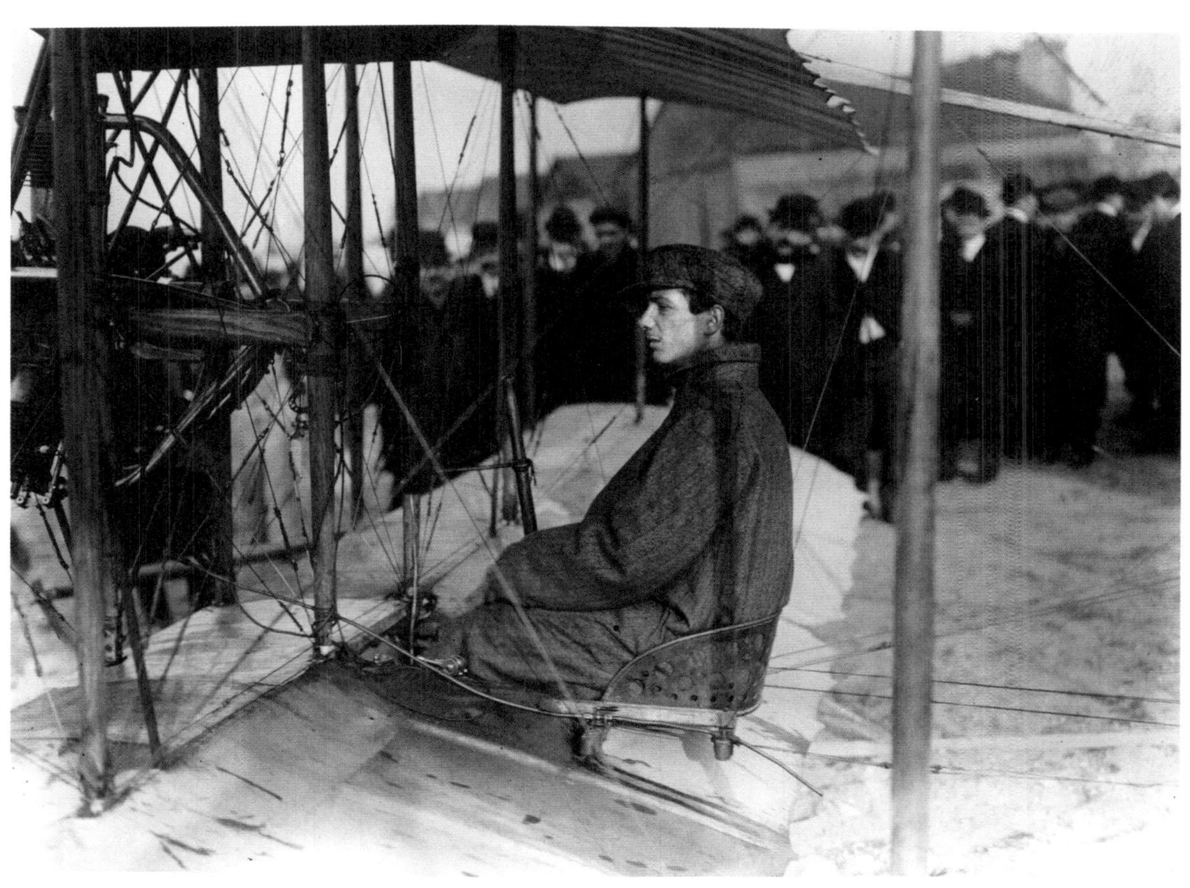

The Italian aviator Giuseppe Cei with his Caudron bi-plane, Issy-les-Moulineaux aerodrome, 1911.

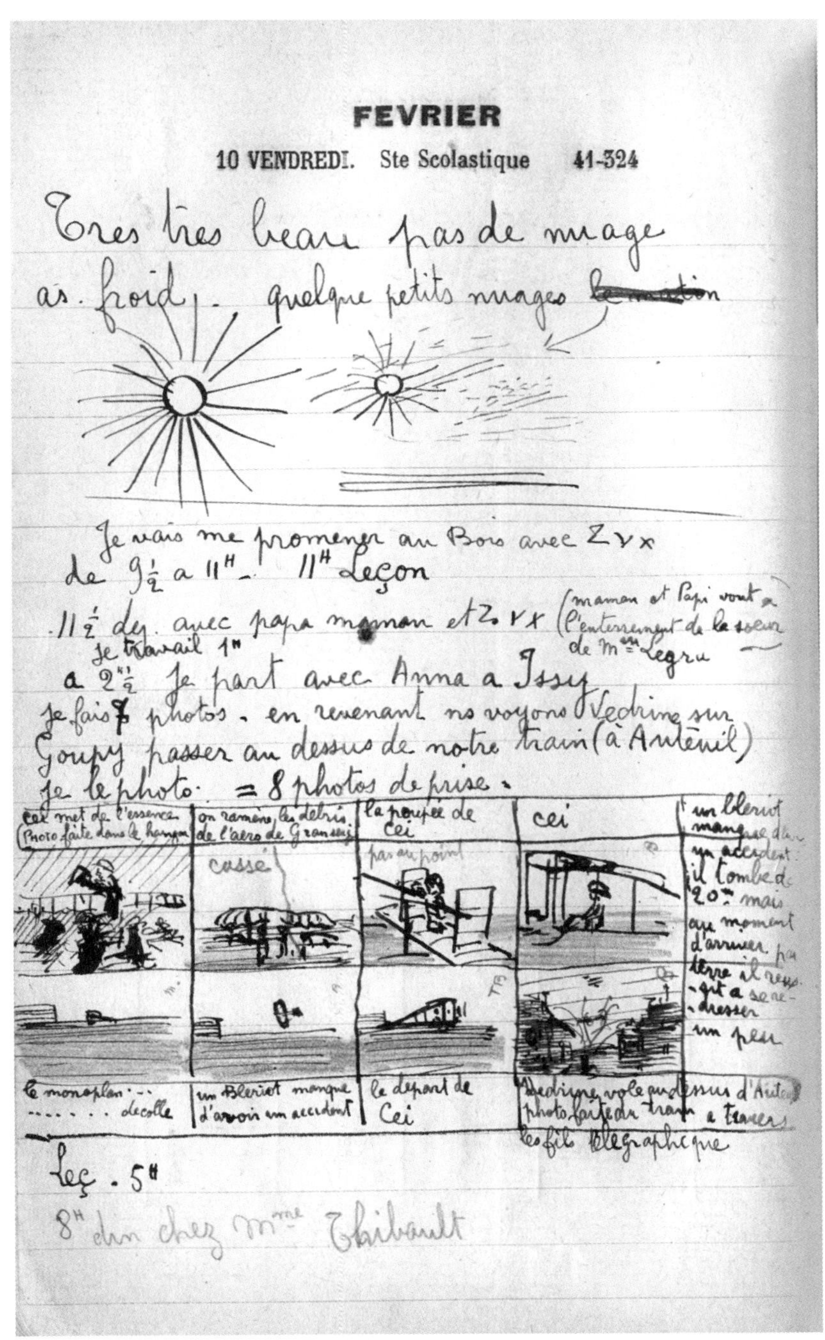

Page from Lartigue's diary, 10 February 1911.

January: 'All of a sudden René Simon (the famous!) goes out of the hangar in his "Blériot" monoplane. He takes off…then he goes up and does some fantastic spirals and turns…. I develop the photos of Simon when I get back. They're a success!'[7] Four days later, Lartigue walked over to *La Vie au Grand Air*: 'They tell me that my photographs will appear full page!'[8] On 10 February 1912, his first published photograph, one of René Simon swooping in the skies, appeared on the cover of the magazine (opposite).

Lartigue first met the Simons brothers when his father and Zissou introduced him to car racing at the Coupe Gordon Bennett on the Circuit d'Auvergne in central France in 1905. France boasted the best roads on both sides of the Atlantic in the early 1900s, contributing to the rapid growth of the car industry. Driving or riding in a motorcar as a leisure pursuit, known

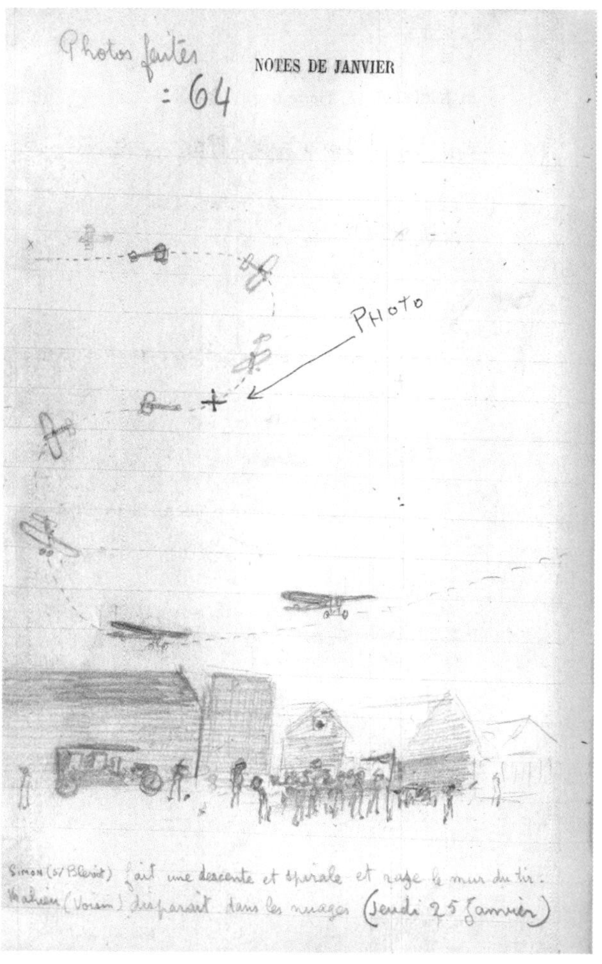

Page from Lartigue's diary, 25 January 1912, featuring René Simon.

as *automobilisme*, required goggles, leather headgear, trench coats (fur-lined in winter) and rubber coats (known as *parapluies de chauffeur*); the ladies were swathed like beekeepers to keep out the dust. Hierarchical as ever, rich sports enthusiasts set themselves apart, turning to costly mechanical sports, whether motorbikes (p. 140), aeroplanes or, more importantly, racing cars. Though car manufacturers financed races like the Coupe Gordon Bennett, it was the press, along with photographers like the Simons, who invented the sport as a spectacle, on this occasion a perilous race through mountain

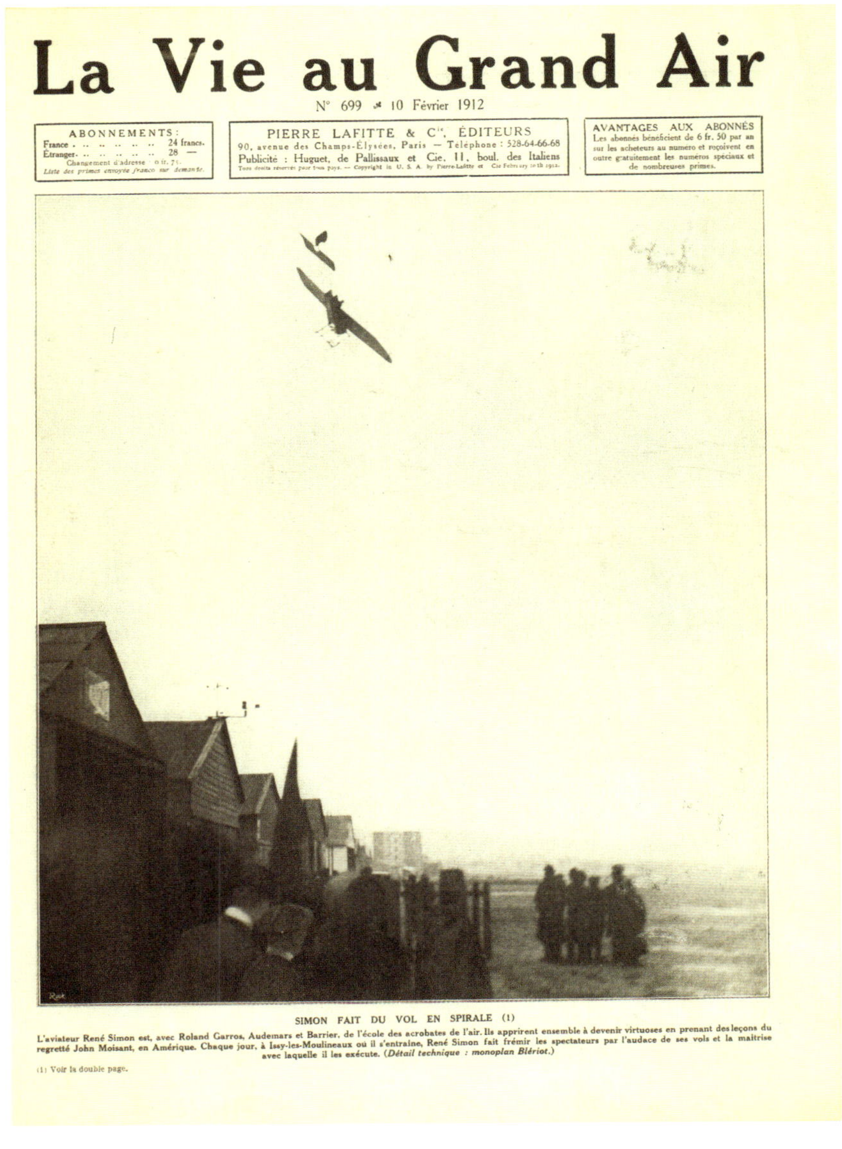

Lartigue's cover of René Simon for *La Vie au Grand Air* magazine, 10 February 1912.

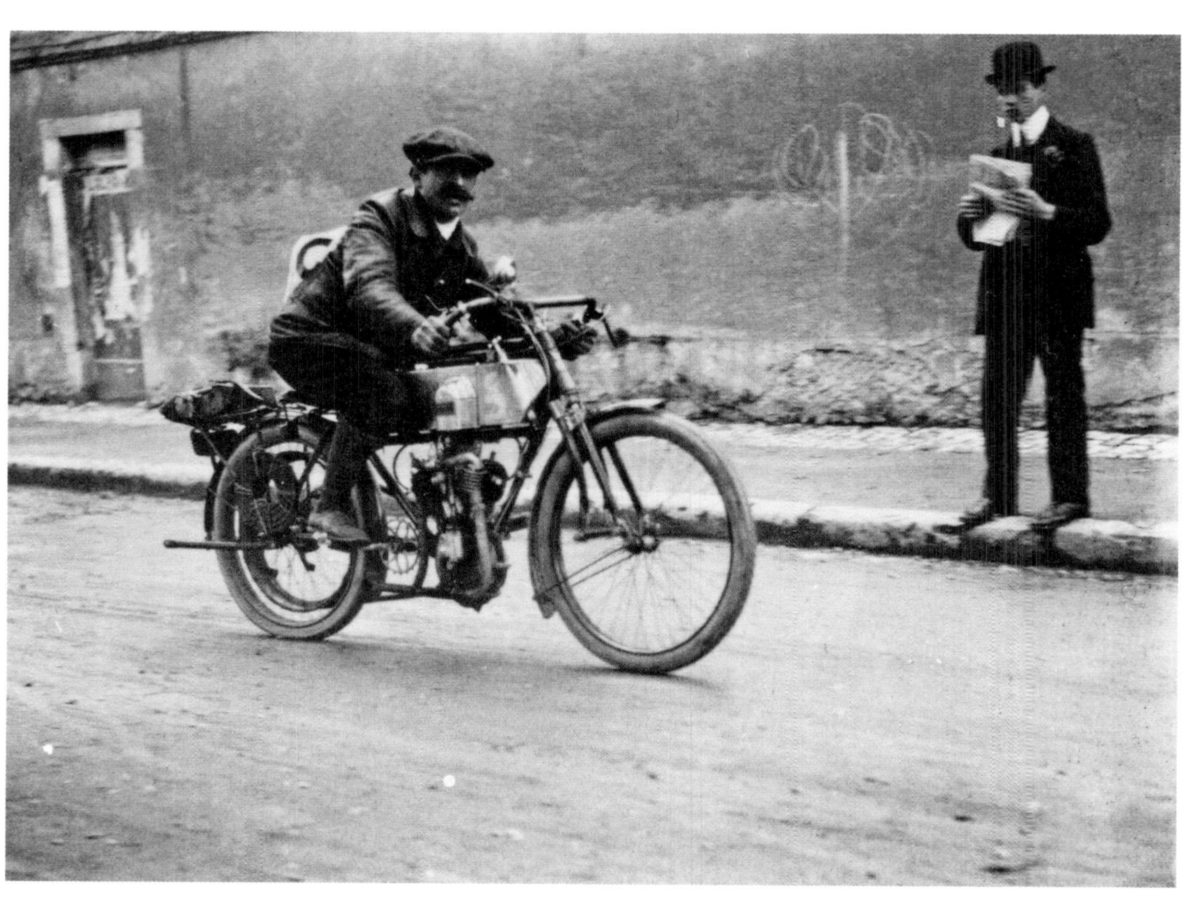

roads: 'At 2.30 o'clock this morning strings of people armed with baskets of provisions and bottles of wine, were trudging up the hillside leading from Clermont to the starting line ten miles out of town...', wrote an American periodical entitled *The Automobile*. 'At each of the sharp bends in the road [Arthur Duray's] mechanic had to hold on to the seat with all his force to prevent being thrown out of the car [sic]....'[9]

The eleven-year-old Jacques stood with his father and Zissou close to a straight-line stretch: 'There are eighteen cars in the race; they leave at three-minute intervals and they have to run four times around the course through the mountains of the Auvergne...along dangerous roads. Papa says the cars will pass us at high speed because we are facing a straight-line stretch.... Again the sound of a horn...of several horns, some far away, one nearby. This time I know I will get a picture – and a good one! It's Jenatzy. There he is in his famous white Mercedes. Click! I have him. I even have time to look at his back.'[10] Unwilling to be limited to three cars, French manufacturers boycotted the Coupe Gordon Bennett the following year, establishing the French Grand Prix under the aegis of the Automobile Club de France instead, racing the cars with their own teams on public roads. Enthralled by their swift progress and changing shapes, the young Lartigue refocused his lens on racing cars. If he came across an image by another photographer that he liked, he would paste it in his album to supplement his own, thus creating a coherent narrative. He also drew innumerable models or sketches of photographs that he had taken on a particular day. To these he added the results of each race, the names of the winners as well as their records.

It was at the 1912 Grand Prix, held at Dieppe, that Lartigue took one of his most memorable photographs (pp. 142–3), Monsieur Folletête and his wife on hand to give the time and numbers.[11] Standing right on the edge of the road, Lartigue captured a driver speeding past, the curtain shutter on his camera rapidly dropping open and closed, registering parts of the scene a millisecond later than others. The tilting trees and spectators, combined with the elliptical wheels of the moving race car, add to the fresh, dynamic sensation of speed. Lartigue describes the scene as follows: 'The first car arrives over there, first on a bend, then it's the straight stretch. It passes us by at great speed. It's amazing! The second one arrives. It's Boillot in a Peugeot. I photograph it at top speed (180 km an hour), pivoting slightly to keep it in my viewfinder as it passes. It was the first time I did that!'[12]

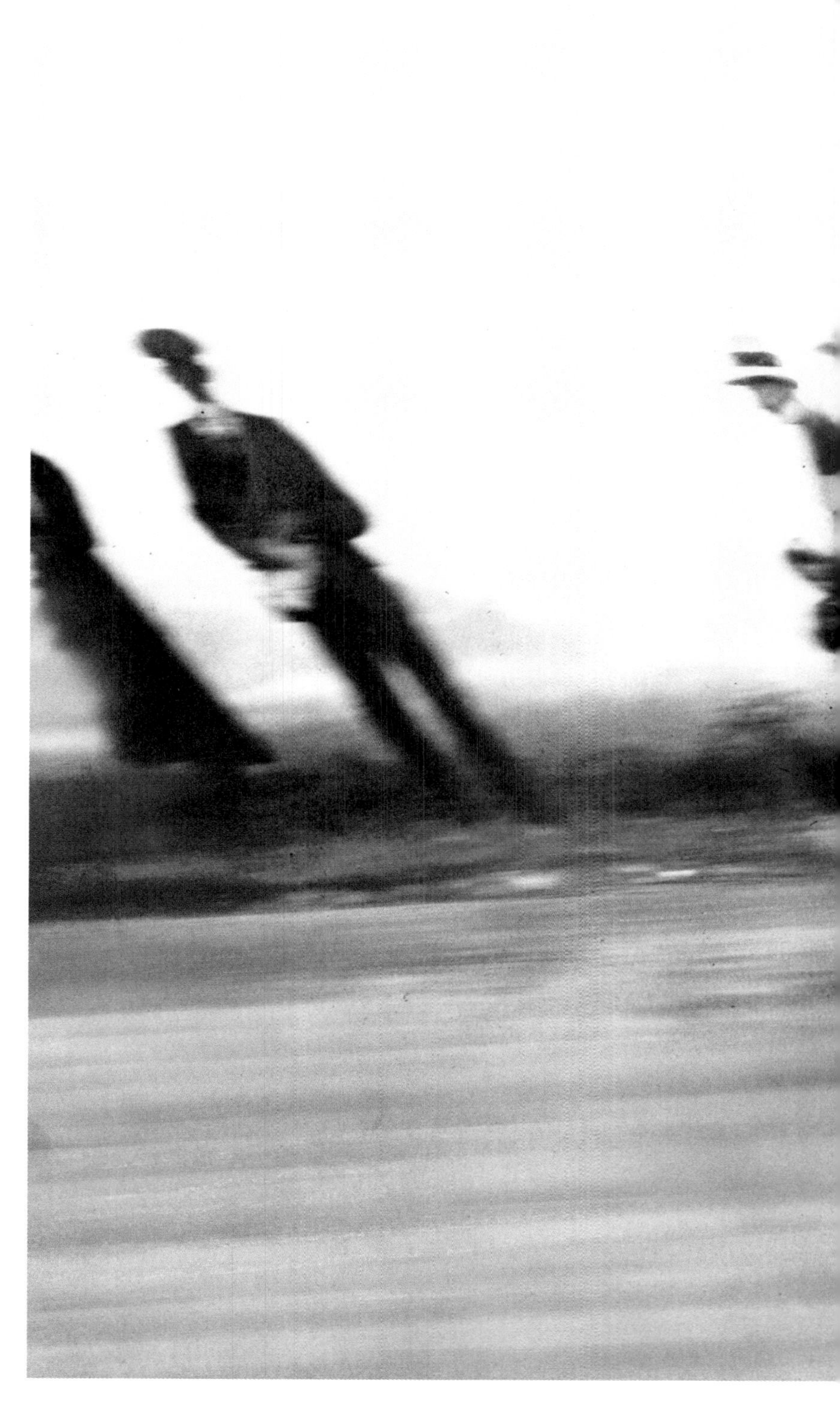

'The French Grand Prix, Circuit
de Dieppe, Normandy, 1912',
as captioned by Lartigue.

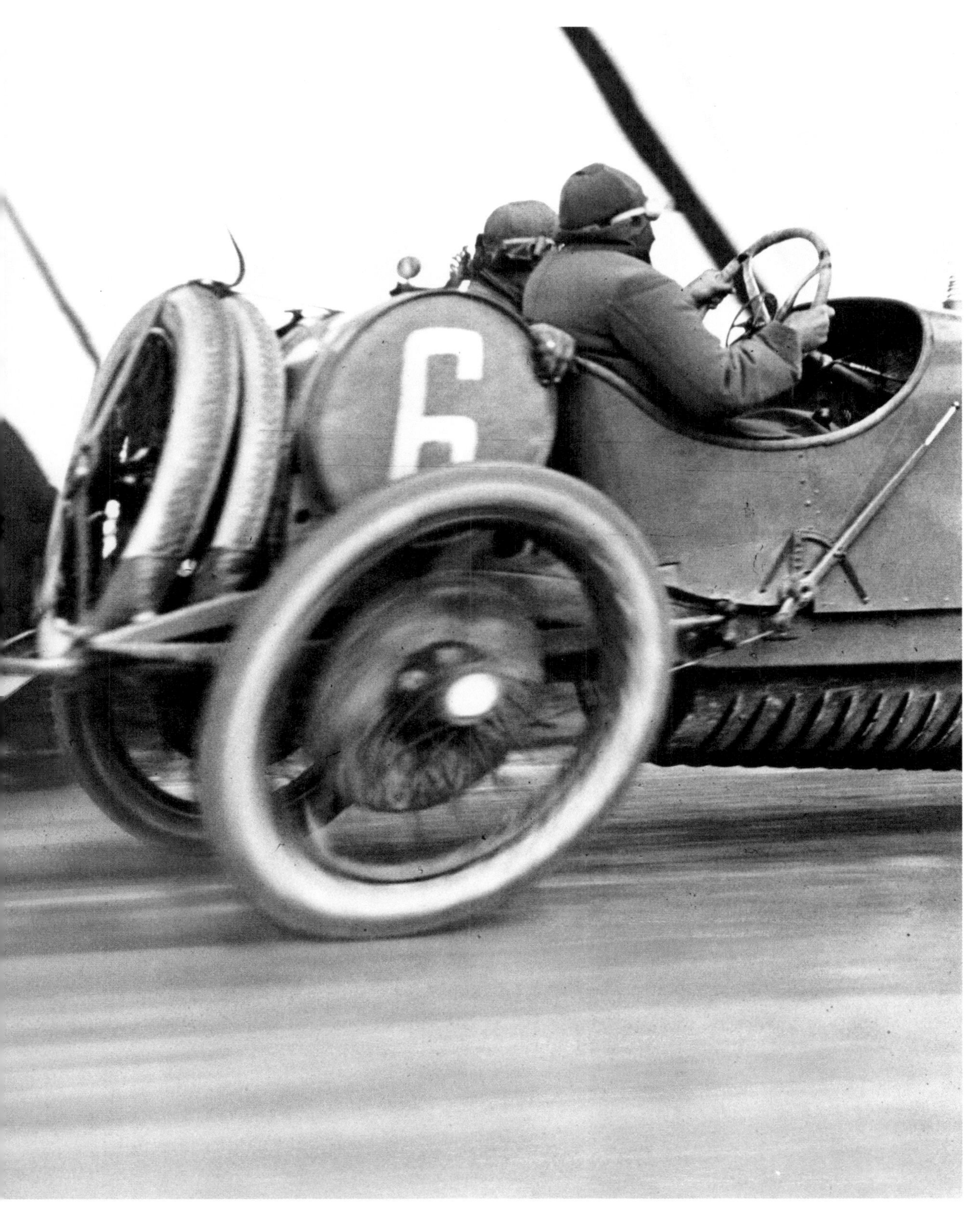

Later that day, Lartigue captured the Italian star racing driver Felice Nazzaro (winner of the 1907 French Grand Prix at the wheel of his Fiat) leaning over a wooden fence as he signals to Louis Wagner in his own Fiat to accelerate (opposite). To no avail: Lartigue's idol Georges Boillot in his Peugeot won an easy thirteen-minute victory over Wagner, who came second. Boillot won the Grand Prix a second time in succession in July 1913

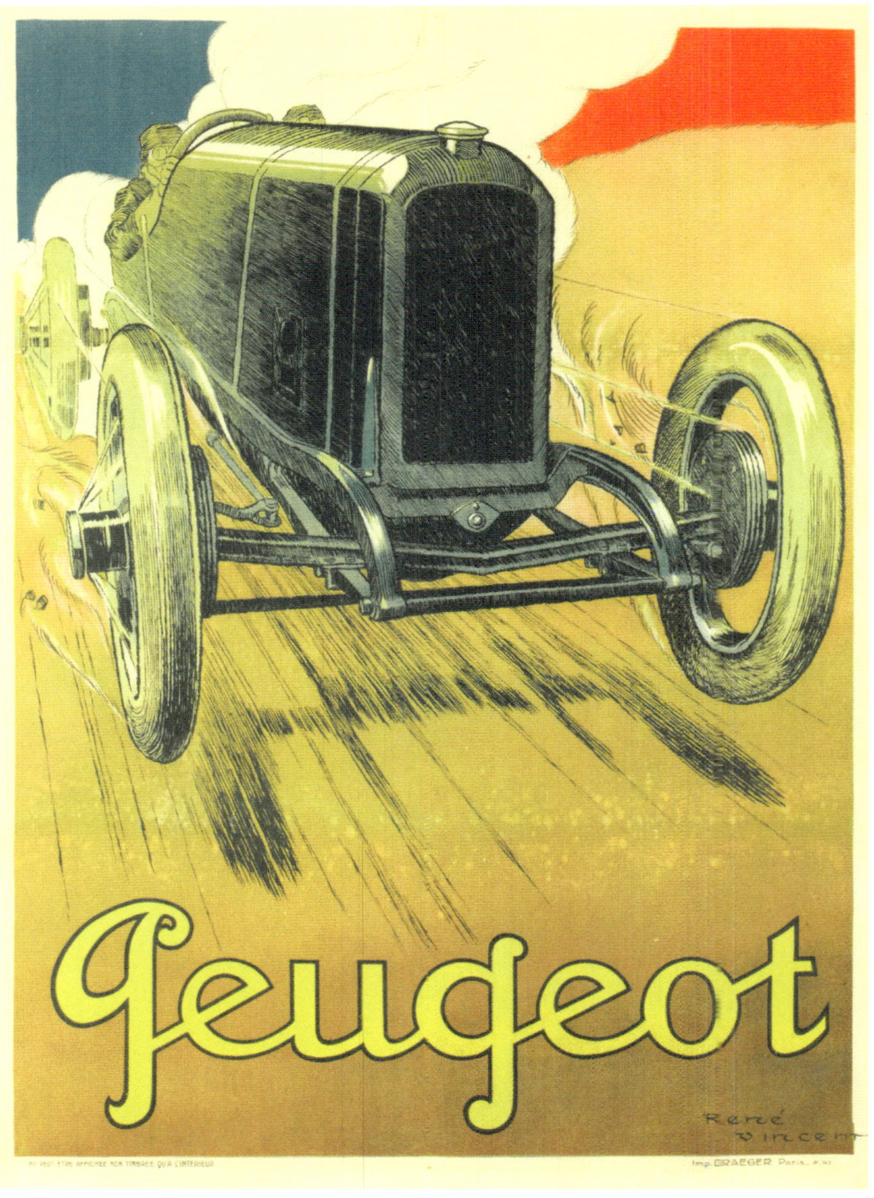

Peugeot poster illustration by René Vincent, 1909.

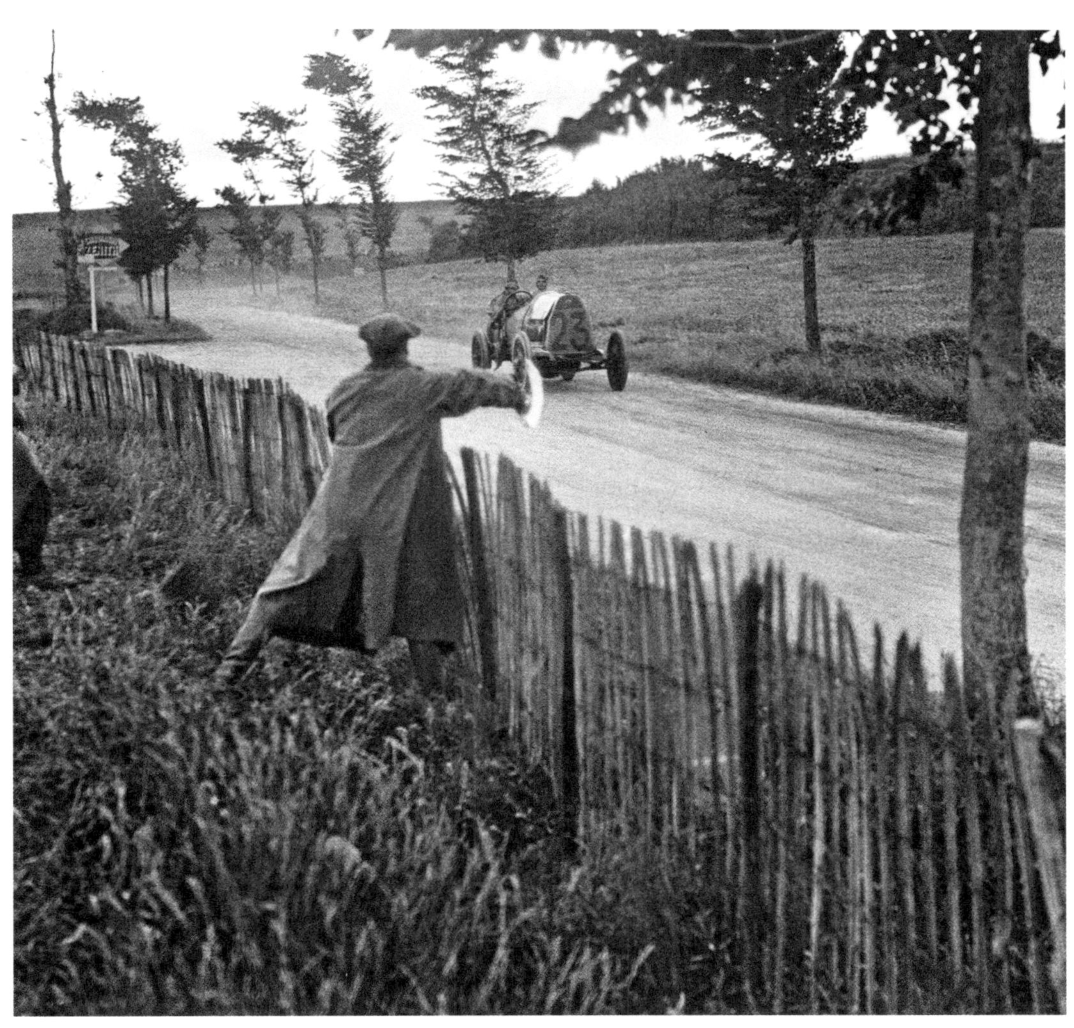

The Italian racing car driver Felice Nazzaro instructing his team-mate Louis Wagner
to accelerate his Fiat, the French Grand Prix, Circuit de Dieppe, Normandy, 1912.

on the Circuit de Picardie, near Amiens. Lartigue photographed him at the wheel of his Peugeot hurtling down a shaded tree-lined road, a second racer in pursuit (opposite). That evening, as so often, he made a precise sketch of the photograph before even developing it, adding in a miniature portrait of a goggled Boillot at the wheel (below). The advent of the First World War, only a year later, saw the destruction of many of the roads in northern France, including the Circuit de Picardie. The French Grand Prix would not return until 1921.

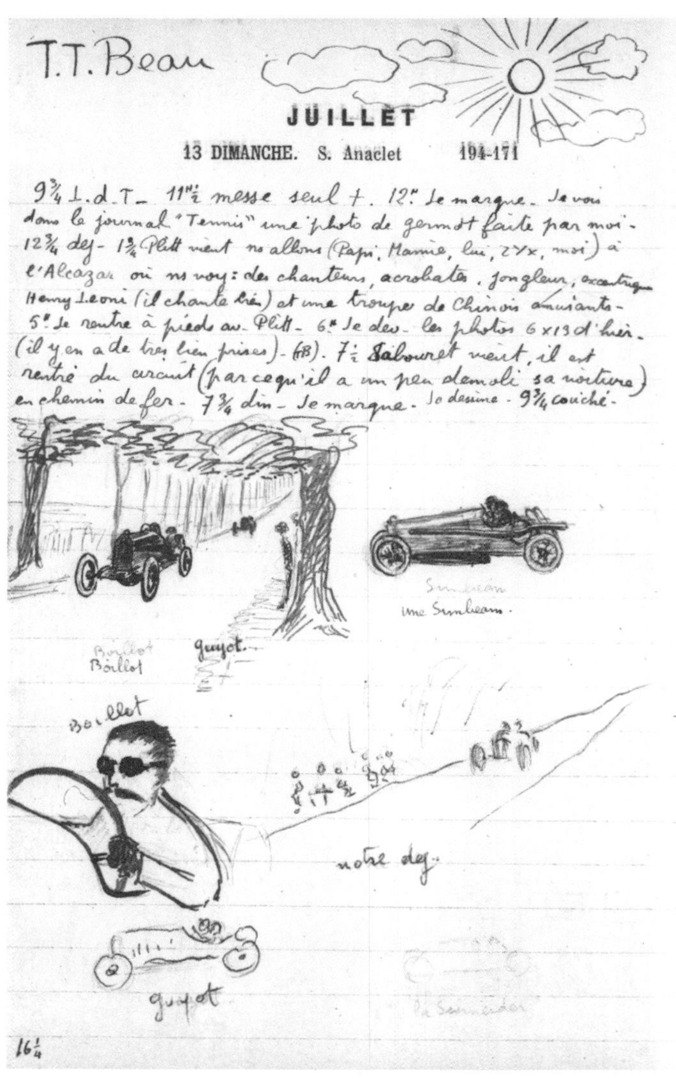

Page from Lartigue's diary, 13 July 1913.

Chapter Six
The Sporting Life

Though a slight figure, Lartigue was an avid amateur sportsman. Swift and agile, he began skating, swimming and playing tennis in his late teens, at a time when outdoor activity among the Parisian elite had become all the rage. France was slow to take up sport, compared to Britain and Germany, but adopted most types in the 1890s. By 1909 the country boasted 1,800 cycling clubs alone (the number one French sport at the time), while tennis gained popularity in about 1911. Étienne-Jules Marey at the Parc des Princes laboratory in the Bois de Boulogne near the Lartigue family home, meanwhile, had started measuring human movement, making the first sports films with the use of a 500-metre track with a black backdrop. The well-heeled now associated physical dynamism with progress and modernity. A growing appreciation of its health benefits further enhanced its prestige.

In 1913, the nineteen-year-old Lartigue joined the Racing Club de France, a multi-disciplinary sports club in the Bois. That summer, the first seaside sports centre with crossbars and other exercise equipment, under the aegis of a doctor, opened at La Baule, a new resort on the west coast of France. Lartigue photographed a couple of friends who, like his brother Zissou, sported a new fashion for striped rowing blazers (p. 152), first spotted at the Henley Regatta in the 1860s. Wearing the correct sporting attire was vital for the smart set, in Lartigue's case often a pair of white pressed trousers and shirt. Young women like the photographer's cousin Simone Roussel enjoyed a new physical freedom: 'Nowadays there is no woman in fashionable society, if she wishes to be absolutely correct or noticed, who does not drive horses or motors (in the near future, probably aeroplanes), ride, cycle well, skate, hunt with the enthusiasm of Diana, or walk like the most austere pedestrian,' wrote the bibliophile, journalist and publisher Octave Uzanne in his book *The Modern Parisienne*, published in 1912.[1]

For Christmas that year, Lartigue received a wooden self-designed photographic storage cabinet with multiple shelves, complete with a special light box to view his stereoscopic images. More importantly, his father gave him a Pathé Professionnel cine-camera for 35 mm films, with a stand so large and heavy it could scarcely be brought to him. 'It's almost unique and, among those that have one, I am in any case the youngest.... The great cinema houses – Pathé, Gaumont, Éclair – receive me as if I, too, were important; and in the sports clubs – tennis, skating, etc. – everybody rushes to be my "friend"....'[2]

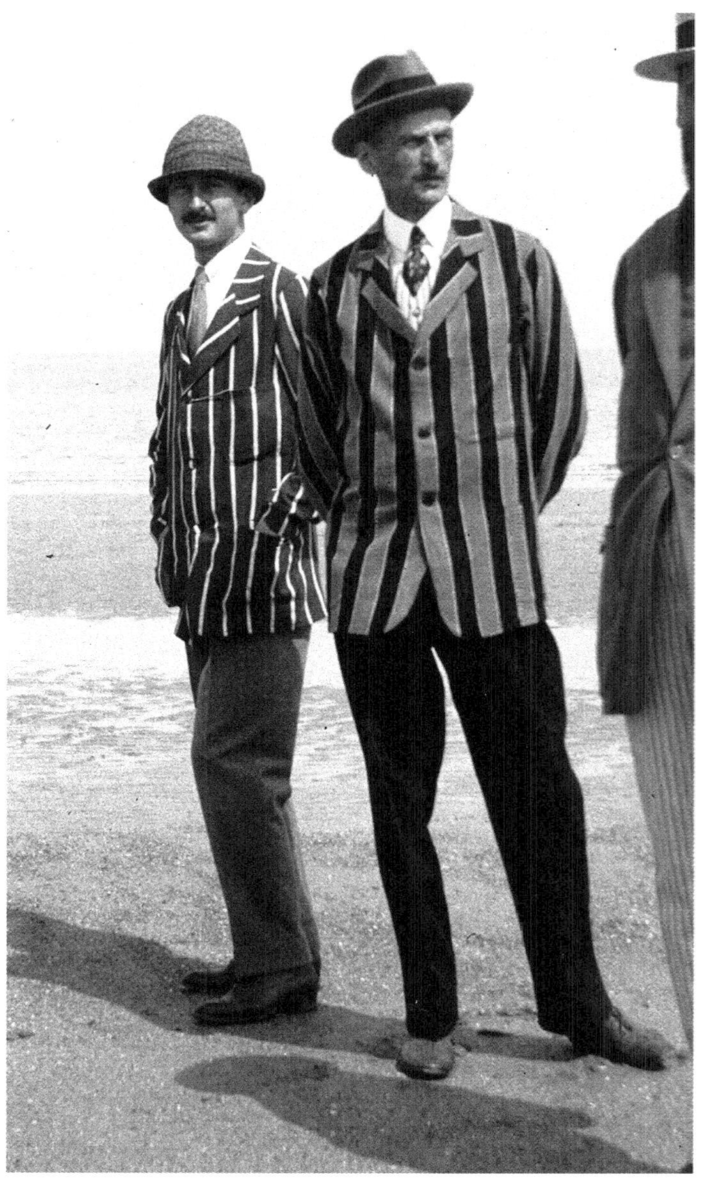

'Stylish men', La Baule, Brittany, 1913.

Armed with a lesson from a film technician at the Pathé headquarters in Vincennes, Lartigue set off three weeks later for St Moritz, winter sports then only in its infancy: 'Going to the mountains in the middle of winter – a lot of people in France say you'd have to be mad!'[3] There he stayed with his parents, Zissou and Monsieur Folletête in a grand hotel with *thés dansants* in the afternoons, noting that most of the guests were German or English, though the Brazilian aviator Alberto Santos-Dumont also appeared. Lartigue began filming with his Pathé Professionnel, also taking copious photographs, interchanging his Klapp Takyr and Klapp Nettel, whether of his father and Folletête in a horse-drawn sleigh (below) or of himself standing next to Zissou at the top of the Cresta Run, their shadows cast far below, as a tobogganer speeds past head-first (p. 154). He also captured the French silent film star, Max Linder, who made short film comedies about Max, a debonair Parisian often in a tight spot on account of his weakness for beautiful women, sliding gently down on a small sled (p. 155).

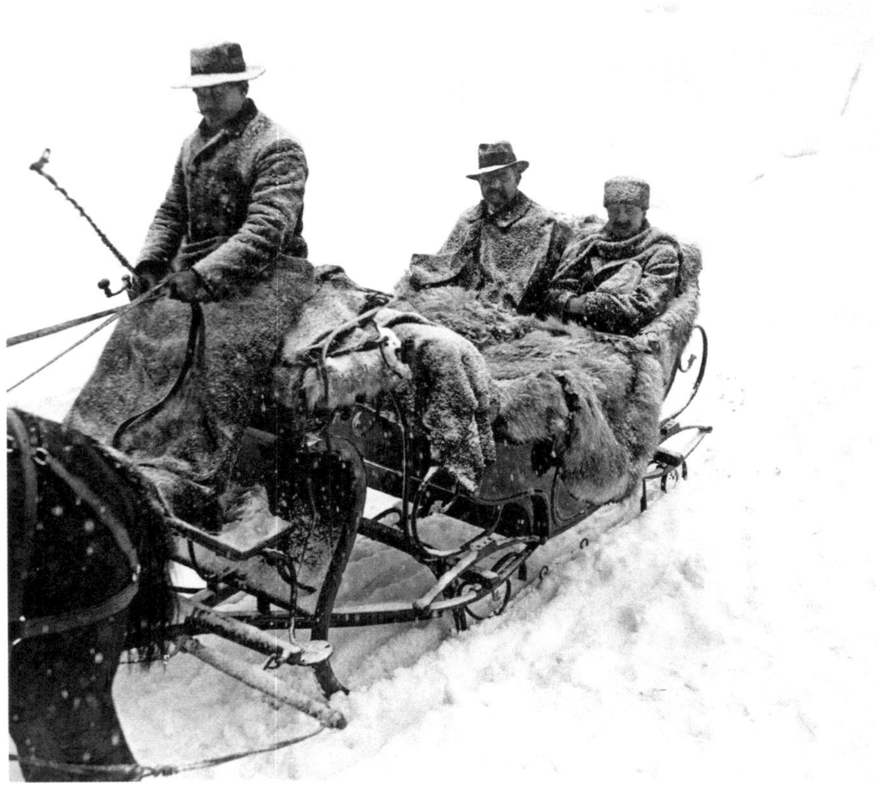

Henri Lartigue and
Monsieur Folletête (Plitt),
St Moritz, January 1913.

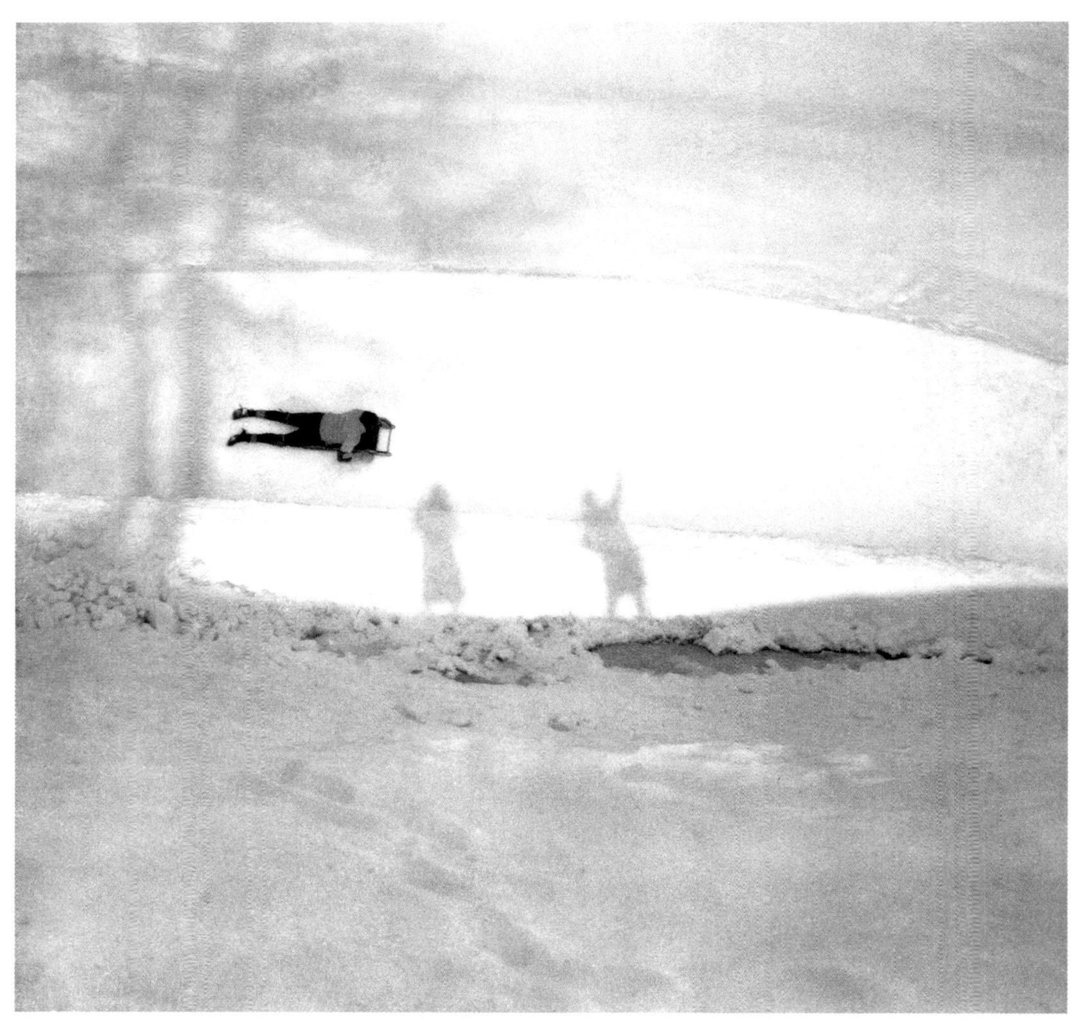

Cresta Run with Jacques Lartigue and Zissou's shadows, St Moritz, 1913.

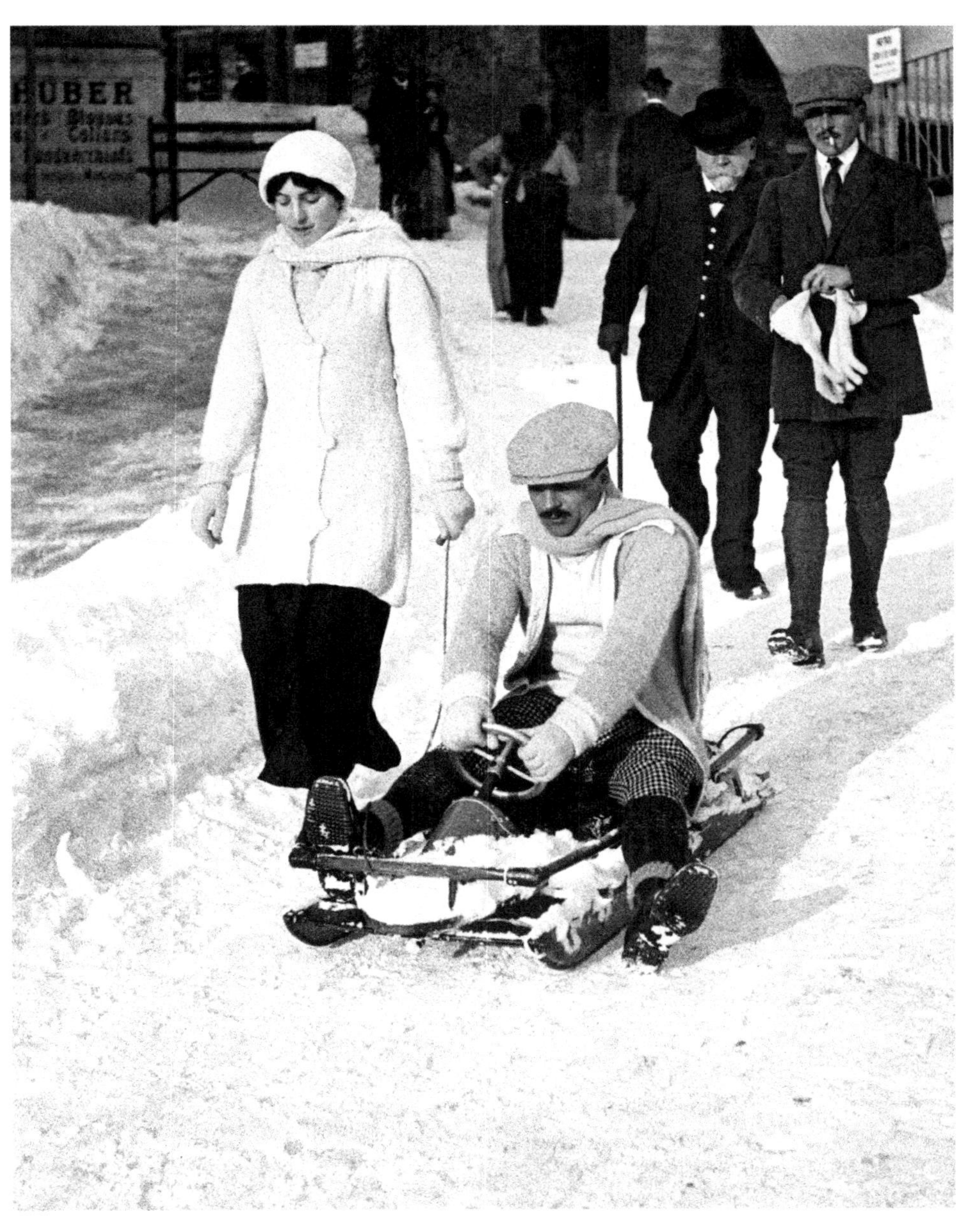

The French silent movie star, director and writer Max Linder, St Moritz, 1913.

Simone Roussel, a skilled skater, who came second in the French skating championships that year, arrived four days later (see below). 'She does so many things well,' commented Lartigue,[4] who photographed his cousin later that year playing tennis (p. 159), or both filmed and photographed her performing gymnastics with her friend Golo in the Forêt de Marly (p. 158), a couple of onlookers (Madame Folletête and Dédé) in the distance. Both young women are fully clothed yet simply dressed in long skirts and blouses, unhampered by the tight corsets, trailing skirts and elaborate undergarments fashionable in the early 1900s. Such a breach of physical decorum beyond the privacy of Rouzat – where Lartigue had once photographed his cousin Bichonnade in an enormous hat, tearing across the courtyard, skirts flying in a game of tag – was also unthinkable only a decade earlier.

Zissou and Simone Roussel, St Moritz, 1913.

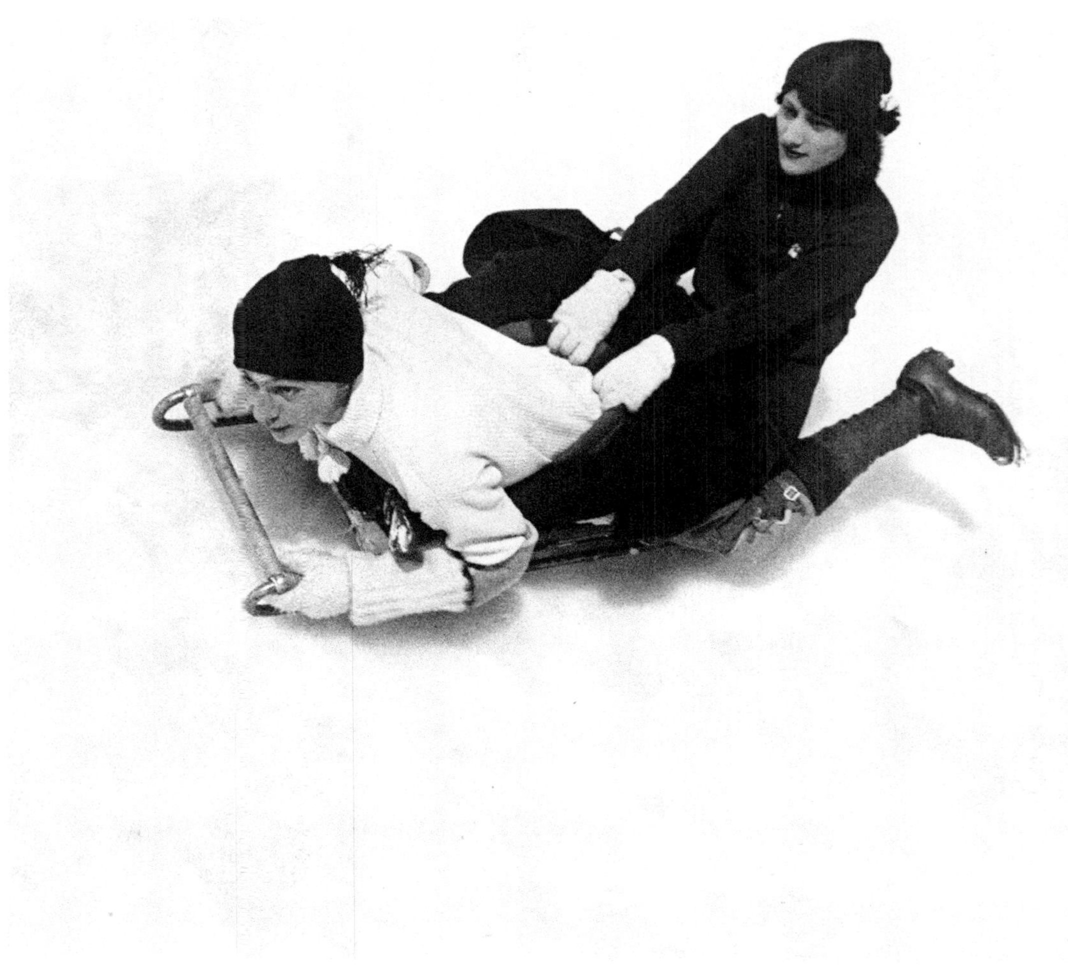

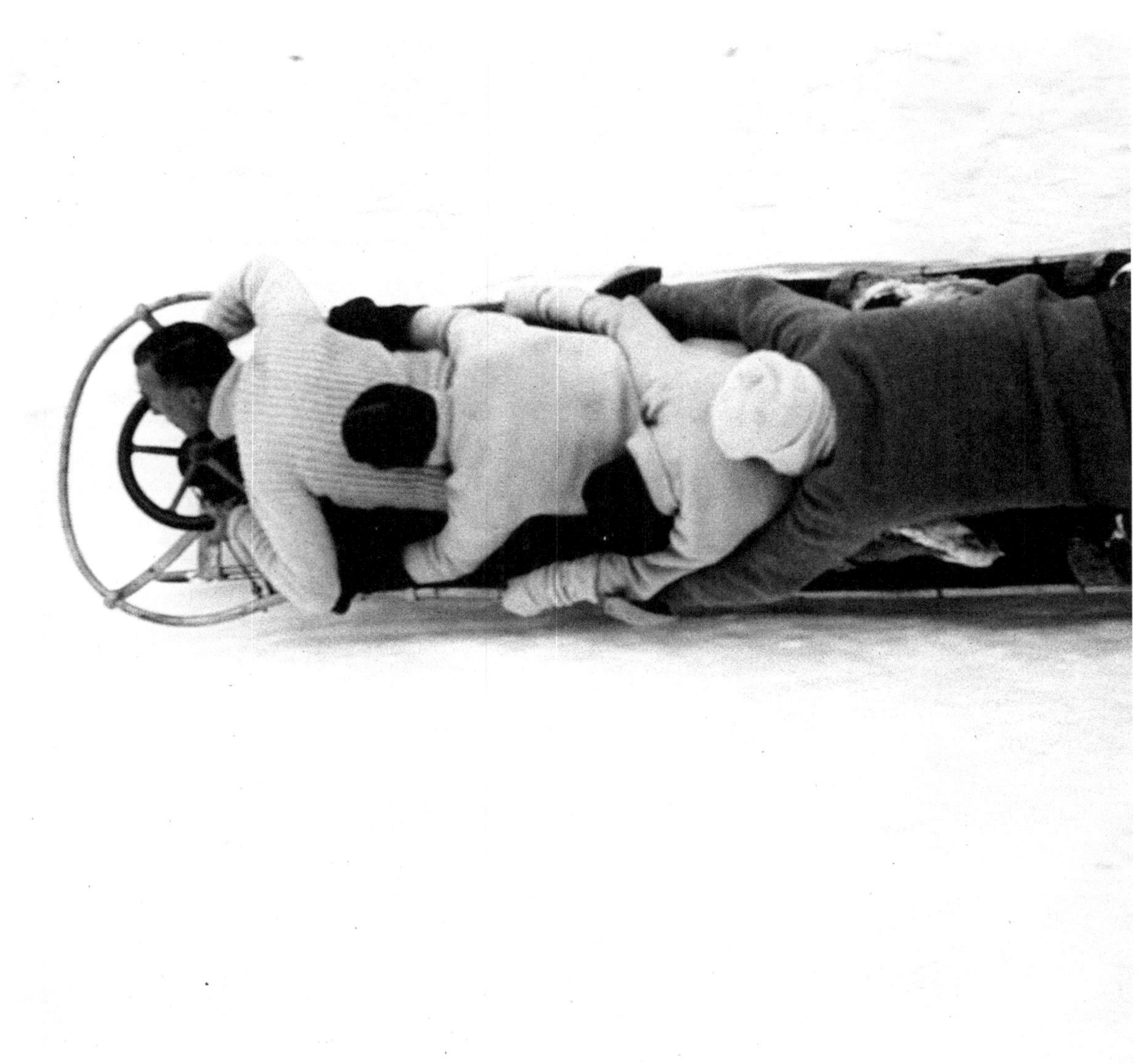

Bobsleigh, St Moritz, 1913.

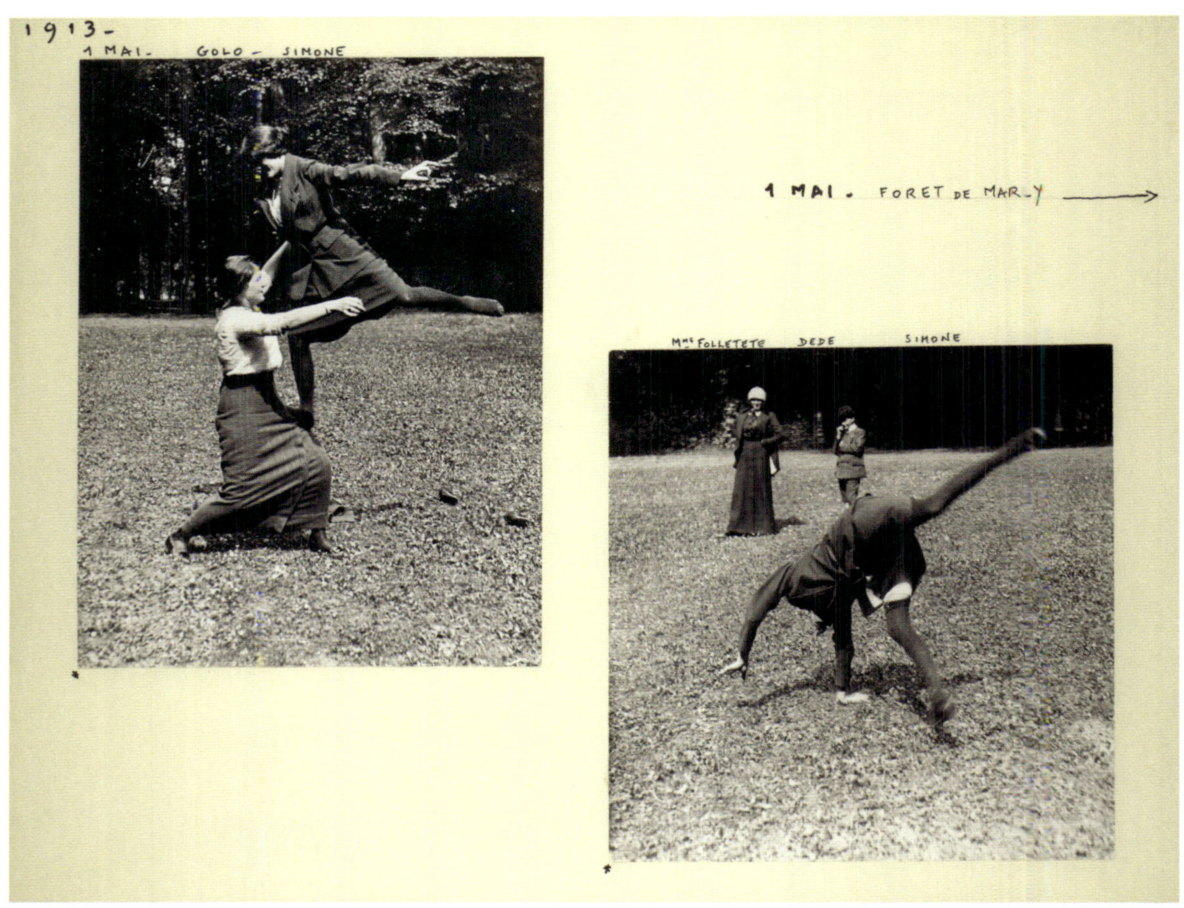

Simone Roussel and her friend Golo in the Forêt de Marly, 1913 (album page).

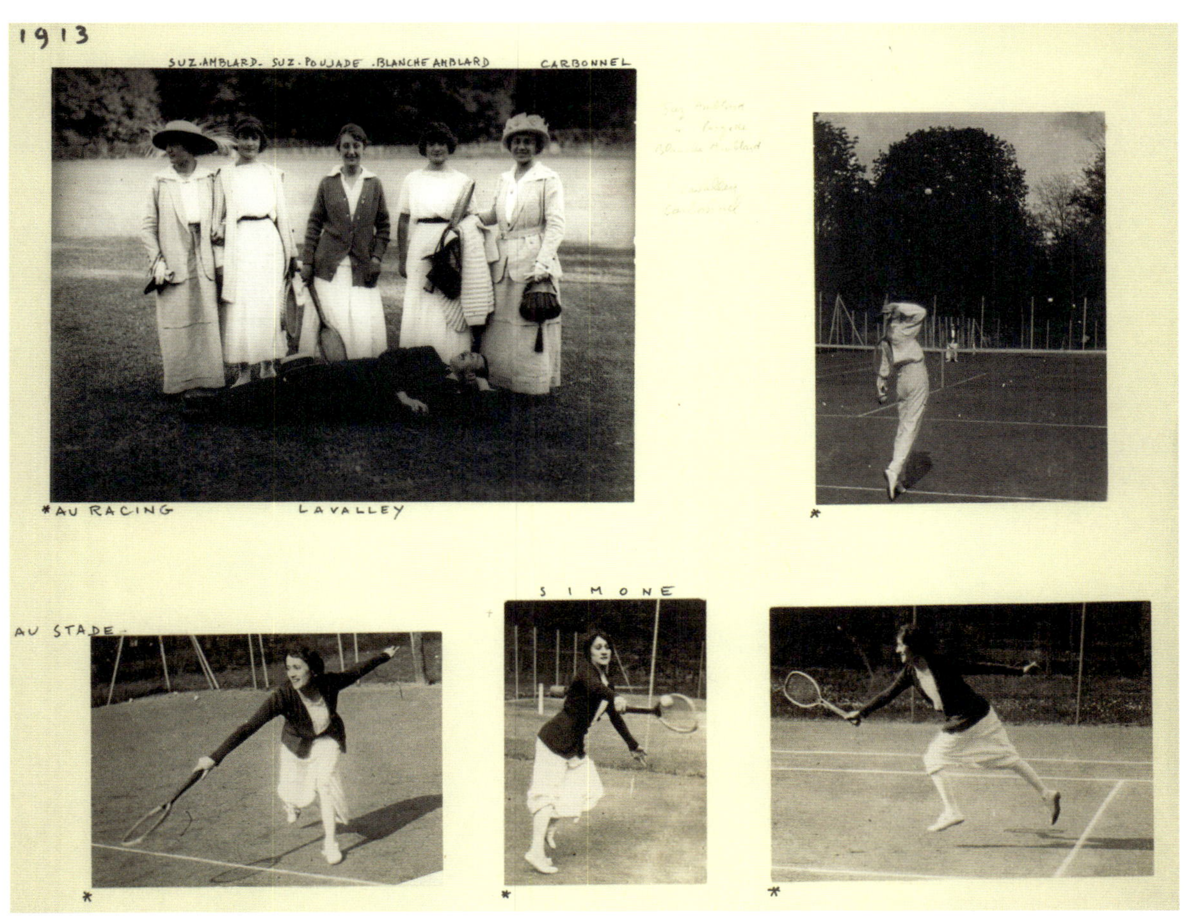

Simone Roussel (album page detail), Paris, 1913.

At St Moritz, Simone was joined by her skating partner, Charles Sabouret, a French figure skater who later took part in the 1924 Olympic Games (first revived in 1896 by Baron Pierre de Coubertin, who valued sportsmanship over material gain). Lartigue filmed and photographed the couple on ice (below, left), or Sabouret flying mid-air on his wooden skis (opposite). 'My love for Simone, I know well I've kept that. But the rest? I console myself with my photos, which catch what they can,' wrote Lartigue, who photographed his cousin in a silent, contemplative portrait in 1913 (below, right).[5] Though he would fall in love often enough, Lartigue in fact had little time for sentiment, preferring, as always, to keep himself barricaded against too much feeling. 'As for me, I'm neither proud nor happy, because it's become a matter of indifference,' he added, when Simone announced her engagement to Sabouret in early 1914.[6] The cousins nevertheless remained lifelong friends, Lartigue photographing Simone leaping in the air on her seventy-fifth birthday in 1970.

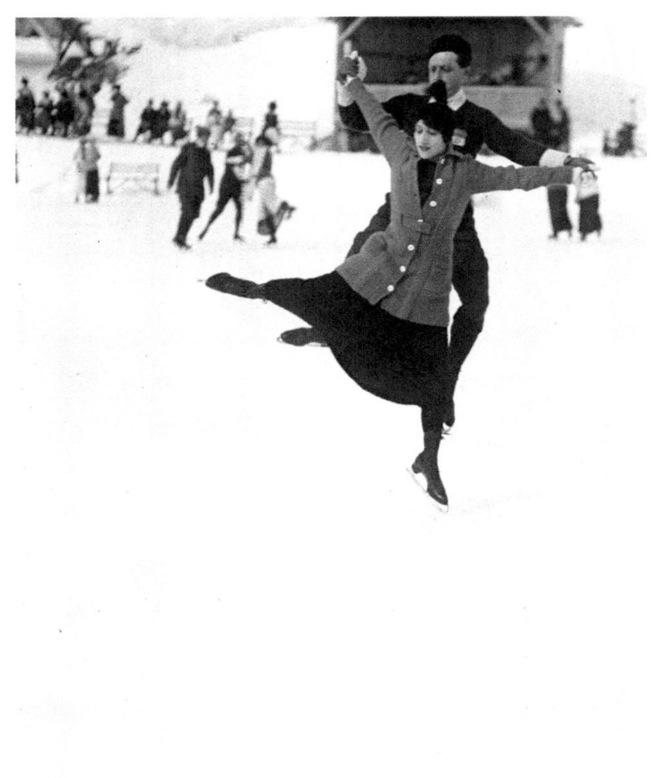

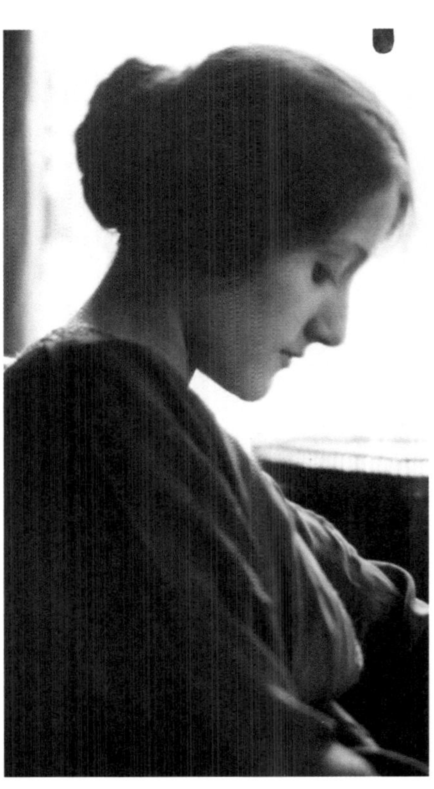

Simone Roussel with Charles Sabouret, St Moritz, 1913.

Simone Roussel, Paris, 1913.

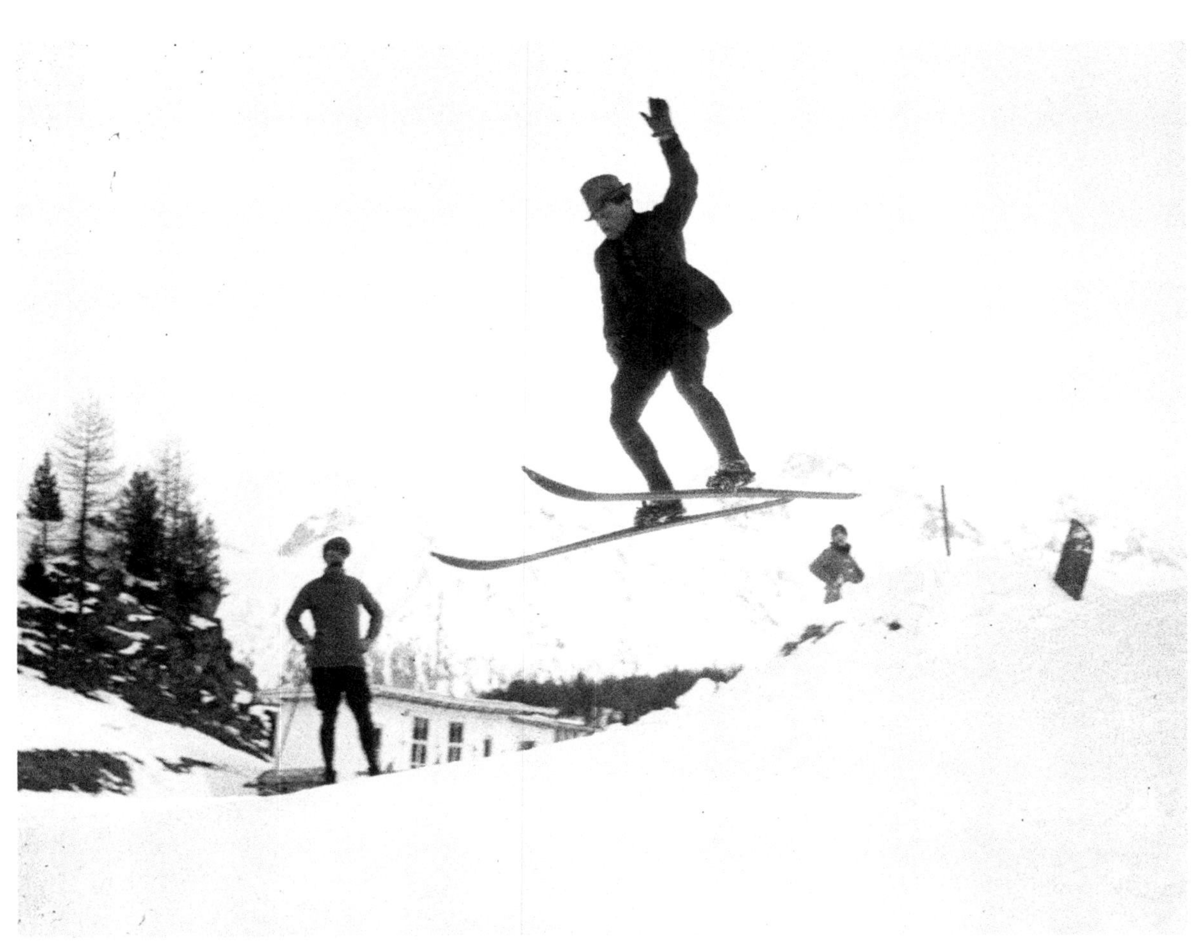

Monsieur Folletête (Plitt) and Charles Sabouret, St Moritz, 1913.

Lartigue's diary sketches, meanwhile, became more detailed and precise during this period, documenting the most compelling images he took each day at St Moritz, filling in the background (below and opposite), sometimes placing himself in the midst of the day's activities. He printed individual frames as images, or sometimes entire cinematic segments, on single pieces of photographic paper, whether skaters at the Vélodrôme Buffalo in 1913 (see pp. 164, 165) or fluttering white figures on court at the Championnat de France in 1914. On rainy days or after dinner, he spliced together segments to create longer reels, titling each topic (tennis, skiing, the Bois de Boulogne or Rouzat), then projecting them as a post-dinner party entertainment upstairs at rue Leroux. His obsession brought him into contact with professional sports photographers and film cameramen, whether at boxing matches or cycle tracks, where professional athletes entered races

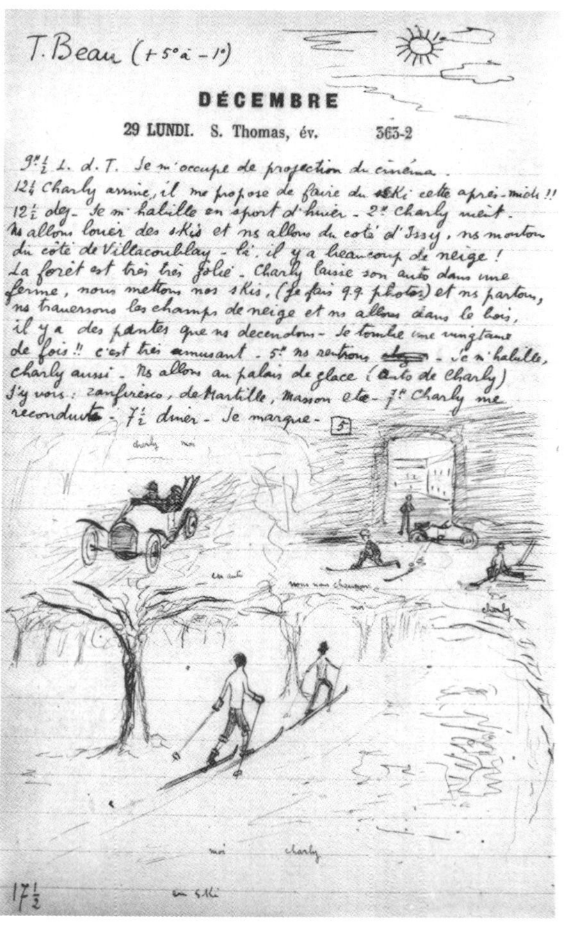

Pages from Lartigue's diary, 29 December 1913, 24 January 1914 and 7 February 1914.

sponsored by bicycle and tyre manufacturers. Sports were the subject of most of his films. On one occasion he joined newsmen filming the Aviette races at the Vélodróme Buffalo, a bicycle racetrack near the Porte Maillot (it was also used for skating in winter). Racers in flat caps attached different-shaped wings to their bicycles, the judges lying flat on their stomachs to check if both Aviette wheels left the ground.

In May 1913, Lartigue took a motor-taxi to the tennis championship semi-finals: '[Le marquis de] Givenchy brought me into the photographers' enclosure. I saw a film cameraman I know. He wanted to film the champions for the Pathé newsreel. I asked Germot and Decugis (the two biggest tennis stars), whom I know, to pose for me. Not only did they accept, but they also asked me to pose in between them!...It will be fun to see myself on a newsreel at the cinema next week.'[7] Pierre Lafitte's periodical *La Vie au*

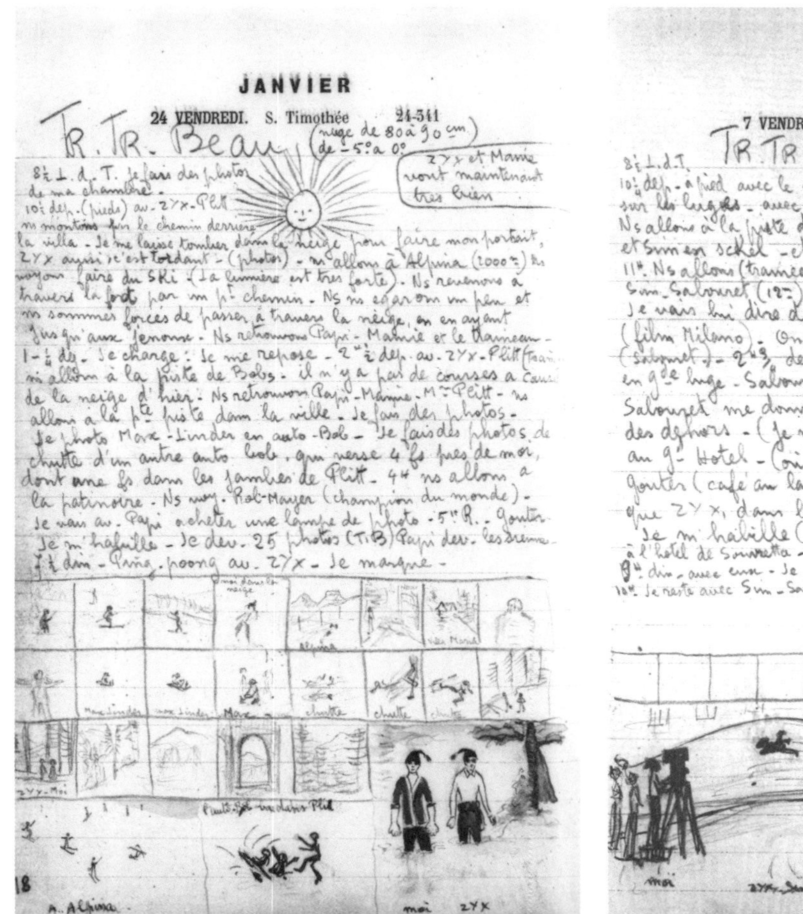

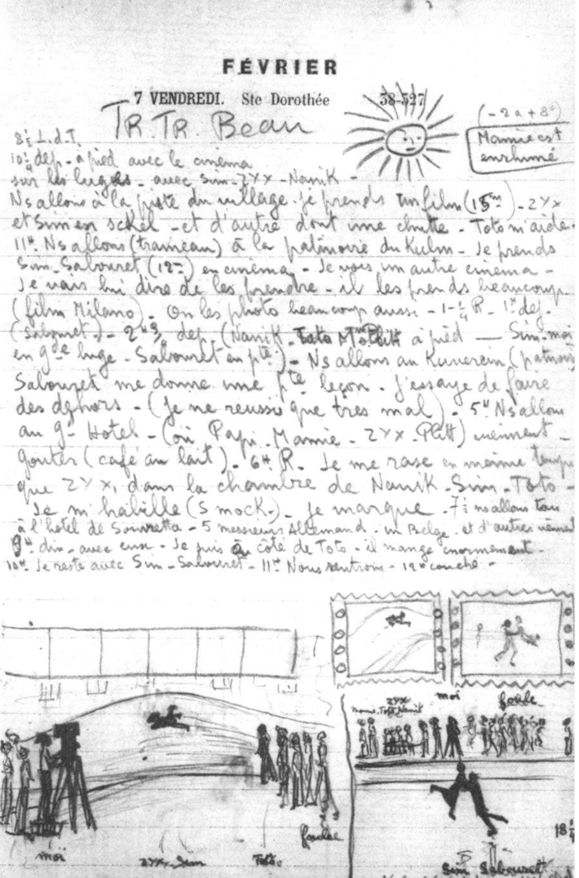

Grand Air later published one of Lartigue's tennis photographs, with the title 'A beautiful smash by Canet'. Lafitte held bi-monthly *galas-sportifs*, while the Racing Club de France gave dinners, strengthening ties between members. Lartigue played with most of the champions. Regular practice on court, as well as matches with players like Maurice Germot, honed his reflexes: 'One has to be quick [with a camera]; I was a champion at tennis, so I've got a keen eye. I react very quickly,' he said.[8] Fascinated, as always, by movement and forms flowing through the air, Lartigue found in sports a new beauty, one that emphasized energy and ease – a theme he would explore in great depth after the First World War. His photographs of fourteen-year-old tennis star Suzanne Lenglen, whom he first spotted at the Nice tennis club, hitting the ball into small squares marked out for her on the court, provide an early example. Trained by her exacting father ('it's easy to see he would really like

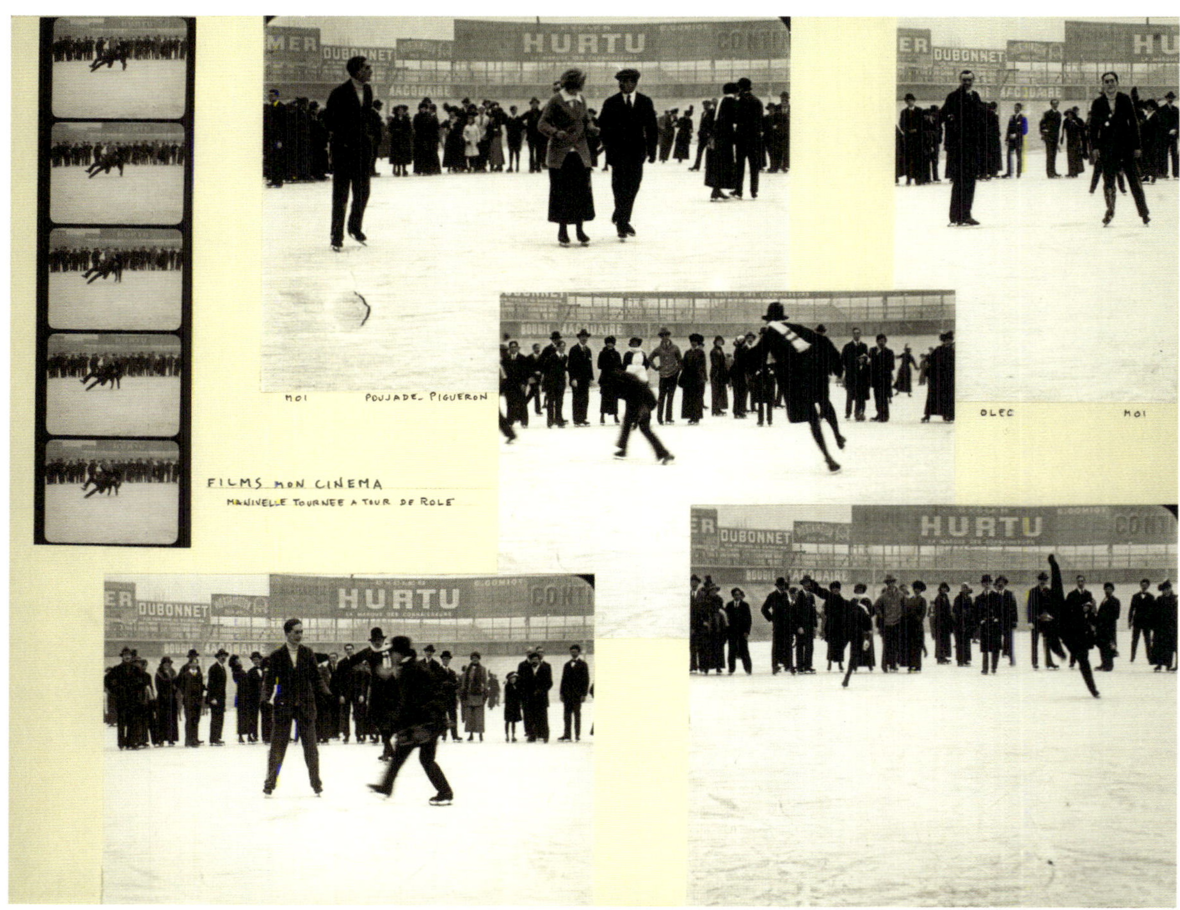

his daughter to be a boy'),[9] Lenglen played in the final of the 1914 French championships. She went on to win thirty-one championship titles after the First World War. Lartigue captured her leaping up to hit a ball with the lithe grace for which she became famous.

At Rouzat in the summer of 1914, Lartigue subjected himself to rigorous daily training: running, jumping, ball-throwing or slicing through the swimming-pool water, competing only against himself. Exempt from military service, on account of his size (at 1.75 metres, or 5 ft 8 in., he weighed only 58 kilos, or 128 pounds), he applied himself to improving his physique with characteristic discipline, noting down improvements as well as taking photographs of himself. In addition to painting, photographing, writing his diaries and working on his albums, exercise proved a life-long habit: 'Every morning, as soon as he got up, [my father] would run to perform his

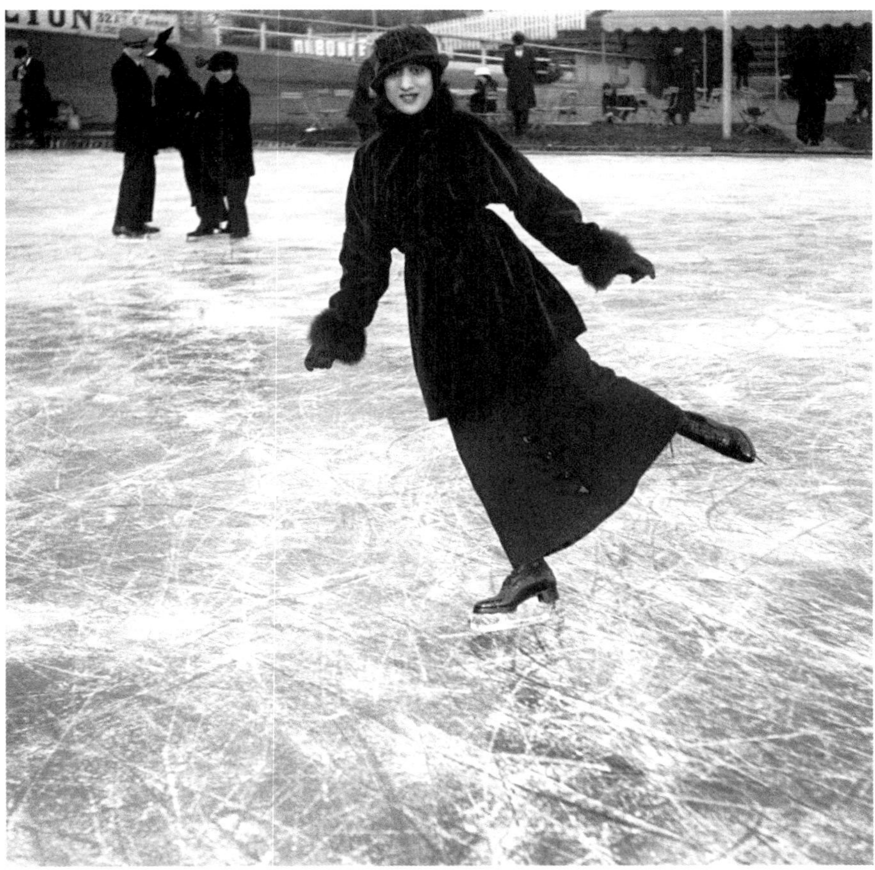

Simone Roussel, Vélodrôme Buffalo, Paris, 1913.

gymnastics on the beach to prove to himself that he was on good form and that the day had started well,' recalled his son Dani.[10]

In January that year, Lartigue had travelled to Chamonix in the French Alps, accompanied by Monsieur Folletête: 'I'm lying on a bunk, with a tiny rented coverlet over me that smells of coal. It's not a good odour, but anything that smells of travel is wonderful.'[11] Dressed in plus-fours, thick socks and an orange pullover, Lartigue set off to buy a pair of skis to join friends from the Palais de Glace. Folletête himself operated Lartigue's Pathé Professionnel to film him skiing down a woodland path (below), though it would not be until the first winter Olympics held in Chamonix in 1924 that the sport took off, tobogganing and bobsleighing being more popular. At that point Lartigue's enthusiasm for cinema (see opposite) appears equal to photography, as the following diary entries reveal: 'January 18th, Sunday [Lartigue having risen at 5 a.m. to go to Mass, in the sincere belief that God would reward him with success with his filming]. 12.00 The bobsleigh races begin. I take photographs and film the bobsleighs speeding past. 1.45 Everyone to the ice rink. I go on foot, because of my cine-camera, which Plitt helps me carry.... [At the French hockey championship] I film up close. 5.00...I send the films to Pathé.... January 21st, Wednesday. 10.00 leave with

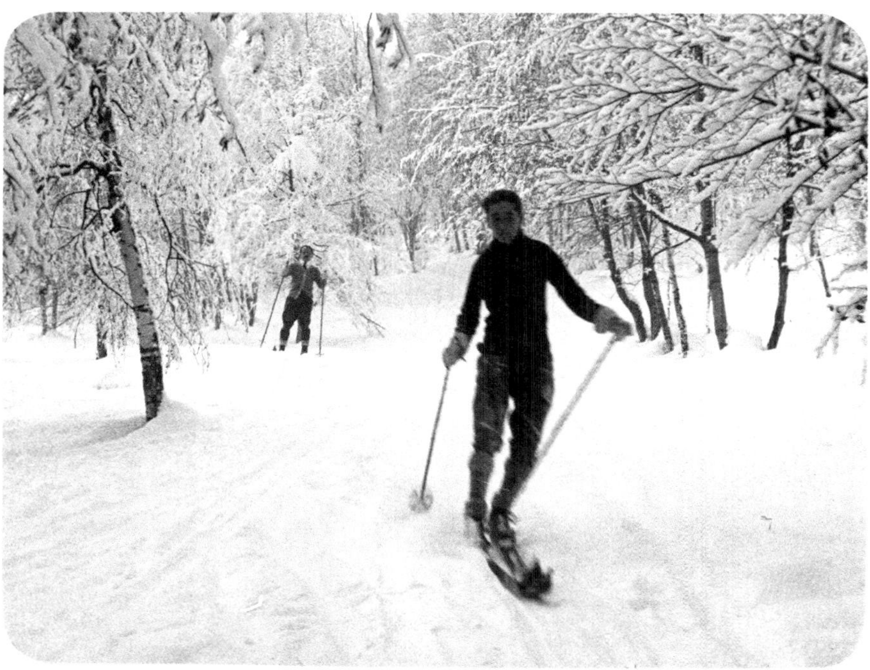

Jacques Lartigue (cine-camera operated by Plitt), Chamonix, 1914.

my cine-camera…. I film and take some colour photographs of us skiing. We are filmed by Gaumont, skiing and skijoring behind sleds (in black and white and in colour)…. 12.30…I write and I try to telephone Pathé. They probably won't take the films of hockey, nor the bobsleighs…. They tell me to re-film some of the others. I load the camera.'[12]

On his return to Paris in late January with a suitcase full of films, Lartigue visited various studios, having already telephoned from Chamonix: 'I go to Pathé where I see M. Gaveau…. He introduces me to the chief operator and I am shown projections of my films [of Chamonix]…. The operator explains their flaws, but several are good. Pathé buys from me: the 606 of Berg at the finish line and various clips of the hockey championships. I am paid

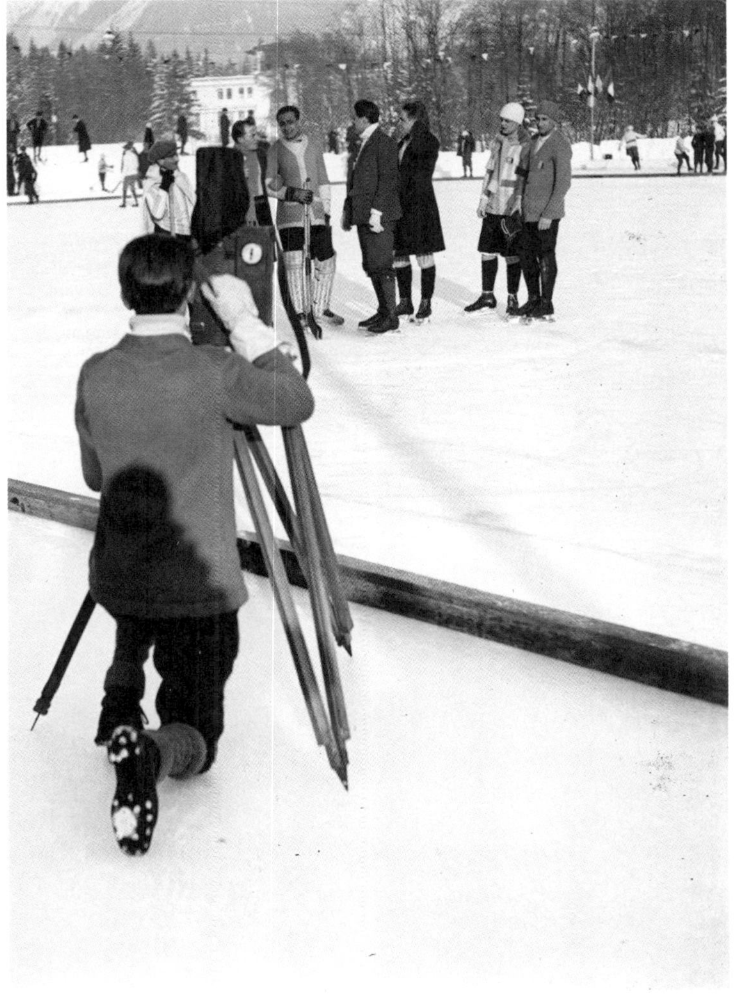

Lartigue operating his cine-camera, Chamonix, 1914.

5 francs per metre. What gives me even greater pleasure is thinking that I will see them in the actual "Pathé Journal" [cinema newsreel]'.[13] On 23 February 1914 he wrote: 'For the first time, news in colour…. It's the film of all of us in Chamonix: skiing, skating, in the street wearing colourful pullovers. All of us together at the enormous Gaumont Palace [cinema] to see ourselves….'[14] Five days later he watched his film of Berg and his team on a bobsleigh at the cinema with his cousin Bichonnade. Yet despite his delight at having sold a series of his short films to Pathé Journal, the novelty of filming sport with his Pathé Professionnel slowly wore off. In the end, Lartigue found he preferred photography: 'You can watch a film two or three times, after which it becomes the same old thing; whereas with photographs, you can look at them with great pleasure time and again.'[15]

Chapter Seven
The End of an Era

On 1 August 1914, just as Germany declared war on Russia, France ordered general mobilization (see pp. 172–3). The first poster went on display on the Place de la Concorde at 4 p.m. Tens of thousands of military-age men prepared to report at designated depots dotted across the capital, only one per cent failing to turn up. Lartigue described the scene at rue Leroux that day: 'I've come downstairs with Oléo [van Weers] to say goodbye to him at the glass door in front of the vestibule. Oléo, my great friend.... He says, "Goodbye, Pic [one of Lartigue's nicknames]. Do you realize you might never see me again?..." [Oléo] who taught me how to shave, who took my photograph at the Racing Club tennis tournaments, who had such fun with me caricaturing the famous people in the Bois or at the theatre. I laugh and tell him he's an idiot to say that. Normally, when I laugh, he starts laughing too, but today he stubbornly refuses, leaving me only with his sad farewell.... His mother and Bouboutte, his sister, arrive later full of sorrow and despair for they too have said goodbye....'[1]

Germany declared war on France only two days later, on 3 August. The Lartigue family had already retreated to Rouzat, their seven-seater open-top Peugeot laden with luggage. Just before setting off, Jacques hurried to buy tennis balls at a sports shop on the Avenue de la Grande Armée, where he spotted a detachment of Zouaves moving towards the Arc de Triomphe. At Rouzat Jacques sought refuge in his darkroom, printing up a handful of photographs left over from an earlier visit. His profound faith in his right to happiness served as a bright shield against the increasingly chaotic world outside. Doubt crept in only when, for the first time in his life, he saw a look of fear in his father's face, a fear of what the war might bring.

In early autumn, the Renault *taximètres* of Paris, once favoured by Madame Lartigue, ferried French soldiers to the front, where the week-long Battle of the Marne began on 6 September. The fight resulted in an Allied victory against the German armies to the west. But 80,000 French soldiers

8½ L. gymn. d. T. Je finis ma malle, je marque.
Je vais acheter des balles de tennis av. de la g^de Armée.
12½ déj. (Mamie, Zyx) Oléo arrive et déj. avec nous.
Il va probablement partir tantôt pour Belfort !!
Papi rentre – Louis vient ns dire aurevoir – T^te Maria et
Marthe viennent (T^te Maria a beaucoup de chagrin du
départ d'Oléo). N^cle Auguste et T^te Gen. viennent –
3^h M. Kennedy vient – Nous partons, Papi, Mamie, Zyx
M. Laroze et moi dans la 35 H.P conduite par Yves et
M. Kennedy et Jeanne (femme de chambre) dans
la 16 H.P. de ville conduite par le beau-frère d'Yves.
Ns partons pour Rouzat – Ns voy. que l'ordre de mobilisation
générale est affiché dans tous les villages !! C'est
pénible de voir toutes les femmes pleurer dans les village.
Ns voy. un train de soldats passer et tous les hommes
et les jeunes-gens s'en vont. 9¼ nous arrivons à
Pouilly où ns dinons – 10½ ns repartons (Je dors de
temps en temps). Ns croisons énormement d'autos –
3^h ns arrivons à Rouzat – Je me lave, je déballe. etc.
4^h couché –

La mobilisation générale est déclarée –

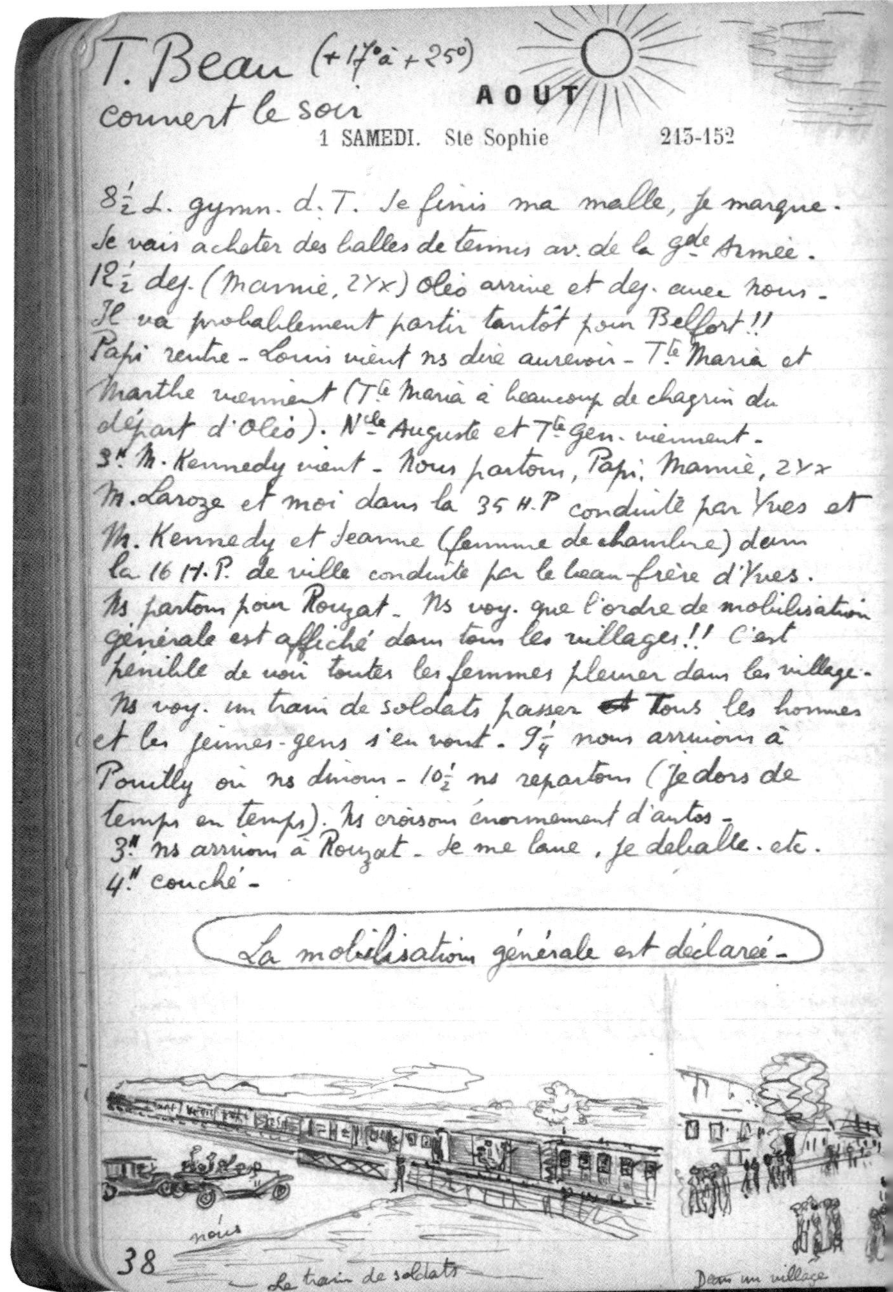

Page from Lartigue's diary, 1 August 1914, showing French Army mobilization.

Beau
(+ 18° à + 25°)

AOUT

(M. Laroze repart pour Paris)

1" couché (voir hier). 10¾ L. gymn. T. Je lis ma messe.
2¾ déj. (Papi. Mammie, ZYx, M. Kennedy.) Pianola - etc.
3" déj. (auto conduite par Yves) avec ~~Pat~~ Mammie, ZYX -
Ns allons à Châtel - Ns allons voir Tᵗᵉ Amélie et les fᵗᵉˢ Bourard.
Ns allons faire q.q. commission (épicier, chocolat etc).
4½ ns allons goûter chez Tᵗᵉ Amélie - 5" Ns allons à Riom
pour tâcher de louer une voiture - Nous voy. gᵈ mère
qui arrive de Bourbon Lancy !!! (par le dernier train)
~~et dont~~) Quelle chance qu'elle ait pu arriver
jusqu'à Riom et que nous l'y ayions rencontrée." Ns
rentrons à Rouzat. ~~Ns~~ Je fais une photo de M. Kennedy
pour un permis de séjour pour les étrangers -
Je reste au jardin etc. 7¾ dîn. (Papi. Mammie, ZYx, gᵈ mᵉ,
M. Kennedy.) Pianola - 9" gymn. c.

> L'auto de ZYx est partie avec le beau-frère d'Yues "
> Yves part demain dans la 35 H.P.

Pas de nouvelles !"
La poste - (téléphones, télégrammes) et les Trains
ne marchent plus !!

40
3

died, including Oléo, the champion chair-jumper of Rouzat. 'Oléo killed, my friend Oléo, so lively! Eccentric! Well turned-out!' wrote Lartigue,[2] decades later, in his 'new-old' album for 1914, around an official photograph of his cousin in army uniform (below), also pasting in a picture he had taken of army manoeuvres at Issy-les-Moulineaux in 1911, to conjure up the declaration of war (opposite).

'This "diary" is not destined for others, so it must contain all my truths. I have no right to say I am enjoying myself in the midst of a cataclysm, but I have even less right to lie by saying to the contrary,' Lartigue confided weeks after Oléo's death.[3] 'The war inevitably made us unhappy, [but] I was happy all the same.... I played sports and we still amused ourselves,' he added in December that year.[4] His wartime photographs reveal a life of carefree continuity (see p. 178), whether in Nice, Biarritz, La Baule or at home in Paris,

Raymond van Weers (Oléc), killed September 1914 (album page).

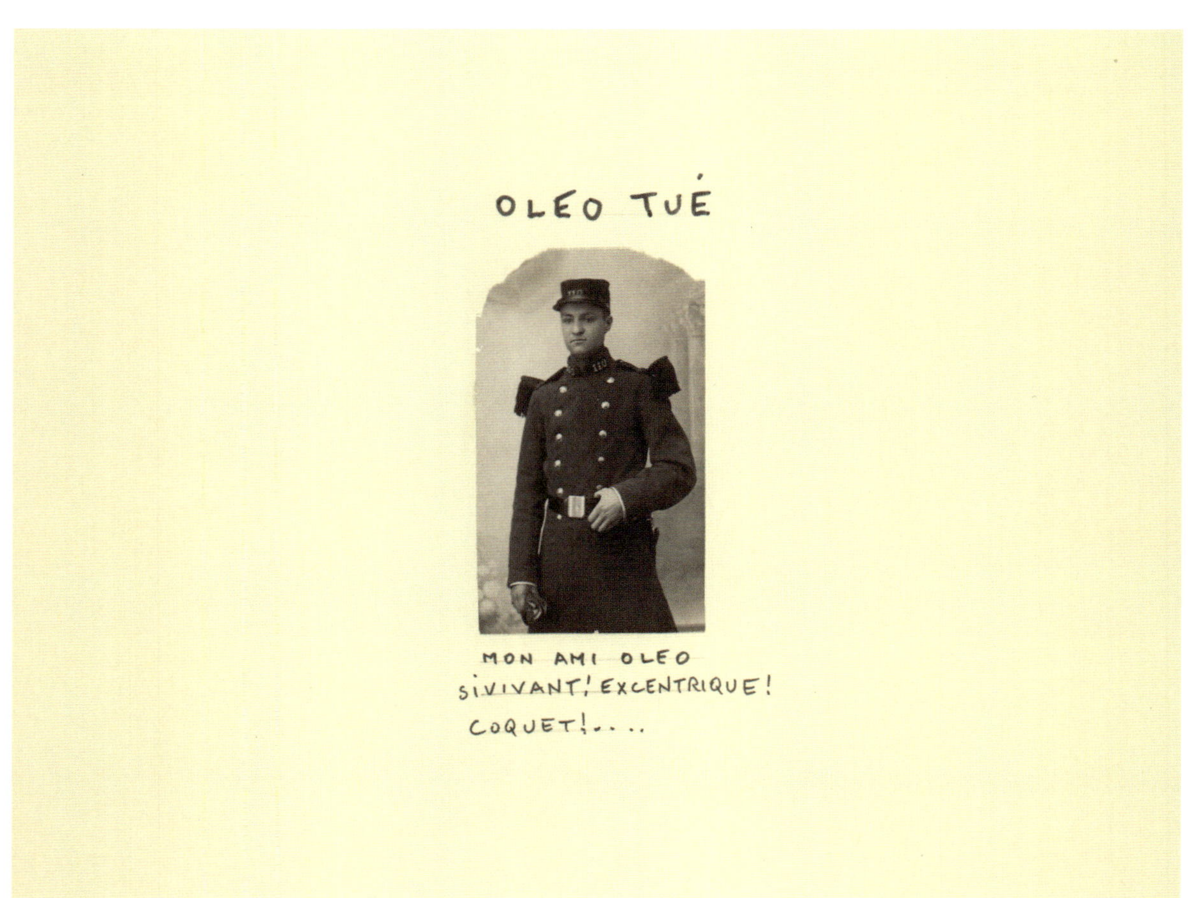

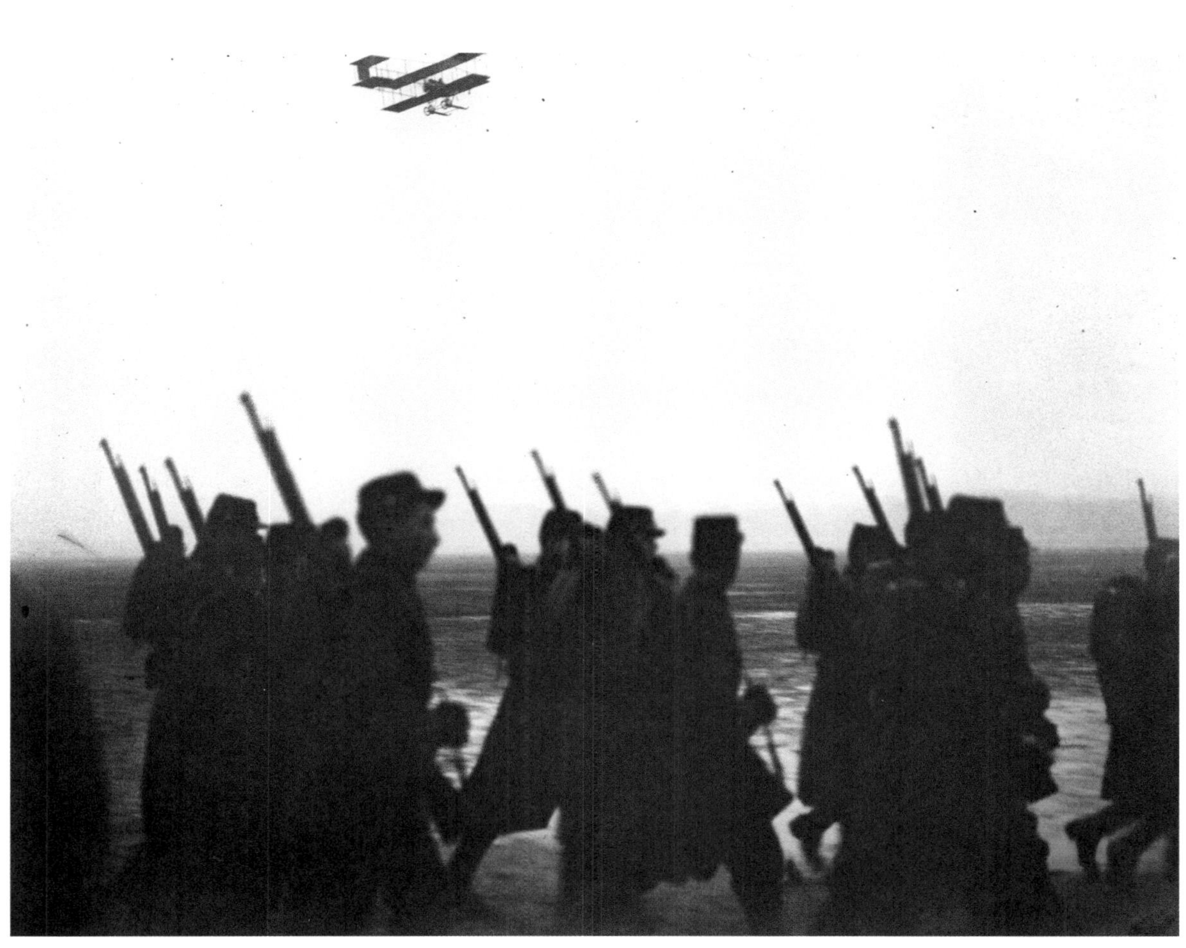

'The War, 1st of August, 1914' (photograph taken in 1911).

where Marthe Chenal, an actress fifteen years his senior, became his first mistress. Separate pages of his diary listing friends or well-known sportsmen killed in battle offer a rare glimpse of the outside world.

Neither he nor Zissou (who also secured an exemption) ever went near the front line. Lartigue wrote that the pair attracted inquisitive stares in public, hinting at an inner moral conflict. Though a tragedy, large Catholic families considered it an honour to lose a son in the First World War, in which almost 1.4 million French combatants died, including Lartigue's hero, the racing driver Georges Boillot, and the aviator Roland Garros, who both joined as fighter pilots. Even the diminutive, underweight, forty-year-old Maurice Ravel entered the Thirteenth Artillery Regiment as a lorry driver, driving munitions at night under heavy bombardment. The composer dedicated each of the six movements of his light-hearted piano suite, *Le Tombeau de Couperin*, written between 1914 and 1917, to evoke the memory of each of his close friends who died at the Front. 'The dead are sad enough in their eternal silence,' he is said to have replied to criticism that the piece lacked a sombre tone.[5]

Lartigue tried to join the Service Photographique Militaire (a photo reconnaissance unit) under the auspices of the Simons brothers in 1916, but he was unsuccessful, much to his parents' relief. Instead, dapper and elegant in his uniform, he chauffeured military officers around Paris in his Pic-Pic 16 HP motor car imported from Switzerland (opposite). 'If this "diary" doesn't mention the war, it is first of all because this is not "a diary",' he wrote in 1917.[6] 'It is my little secret ruse for trying to preserve joys or my happiness, my immense Happiness,' he continued, swiftly excising any unpleasant thoughts or memories. 'I don't like to preserve tragic moments, not even in my memory.... They hurt me,' he explained towards the end of his life.[7] The Belle Époque withered in the First World War trenches. Disillusionment soon crept into daily life. But Lartigue emerged intact, plunging into life with the passions of a child, refusing ever to grow up.

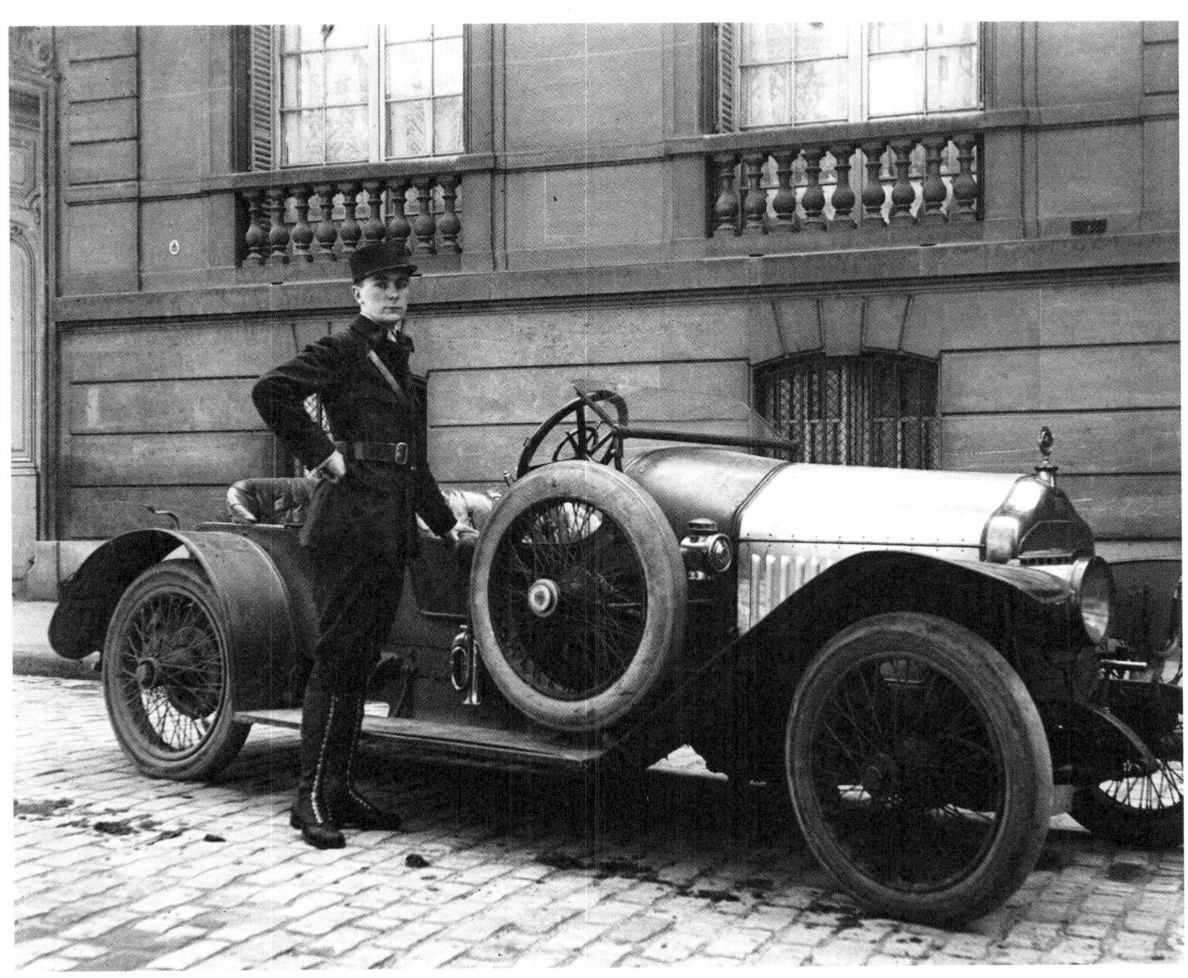

Lartigue with his Pic-Pic 16 HP car in front of 17 rue Leroux, 1916.

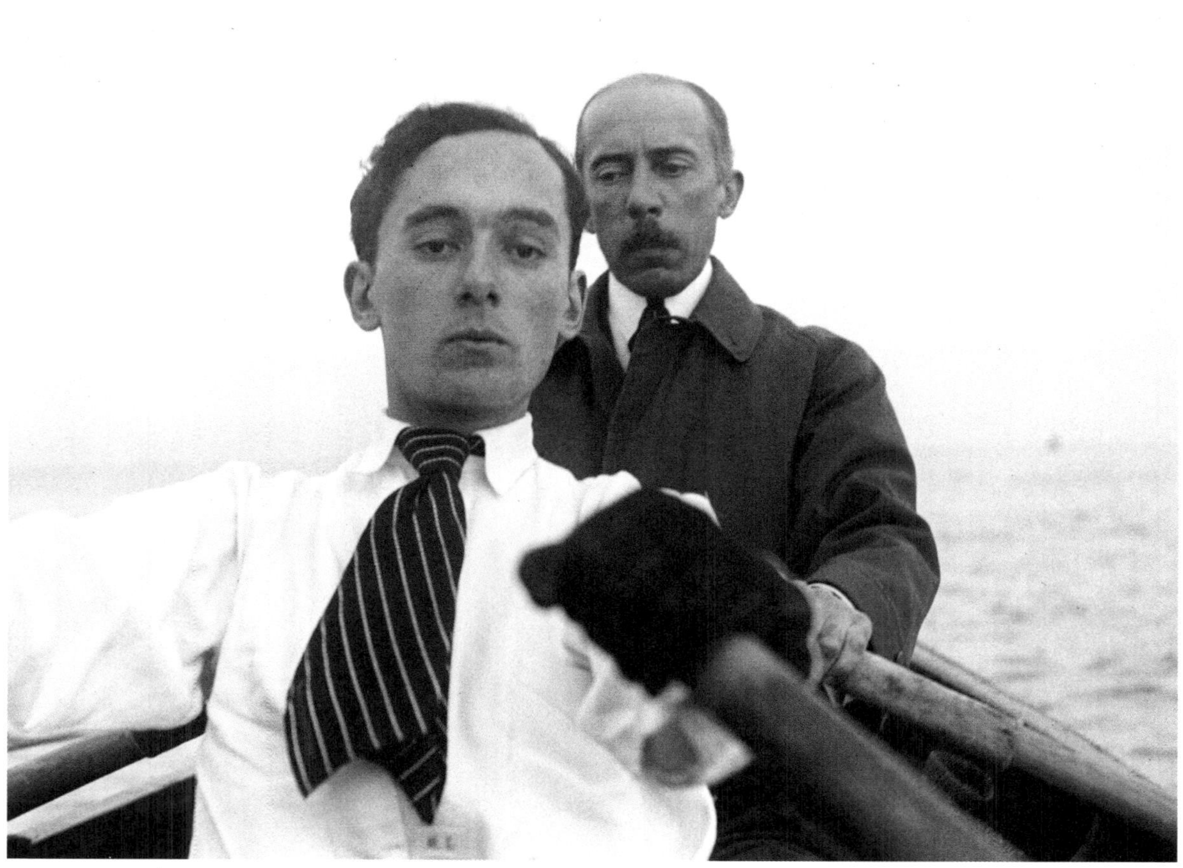

Zissou and the aviator Alberto Santos-Dumont, Arcachon, 1914.

Notes

CHAPTER ONE

1. The Richard Avedon Foundation, New York. Quoted in the *New York Times*, 27 August 2006.

2. Jacques Henri Lartigue, 1897, in *Mémoires sans mémoire* (Paris: Robert Laffont, 1975), p. 19.

3. *The Photographs of Jacques Henri Lartigue* (New York: Museum of Modern Art, 1963), introduction by John Szarkowski, p. 4.

4. Jacques Henri Lartigue, 1896, in *Mémoires sans mémoire*, p. 15.

5. Theodore Zeldin, *A History of French Passions*, Vol. 1, *Ambition and Love* (Oxford: Oxford University Press, 1973), p. 17.

6. Quoted in Philippe Bernet, 'Le Secret du Photographe de Giscard', *L'Aurore*, 25 August 1975.

7. Jacques Henri Lartigue, February 1902, in *Mémoires sans mémoire*, p. 45.

8. Ibid., p. 44.

9. Charles Péguy, *L'Argent*, essay, first part published 16 February 1913 (Paris: Éditions des Équateurs, 2008).

10. Jacques Henri Lartigue, 1900, in *Mémoires sans mémoire*, p. 25.

11. Ibid., p. 32.

12. Ibid., 1901, p. 34.

13. *Master Photographers: Jacques Henri Lartigue*, BBC, 1983 [18:03].

14. Lartigue sometimes printed these stereos as single images, while he printed others for three-dimensional viewing on glass just after he exposed the negatives. He could then examine the latter with special viewers (such as the ones that came with the multi-tiered storage cabinet Henri Lartigue gave him for Christmas; see p. 151) or project them and look at them with specially designed spectacles.

15. Jacques Henri Lartigue, 1907, in *Mémoires sans mémoire*, p. 71.

16. Émile Zola, *Photo Miniature*, no. 21, December 1900.

17. Jacques Henri Lartigue, 1907, in *Mémoires sans mémoire*, p. 71.

18. Ibid., 1912, p. 128.

19. Ibid., p. 117.

20. Ibid.

21. Ibid., p. 109.

22. *Master Photographers*, BBC, 1983 [9:40].

23. Donation Jacques Henri Lartigue, Paris, 'garnet' diary, December 1914.

24. Donation Jacques Henri Lartigue, Paris, diary, 1 February 1914.

25. Jacques Henri Lartigue, August 1938, Paris, in *L'Œil de la mémoire 1932–1985* (Paris: Éditions Carrere-Michel Lafon, 1986), p. 138.

26. Kevin Moore, *Jacques Henri Lartigue: The Invention of an Artist* (PhD thesis), Princeton University Press, 2004, p. 22.

27. Jacques Henri Lartigue, 1907, in *Mémoires sans mémoire*, p. 108.

28. Hervé Guibert, conversation with Jacques Henri Lartigue, *Le Monde*, 24 January 1985.

29. Albert Plécy, *Point de Vue – Images du Monde*, 15 July 1954.

30. Kevin Moore, *Jacques Henri Lartigue: The Invention of an Artist*, p. 192.

31. Ibid., p. 11.

32. Dani Lartigue, Portrait of his father, 18 April 2003, sent to Martine d'Astier, former director of the Donation Jacques Henri Lartigue.

33. Michel Frizot, *The New History of Photography* (Cologne: Könemann, 1998), p. 342.

CHAPTER TWO

1. Alain Corbin, *The Lure of the Sea: The Discovery of the Seaside in the Western World, 1750–1840*, trans. Jocelyn Phelps (Berkeley and Los Angeles: University of California Press, 1994), p. 53.

2. Jacques Henri Lartigue, *Mémoires sans mémoire* (Paris: Robert Laffont, 1975), p. 70.

3. Ibid., p. 19.

4. Ibid., p. 17.

5. Ibid., p. 20.

6. Vladimir Nabokov, *Speak Memory: An Autobiography Revisited* (London: Penguin Books, 1967), p. 118.

7. Edmond de Goncourt, *Mémoires de la vie littéraire*, 24 July 1886 (Paris: Fasquelle & Flammarion, 1956).

8. Pompon, 'La Bonne Comtesse', *Gil Blas*, 22 August 1901.

9. Rémy Campos, *Debussy à la plage* (Paris: Éditions Gallimard, 2018), p. 179.

10. Jacques Henri Lartigue, *Mémoires sans mémoire*, p. 165.

11. *La Grande Vie*, 1901, quoted in Catherine Guigon, *Les Cocottes, reines du Paris, 1900* (Paris:

Parigramme, 2012), p. 107.

12. Jacques Henri Lartigue, 1911, in *Mémoires sans mémoire*, p. 98.

13. Ibid.

14. Donation Jacques Henri Lartigue, Paris, diary, 1927.

CHAPTER THREE

1. Jacques Henri Lartigue, *Mémoires sans mémoire* (Paris: Robert Laffont, 1975), pp. 59–60.

2. Theodore Zeldin, *A History of French Passions*, Vol. 1, *Ambition and Love* (Oxford: Oxford University Press, 1973), p. 17.

3. Jacques Henri Lartigue, *Mémoires sans mémoire*, p. 73.

4. *Master Photographers: Jacques Henri Lartigue*, BBC, 1983 [24:30].

5. Jacques Henri Lartigue, *Mémoires sans mémoire*, p. 32.

6. Florette Lartigue, *La Traversée du siècle* (Paris: Bordas, 1990), p. 33.

7. Jacques Henri Lartigue, *Diary of a Century*, ed. Richard Avedon (New York: Viking Press, 1970), unpaginated.

8. Jacques Henri Lartigue, *Mémoires sans mémoire*, p. 58.

9. Ibid., p. 56.

10. Ibid., p. 75.

11. Ibid., p. 106.

12. Kevin Moore, *Jacques Henri Lartigue: The Invention of an Artist* (PhD thesis), Princeton University Press, 2004, p. 85.

13. Jacques Henri Lartigue, *Mémoires sans mémoire*, p. 107.

14. Jacques Henri Lartigue, *Mémoires sans mémoire*, p. 93.

15. Ibid., p. 73.

16. Florette Lartigue, *La Traversée du siècle*, p. 33.

17. Jacques Henri Lartigue, diary, August 1923, quoted in Martine d'Astier, *Jacques Henri Lartigue: Une vie sans ombre* (Paris: Découvertes Gallimard, 2009), p. 68.

CHAPTER FOUR

1. Jacques Henri Lartigue, *Diary of a Century*, ed. Richard Avedon (New York: Viking Press, 1970), unpaginated.

2. Jacques Henri Lartigue, *Mémoires sans mémoire* (Paris: Robert Laffont, 1975), p. 81.

3. Colette, *Chéri and The Last of Chéri* (London: Penguin Twentieth Century Classics, 1995), p. 103.

4. Jacques Henri Lartigue, *Mémoires sans mémoire*, p. 94.

5. *Master Photographers: Jacques Henri Lartigue*, BBC, 1983 [8:04].

6. Jacques Henri Lartigue, *Mémoires sans mémoire*, p. 80.

7. Ibid., p. 81.

8. *Master Photographers*, BBC, 1983 [8:21].

9. Jacques Henri Lartigue, *Mémoires sans mémoire*, p. 82.

10. *Master Photographers*, BBC, 1983 [8:38].

11. Jacques Henri Lartigue, *Mémoires sans mémoire*, p. 81.

12. Ibid., p. 161.

13. Ibid., pp. 96–7.

14. *Master Photographers*, BBC, 1983 [10:20, 10:42].

15. Jacques Henri Lartigue, *Mémoires sans mémoire*, p. 146.

16. Madame Carette, *Femina*, 15 July 1901.

17. Jacques Henri Lartigue, *Mémoires sans mémoire*, p. 44.

18. Ibid., p. 128.

19. Ibid., p. 97.

20. Colette, *Gigi* (London: Penguin Books, 1958), p. 34.

21. Jacques Henri Lartigue, *Mémoires sans mémoire*, p. 97.

22. Émilienne d'Alençon, cited in exh. cat. *Splendeurs et Misères : Images de la Prostitution 1850–1910* (Paris: Musée d'Orsay, 2015).

23. Liane de Pougy, cited in Catherine Authier, *Femmes d'exception, femmes d'influence : Une histoire des courtisanes au XIXe siècle* (Paris: Armand Colin, 2015).

24. Jacques Henri Lartigue, *Mémoires sans mémoire*, p. 99.

25. *Le Figaro*, 23 December 1893.

26. Jacques Henri Lartigue, *Mémoires sans mémoire*, p. 143.

27. Claude Arnaud, *Jean Cocteau: A Life* (New Haven: Yale University Press, 2016), p. 19.

28. Colette, *Gigi*, p. 27.

29. Ibid., p. 11.

30. Edmond Benjamin and Paul Desachy, *Le Boulevard : Croquis parisiens* (Paris: E. Marpon & E. Flammarion, 1893), p. 18, quoted

in Charles Rearick, *Pleasures of the Belle
Époque: Entertainment and Festivity in Turn-of-the-
Century France* (New Haven: Yale University
Press, 1985).

31. Jacques Henri Lartigue, *Mémoires sans
mémoire*, p. 108.

32. Hugo, *Vingt ans maître d'hôtel chez Maxim's*
(Paris: Amiot Dumont, 1951), quoted
in Catherine Authier, *Femmes d'exception,
femmes d'influence*, p. 103.

33. Jacques Henri Lartigue, *Mémoires sans
mémoire*, p. 147.

34. *Master Photographers*, BBC, 1983 [15:05].

35. Marcel Proust, *Swann's Way*, cited in Dora
Zhang, 'A Lens for an Eye: Proust and
Photography', in *Representations*, Vol. 118,
No. 1, Spring 2012.

36. Hervé Guibert, 'Conversation with Jacques
Henri Lartigue', *Le Monde*, 24 January 1985.

37. Marcel Proust, *Within a Budding Grove*, cited
in Dora Zhang, 'A Lens for an Eye: Proust
and Photography'.

38. Marcel Proust, *Swann's Way*, cited in ibid.

CHAPTER FIVE

1. Jacques Henri Lartigue, *Mémoires sans mémoire*
(Paris: Robert Laffont, 1975), p. 78.

2. *Master Photographers: Jacques Henri Lartigue*,
BBC, 1983 [23:55].

3. Jacques Henri Lartigue, *Mémoires sans
mémoire*, pp. 77–8.

4. Ibid., p. 71.

5. Ibid., p. 103.

6. Ibid., p. 113.

7. Ibid., p. 121.

8. Ibid., p. 122.

9. *The Automobile*, 20 July 1905.

10. Jacques Henri Lartigue, *Diary of a Century*,
ed. Richard Avedon (New York, Viking
Press, 1970), unpaginated.

11. Lartigue may, however, have mislabelled
the photograph. No number 6 car ran in
the Dieppe race, but there was one the
following year – a Th. Schneider, driven
by a M. René Croquet – so the photograph
must have been taken at the Circuit de
Picardie in 1913.

12. Jacques Henri Lartigue, *Mémoires sans
mémoire*, p. 127.

CHAPTER SIX

1. Octave Uzanne, *The Modern Parisienne*
(London: William Heinemann, 1912), p. 159.

2 Jacques Henri Lartigue, *Mémoires sans mémoire*
(Paris: Robert Laffont, 1975), p. 136.

3. Ibid., p. 137.

4. Jacques Henri Lartigue, *Diary of a Century*,
ed. Richard Avedon (New York: Viking
Press, 1970), unpaginated.

5. Jacques Henri Lartigue, April 1913,
in *Mémoires sans mémoire*, p. 146.

6. Ibid., p. 180.

7. Ibid., p. 149.

8. *Master Photographers: Jacques Henri Lartigue*,
BBC, 1983 [5:05].

9. Jacques Henri Lartigue, *Diary of a Century*,
unpaginated.

10. Dani Lartigue, 'Portrait of his father',
18 April 2003, sent to Martine d'Astier,
former director of the Donation Jacques
Henri Lartigue.

11. Jacques Henri Lartigue, January 1914,
in *Mémoires sans mémoire*, p. 168.

12. Jacques Henri Lartigue, diary pages for
18 and 21 January 1914.

13. Ibid., p. 176.

14. Ibid., pp. 183–4.

15. Martine d'Astier, *Jacques Henri Lartigue: Une
vie sans ombre* (Paris: Découvertes Gallimard,
2009), p. 41.

CHAPTER SEVEN

1. Jacques Henri Lartigue, *Mémoires sans mémoire*
(Paris: Robert Laffont, 1975), p. 201.

2. Jacques Henri Lartigue, photograph
album, 1914.

3. Donation Jacques Henri Lartigue, Paris,
November 1917, in Lartigue's unpublished
diary, p. 55.

4. Donation Jacques Henri Lartigue, document.

5. Maurice Ravel, *Le Tombeau de Couperin
and Valses Nobles et Sentimentales in Full
Score* (Mineola, NY: Dover Publications,
repr. 2001).

6. Jacques Henri Lartigue, *Mémoires sans
mémoire*, p. 273.

7. *Master Photographers: Jacques Henri Lartigue*,
BBC, 1983 [16:12].

Chronology

1894 ‣ Jacques Henri Lartigue is born on 13 June at the house of his parents, Henri and Marie Lartigue, in Courbevoie on the outskirts of Paris. His older brother Maurice (Zissou) was born on 2 August 1890.

1899 ‣ The Lartigue family moves from Courbevoie to the Boulevard Émile-Augier in Paris.

1901 ‣ The family moves again, to a *hôtel particulier* at 40 rue Cortambert in the 16th *arrondissement*.
‣ Henri Lartigue buys a country house from the composer Jules Massenet at Pont-de-l'Arche in Normandy.

c.1902 ‣ Henri Lartigue gives Jacques his first camera, a wooden 13 × 18 cm plate camera.

1904 ‣ Henri Lartigue starts giving Jacques a series of increasingly lightweight, flexible and sophisticated cameras (see p. 187).

1905 ‣ Henri Lartigue buys the Château de Rouzat in the Puy-de-Dôme region of the Auvergne.
‣ He takes his family to the Coupe Gordon Bennett motor race on the Auvergne Circuit.
‣ Jacques meets one of the Simons brothers, star photographers at *La Vie au Grand Air* magazine.

1907 ‣ Jacques receives his first Holy Communion.

1908 ‣ Wilbur Wright demonstrates the engine-powered Wright aeroplane at Le Mans.
‣ Jacques starts photographing aviation pioneers.

1909 ‣ Louis Blériot makes the first flight across the English Channel from Calais to Dover.

1910 ‣ Jacques begins photographing fashionable women in the Bois de Boulogne.

1911 ‣ The family moves to a *hôtel particulier* at 17 rue Leroux in the 16th *arrondissement*.
‣ Jacques sells his first photographs to *La Vie au Grand Air*.
‣ He shoots his first film in the Bois de Boulogne with a cinematograph given to him by his father.
‣ He starts writing his diaries.
‣ He starts arranging his photographs in albums.

1913 ‣ Jacques travels with his family to St Moritz.

1914 ‣ Jacques travels to Chamonix.
‣ He sells his winter sports films to Pathé.
‣ He is exempted from military service.
‣ French troops are mobilized on 1 August.
‣ Germany declares war on France on 3 August.
‣ Jacques starts spending time on the Riviera between 1914 and 1918.

Cast of Characters

Tante Amélie
　Surname and relationship to Lartigue family
　unknown; possibly close family friend.

Georges Bourard
　Family friend.

Henry S. Broadwater (Rico)
　American friend of Jacques and Zissou.

Louis Ferrand (Loulou)
　Son of Eugène Ferrand, mayor and notary at
　Pont-de-l'Arche; brother of Robert (Bobino).

Robert Ferrand (Bobino)
　Son of Eugène Ferrand, mayor and notary at
　Pont-de-l'Arche; brother of Louis (Loulou).
　Killed in the First World War.

André Haguet (Dédé)
　Jacques' cousin, son of Auguste
　(Nononcle Auguste) and Geneviève Haguet,
　brother of Marcelle.

Auguste Haguet
　Jacques' maternal grandfather, married
　to Eugénie Haguet.

Auguste Haguet (Nononcle Auguste)
　Jacques' uncle (brother of Jacques' mother,
　Marie), husband of Geneviève (née Lartigue,
　sister of Jacques' father, Henri), father of
　Marcelle and André (Dédé).

Eugénie Haguet, née Coulon
　Jacques' maternal grandmother,
　mother of Maria, Auguste, Henri and Marie
　(Jacques' mother).

Geneviève Haguet (Tante Yéyé)
　Jacques' aunt (née Lartigue, sister of Jacques'
　father, Henri), wife of Auguste (brother of
　Jacques' mother, Marie), mother of Marcelle
　and André (Dédé).

Henri Haguet
　Jacques' uncle (brother of Jacques' mother,
　Marie), husband of Marguerite (née
　Lartigue, sister of Jacques' father, Henri),
　father of Jean (Biclo).

Jean Haguet (Biclo)
　Jacques' cousin, son of Henri and
　Marguerite Haguet.

Marcelle Haguet
　Jacques' cousin, daughter of Auguste
　(Nononcle Auguste) and Geneviève Haguet,
　sister of André (Dédé).

Marguerite Haguet
　Jacques' aunt (née Lartigue, sister of
　Jacques' father, Henri), married to Henri
　(brother of Jacques' mother, Marie),
　mother of Jean (Biclo).

Hubert Laroze
　Friend of Jacques' parents.

Charles Lartigue
　Jacques' paternal grandfather, father of
　Maurice, Henri (Jacques' father), Marguerite,
　Marcel, Geneviève and Raymond.

Dani Lartigue
　Son of Jacques Henri Lartigue and his first
　wife, Madeleine Messager (known as Bibi);
　born 1921, died 2017.

Emilie Lartigue
　Jacques' paternal grandmother, wife of
　Charles Lartigue, mother of Maurice,
　Henri (Jacques' father), Marguerite, Marcel,
　Geneviève and Raymond Lartigue.

Henri Lartigue
　Father of Jacques and Maurice (Zissou),
　husband of Marie Lartigue.

Henry (or Henri) Lartigue
　Jacques' great uncle, and grandfather of
　Caroline (Caro) and Simone Roussel.

Marie Lartigue, née Haguet
　Mother of Jacques and Maurice (Zissou),
　wife of Henri Lartigue, daughter of Auguste
　and Eugénie Haguet.

Maurice Lartigue (Zissou, Zyx)
　Brother of Jacques Henri Lartigue,
　son of Henri and Marie Lartigue.

Raymond Lartigue (Nononcle Raymond)
　Jacques' uncle (brother of Jacques' father,
　Henri), husband of Cécile Lartigue, father
　of Raymonde Lartigue.

Caroline Roussel (Cousin Caro, Nanik)
　Jacques' cousin, older sister of
　Simone Roussel, daughter of Paul
　and Caroline Roussel.

Paul Roussel (Toto)
　Father of Jacques' cousins Caroline
　(Caro) and Simone Roussel, husband
　of Caroline Roussel (née Lartigue,
　daughter of Henry Lartigue). Poet and
　newspaper director.

Simone Roussel (Cousin Simone, Sim)
　Jacques' cousin, younger sister of Caroline
　(Caro) Roussel, daughter of Paul and

Caroline Roussel; married to Charles
Sabouret, skating champion.

Charles Sabouret (Charley)
Friend of Jacques, married to Jacques' cousin
Simone Roussel. In 1920 he competed and
came seventh in the Olympics pair skating
in Antwerp, Belgium, with Simone.

Henry van Weers (Nononcle van Weers)
Uncle of Jacques' mother, married to
Maria van Weers, father of Madeleine
(Bichonnade), Marthe (Bouboutte) and
Raymond (Oléo).

Madeleine van Weers (Bichonnade)
Daughter of Henry and Maria van
Weers, sister of Marthe (Bouboutte)
and Raymond (Oléo).

Marcel van Weers
Cousin of Jacques' mother, Marie Lartigue.

Marthe van Weers (Bouboutte)
Daughter of Henry and Maria van Weers,
sister of Madeleine (Bichonnade) and
Raymond (Oléo).

Raymond van Weers (Oléo)
Son of Henry and Maria van Weers, brother
of Madeleine (Bichonnade) and Marthe
(Bouboutte). Killed in the Battle of the
Marne, September 1914.

LARTIGUE HOUSEHOLD

Marius Aubert
Mathematics tutor to Jacques and Maurice
(Zissou). Professor of mathematics at the
Sorbonne. Assistant to Gabriel Lippmann,
winner of the Nobel Prize for Physics in
1908 for his method of reproducing colours
in photography.

Ernest Boudisseau
Valet.

Noémie Boudisseau
Cook.

Monsieur Folletête (Plitt)
Henri Lartigue's private secretary.

Julie Giquel (Dudu)
Housekeeper/nanny.

Kätchen
Maid.

Yves Lecouster
Driver for the Lartigues until Jacques turned
sixteen.

Louis
Butler.

RACING DRIVERS

Georges Boillot
Racing car driver for Peugeot, Grand Prix de
l'ACF in Dieppe on 25–26 June 1912. He also
won the Grand Prix de l'ACF in Amiens on
12 June 1913. Died in air combat during the
First World War.

Camille Jenatzy
Belgian racing car driver; first man to break
the 100 km/hr barrier.

Felice Nazzaro
Italian racing car driver; won all the great
races of the day, including the French Grand
Prix twice.

Louis Wagner
French racing car driver; won second place in
the Grand Prix de l'ACF on 25–26 June 1912.

AVIATORS

Louis Blériot
French aviation pioneer, inventor
and engineer, first to fly across the
English Channel.

Giuseppe Cei
Italian aviator, killed when his aeroplane
crashed in 1911.

Henry Farman
Anglo-French aviator, aircraft designer and
manufacturer; first to make circular flight
of one kilometre.

Roland Garros
Pilot and aviation pioneer. On 23 September
1913 he became the first person to cross the
Mediterranean non-stop. He was shot down
and killed one month before the end of the
First World War.

Alberto Santos-Dumont
Brazilian inventor and aviation pioneer.

René Simon
French aviator, known for his daring tactics.

Gabriel Voisin
French aviation pioneer.

Wilbur Wright
American aviator and inventor; along with
his brother Orville, credited with building
the first successful powered aeroplane.

Camera Equipment

From 1902 to 1914, Jacques Henri Lartigue used the following:

WOODEN VIEW CAMERA with lens cap, without shutter, mounted on a tripod, by J. Audouin
   for 13 × 18 plates.
JUMELLE CAMERA for 9 × 12 plates, shutter speed 1/50.
STÉRÉO-SPIDO CAMERA by L. Gaumont for 6 × 13 plates, shutter speed 1/300 (borrowed from
   his father, Henri Lartigue).
BLOCK-NOTES CAMERA by L. Gaumont for 4.5 × 6 plates, shutter speed 1/100.
NO. 2 BROWNIE FOLDING CAMERA by Eastman Kodak for 6 × 9 film, shutter speed 1/100.
KLAPP TAKYR CAMERA by E. Krauss for 9 × 12 plates, Zeiss lenses, shutter speed 1/1000.
NO. 1 FOLDING POCKET CAMERA by Eastman Kodak for 6 × 9 plates, shutter speed 1/100.
KLAPP STEREO-CAMERA by Nettel for 6 × 13 plates, Zeiss Tessar lenses, shutter speed 1/1200.
VÉRASCOPE STEREO-CAMERA by Jules Richard for 45 × 107 mm plates, shutter speed 1/200
   (borrowed from Henri Lartigue's private secretary, Monsieur Folletête).
PATHÉ CINÉMATOGRAPHE, HAND-CRANKED CINE-CAMERA (35 mm).
PATHÉ PROFESSIONNEL HAND-CRANKED CINE-CAMERA (35 mm).

Diaries

Jacques Henri Lartigue kept a meticulous written record of his daily life for over seventy years.
As a nine-year-old, he dictated his *Livre de rêves de Coco* (Coco's Book of Dreams, 1903) to his paternal
aunt Yéyé (Geneviève). Just before his first Holy Communion, he wrote *Sentiments de retraite* (Feelings
on Retreat, 1907), aided by his family and tutors. This was followed by jottings in a garnet-coloured
notebook entitled *Raisons pour lesquelles je suis si heureux* (Reasons Why I am so Happy, 1910–11).

In 1911, annoyed by his entourage's incessant complaints about the weather, the seventeen-
year-old began writing a daily diary with a small drawing of the weather (sun, rain, wind, storm,
etc.), plus the temperature, rating the day on a scale from 1 to 20. He often used the bottom of
the page for drawings or sketches of the photographs he had taken that day. These early diaries
focus on Lartigue's daily life: what time he got up, prayers, washing, breakfast, lunch, photographs
(he noted the number of photographs taken per month), exercise, amusements, outings, and so
on. As time wore on, these private diaries became more detailed and reflective. From 1917, Lartigue
replaced them with a proper journal written on loose sheets of paper.

Lartigue later expanded, edited and embellished his written fragments and journals to create
an autobiography in diary form. The first – and, to date, only – printed volume (1911–1921) was
published, in French, as *Mémoires sans mémoire* by Robert Laffont, Paris, in 1975.

Bibliography

Diary of a Century: Jacques Henri Lartigue. Edited by Richard Avedon. New York: Viking Press, 1970.

Les Forcenés de l'image. Mary Bertrand. 'Jacques Henri Lartigue ou les archives de l'indolence', pp. 35–57. Paris: Éditions Métailié, 2000.

Debussy à la plage. Rémy Campos. Paris: Éditions Gallimard, 2018.

Jacques Henri Lartigue : Une vie sans ombre. Text by Martine d'Astier. Paris: Découvertes Gallimard, 2009.

Lartigue: Album of a Century. Edited by Martine d'Astier, Quentin Bajac and Adrian Sayag. Text by Martine d'Astier, Clément Chéroux, Maryse Cordesse and Kevin Moore. London: Thames & Hudson, 2004.

Lartigue: Life in Color. Martine d'Astier and Martine Ravache. New York: Harry N. Abrams, 2015.

Trois Grâces de la Belle Époque. Claude Dufresne. Paris: Éditions Bartillat, 2003.

The New History of Photography. Michel Frizot. Cologne: Könemann, 1998.

Jacques Henri Lartigue: Photographer. Introduction by Vicki Goldberg. London: Thames & Hudson, 1998.

Les Cocottes, reines du Paris, 1900. Catherine Guigon. Paris: Parigramme, 2012.

Jacques-Henri Lartigue : La Traversée du siècle. Florette Lartigue. Paris: Bordas, 1990.

Mémoires sans mémoire. J. H. Lartigue. Paris: Robert Laffont, 1975.

Lartigue, l'élégance photographique. Marianne Le Galliard. Paris: Somogy éditions d'art, 2016.

Reading Boyishly: Roland Barthes, J. M. Barrie, Jacques Henri Lartigue, Marcel Proust and D. W. Winnicott. Carol Mavor. Durham, NC, and London: Duke University Press, 2007.

Jacques Henri Lartigue: The Invention of an Artist. Kevin Moore (PhD thesis), Princeton University, 2004.

Jacques-Henri Lartigue : Le Choix du bonheur. Texts by Bertrand Poirot-Delpech, Richard Avedon, Shelley Rice and John Szarkowski. Besançon: Éditions La Manufacture, 1992.

Pleasures of the Belle Époque: Entertainment and Festivity in Turn-of-the-Century France. Text by Charles Rearick. New Haven, CT: Yale University Press, 1985.

The Photographs of Jacques Henri Lartigue. Introduction by John Szarkowski. New York: Museum of Modern Art, 1963.

Jacques Henri Lartigue: A Sporting Life. Thierry Terret. Arles: Actes Sud/Hermès, 2013.

Jacques Henri Lartigue : Un dandy à la plage. Text by Bernard Toulier. Paris: Éditions La Découverte, 2016.

La Belle Époque : La France de 1900 à 1914. Michel Winock. Paris: Perrin, 2003.

A History of French Passions, Volume 1, *Ambition and Love.* Theodore Zeldin. Oxford: Oxford University Press (The Oxford History of Modern Europe series), repr. 2003.

Picture Credits

pp. 2, 11, 18, 19, 22, 23, 24 (left), 25, 26, 29, 30, 31, 32, 33, 35, 44, 45, 47, 48–9, 50, 51, 52, 53, 54, 57, 58, 62, 63, 64, 66, 67, 68, 69, 70, 72 (above), 72 (below), 73, 74, 76 (above), 76 (below), 77, 79 (above), 79 (below), 81, 82, 83, 85, 86, 91, 94, 95, 96, 97, 98, 99, 100–1, 102, 103, 104–5, 108, 109, 110, 111, 113, 114, 116, 117, 118–19, 120, 122, 125, 130, 131, 132 (below), 133 (above), 133 (below), 134 (above), 134 (below), 136, 140, 142–3, 145, 147, 148, 152, 153, 154, 155, 156, 157, 158, 159, 160 (left), 160 (right), 161, 164, 165, 166, 167, 175, 178 Photographs by Jacques Henri Lartigue © 2020 Ministère de la Culture – France/AAJHL

pp. 13, 14, 15, 21, 27, 34, 55, 65, 71, 75, 89, 90, 92, 93, 137, 138, 139, 146, 162, 163 (left), 163 (right), 172–3, 174, 177 Donation Jacques Henri Lartigue

p. 17 Bibliothèque nationale de France

p. 24 (right) The Metropolitan Museum of Art, New York. Robert Lehman Collection, 1975 (1975.1.224). Photo 2019 The Metropolitan Museum of Art/ Art Resource/Scala, Florence.

pp. 107, 115 and 121 Roger-Viollet/TopFoto

p. 132 (above) Ullsteinbild/TopFoto

p. 144 Fonds de Dotation Peugeot pour la Mémoire de l'Histoire Industrielle. Photo Centre d'Archives de Terre Blanche.

The illustrations in this book are unretouched, preserving any original markings, age spots and tonal variations with regard to Lartigue's photographs, diary pages and album pages.

Acknowledgments

The publisher wishes to thank Marion Perceval and Charles-Antoine Revol at the Donation Jacques Henri Lartigue for their help and support with the Lartigue illustrations for this book. The author, in addition, would like to thank Martine d'Astier, former director of the Donation Jacques Henri Lartigue, as well as Aris Kourkoumelis.

Index

Page numbers in *italics* refer to illustrations.